MW01709799

english@eleven

VCE ENGLISH UNITS 1 & 2

2ND EDITION

english@ eleven

VCE ENGLISH UNITS 1 & 2

2ND EDITION

TONI GLASSON

BICENTENNIAL 1807 WILEY 2007

jacaranda
jaconline.com.au

Second edition published 2007 by
John Wiley & Sons Australia, Ltd
42 McDougall Street, Milton, Qld 4064

Offices also in Sydney and Melbourne

Typeset in 10/12.5 pt Electra LT

National Library of Australia
Cataloguing-in-publication data

Glasson, Toni.
English at eleven: VCE English units 1 & 2, 2E.

Year 11 students.
ISBN 978 0 7314 0478 0.

1. English language — Rhetoric — Juvenile literature.
2. English literature — History and criticism — Juvenile literature. I. Title.

808.042

Front and back cover images: © Digital Vision, © Fancy, © Photodisc

Illustrated by Lisa Coutts, Steve Hunter, James Hart, Jonathan Passamani and Glenn Lumsden
Anniversary logo design: Richard Pacifico

Typeset in India by TechBooks
Layout by Wiley Composition Services

Printed in Singapore by
Craft Print International Ltd

10 9 8 7 6 5 4 3 2 1

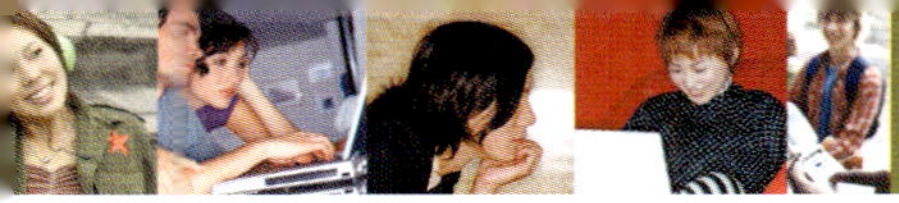

Contents

Introduction

This text has been written to support teachers in the implementation of Units 1 and 2 of the reaccredited VCE English Study Design.

Chapters One and Two link directly to Area of study 1: Reading and responding. These chapters focus on the analysis of a variety of print, non-print and multimodal texts, with a view to encouraging in students the ability to identify and discuss the key aspects of these texts and, in particular, to understand the ways in which authors and readers create meaning. The learning activities in these chapters can be used to support similar learning activities related to the set text/s selected by the school.

Chapters Three, Four and Five link to Area of study 2: Creating and presenting. The focus of this area of study is on the analysis and production of texts within a selected context — themes and ideas, technology and communication or workplace communication. (Teachers choose one context as the focus for each unit, or one context as the focus for both units.) These chapters feature a variety of texts relevant to each of the contexts and provide opportunities to analyse purpose and intended audience, as well as the authorial choices related to structure and linguistic features. These texts are designed to support the set text/s selected by the school.

Chapters Six, Seven and Eight focus on Area of study 3: Using language to persuade. Chapters Six and Seven examine the use of language in print, non-print and multimodal texts (including texts from the media as well as other contexts) that seek to present a point of view, while Chapter 8 examines the identification of appeals to logic and the construction of a reasoned argument.

Each chapter contains a variety of learning activities, each specifically linked to a short text. In addition, there is a comprehensive list of assessment tasks, covering oral, written and multimodal modes of responding. Teachers can choose from these assessment tasks according to the interests and prior experiences of their students. The criteria for assessment, provided at the end of each chapter, reflect the knowledge and skills outlined in the Study Design and offer examples (in the listed dot points) of how the knowledge and skills could be evident in the completed assessment task, depending on the chosen mode.

Another feature of this text is the provision throughout the chapters of suggested strategies such as for preparing to read a text, for making an oral presentation, for checking the meaning of unfamiliar vocabulary, for beginning a short story, for active listening, for reading playscripts, poems and websites, and for writing an analytical response.

The VCE English Study Design provides opportunities for teachers to design courses that reflect the ways in which their students learn and to engage their interest. I hope that this textbook can be used to assist in this regard.

Toni Glasson

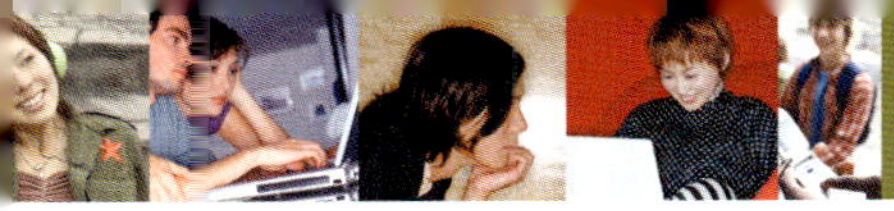

Outcomes grid: VCE ENGLISH STUDY DESIGN

English @ Eleven, 2E chapters, learning activities, assessment tasks and criteria for assessment for Units 1 and 2.

Unit 1 Outcomes	Unit 2 Outcomes	Chapters and Learning activities	Assessment tasks	Criteria for assessment
Area of study: Reading and responding				
Identify and discuss key aspects of a set text, and construct a response in oral or written form.	Discuss and analyse how texts convey ways of thinking about the characters, ideas and themes, and construct a response in oral or written form.	**CHAPTER 1:** Print and non-print texts 1.1–1.8 (Novels) 1.9 (Non-fiction texts) 1.10 (Short stories) 1.11–1.15 (Drama) 1.16–1.19 (Poetry) 1.20 (Speeches)	Responding creatively to a novel in writing p. 14 Responding to a novel in oral form p. 14 Responding to non-fiction p. 18 Responding to short stories p. 22 Responding to drama p. 27 Responding to Shakespearean plays p. 32 Responding to poems p. 41 Responding to a speech p. 43	Chapter 1, p. 44
		CHAPTER 2: Multimodal texts 2.1–2.12 (Narrative films) 2.13–2.17 ('Reality' TV) 2.18 (Hypertext) 2.19 (Picture books)	Responding to film as text p. 64 Responding to documentary films p. 65 Responding to 'reality' TV programs p. 72 Responding to a hypertext p. 73 Responding to websites p. 75	Chapter 2, p. 76
Area of study: Creating and presenting				
Create and present texts, taking account of audience, purpose and context.	Create and present texts, taking account of audience, purpose and context.	**CHAPTER 3:** Exploring and presenting themes or ideas 3.1–3.9 (Exploring and presenting: Who am I?) 3.10–3.12 (Editing and proofreading) 3.13–3.23 (Exploring and presenting: It's not fair!)	Exploring and presenting themes or ideas p. 97 Exploring and presenting themes or ideas p. 117	Chapter 3, p. 117
		CHAPTER 4: Exploring technology and communication 4.1 (The digital divide) 4.2–4.3 (SMS) 4.4–4.8 (Online communication) 4.9 (Ezines) 4.10–4.12 (Websites) 4.13 (Blogs) 4.14–4.15 (Datashow presentations)	Creating and presenting with communication technology p. 139	Chapter 4, p. 140

(continued)

English @ Eleven, 2E chapters, learning activities, assessment tasks and criteria for assessment for Units 1 and 2.

Unit 1 Outcomes	Unit 2 Outcomes	Chapters and Learning activities	Assessment tasks	Criteria for assessment
Area of study: Creating and presenting (*continued*)				
Create and present texts, taking account of audience, purpose and context.	Create and present texts, taking account of audience, purpose and context.	**CHAPTER 5:** | Exploring the workplace 5.1 (What is a workplace?) 5.2–5.10 (What are some of the issues surrounding the workplace?) 5.11 (Form, context, audience and purpose) 5.12–5.16 (Workplace texts)	Creating and presenting workplace texts p. 169	Chapter 5, p. 171
Area of study: Using language to persuade				
Identify and discuss, either in writing and/ or orally, how language can be used to persuade readers and/or viewers.	Identify and analyse how language is used in a persuasive text, and present a reasoned point of view in an oral or a written form.	**CHAPTER 6:** | Using language to persuade in print and non-print texts 6.1–6.9 (Verbal language)	Analysing language used to persuade p. 196	Chapter 6, p. 202
		CHAPTER 7: | Using language to persuade in multimodal texts 7.1 (Cartoons) 7.2 (Photographs) 7.3 (Graphs) 7.4 (Posters) 7.5–7.7 (Print advertisements) 7.8 (Television advertisements) 7.9–7.10 (Television current affairs programs) 7.11 (Documentaries) 7.12 (Websites)	Evaluating a controversial documentary p. 219 Analysing persuasive multimodal texts p. 221	Chapter 7, p. 224
		CHAPTER 8: | Presenting a point of view 8.1–8.6 (Examining the arguments of others) 8.7–8.8 (Constructing a written argument) 8.9 (Other ways of arguing in writing) 8.10 (Constructing an oral argument)	Constructing an argument on an issue of personal interest to you p. 250	Chapter 8, p. 250

Acknowledgements

The author and publisher would like to thank the following copyright holders, organisations and individuals for their assistance and for permission to reproduce copyright material in this book.

Internal design

• © Digital Vision • © Fancy • © Photodisc

Images

• ABC: page **215** • Age Syndications: page **183**/Poster 'How what you eat affects the Earth' taken from *The Age* 2/6/06, p. 98 • Amnesty International Australia: page **116** • © Andrew Weldon: page **112**/*The Age* 20/12/05 p. 52 • Arts Victoria: page **207** (bottom)/Arts Council Research Bulletin, June 1997, data source ABS; (top)/ABS, Leisure participation Victoria, October 1996 • Austral International: pages **52–3** (centre) • Australian Picture Library: pages **29**/The Kobal Collection/20th Century Fox; **42**/Corbis/Bettmann; **46**, **47** (top left), **48** (bottom left), **48** (bottom right), **49** (top right)/APL; **54** (top)/Bureau L.A. Collection/Corbis; **55** (bottom), **63** (bottom), **63** (top), **218** (bottom)/APL • © Brand X Pictures: page **227** • Cartoon Stock Ltd: page **159**/Mike Baldwin • Dairy Australia: page **211** (left) • David Pannett: page **91** • © Digital Vision: page **101** • Eastgate Systems Inc.: page **73**/Deena Larsen • Getty Images: page **249**/Taxi • © Image Disk Photography: page **181** • Incredible Adventures: page **223** • J.K Wright: page **71**/*The Age* • © John Wiley & Sons Australia: pages **148**, **169** (right)/Taken by Kari-Ann Tapp • Kenley Arndt: page **155** • Kobal Collection: pages **47** (bottom left), **54** (bottom)/Warner Brothers; **47** (right)/Archer Street/Delux/Lion's Gate/Buitendijk, Jaap; **48** (top left), **52** (top), **57** (left), **63** (centre), **218** (top)/The Kobal Collection; **49** (bottom left)/Universal/Wing Nut Films; **49** (bottom right), **55** (centre)/20th Century Fox; **52** (bottom)/Big Talk/WT2; **55** (top)/Lucas Film; **65**/Blitz/Welch • Lothian Books Publishing: page **74**/Shaun Tan and John Marsden • Mark Knight: page **204** (bottom, top) • Melbourne GPO: page **211** (right) • Newspix: pages **67** (left)/Craig Greenhill; **67** (right)/Peter Clark; **68**/Steve Pohlner; **175**/Colin Murty; **180**/Raoul Kochanowski; **184**/Grainger John; **186**/Evan Agostini/Getty Images; **194**/James Knowler • Nokia Telecommunications Australia: page **120** (right) • NRH Regional Rehab Outpatient Network: page **157** • PeTA: page **220**/From www.peta.org/actioncentre//clothing.asp • Peter Nicholson: page **205** (top)/Cartoon by Nicholson from *The Australian*, www.nicholsoncartoons.com.au • Photodisc: pages **131**, **141** (left, centre, right), **169** (bottom centre)/© 1997, **169** (bottom left, top left), **176**, **183** (bottom left), **183** (centre right)/© 2002, **183** (top left, top right), **199**, **200**, **201**, **231**, **246** • Photolibrary: page **208** (bottom)/Roy Charlie • Playgroup Victoria: page **222** • Random House Group UK: page **3** (bottom centre, bottom left)/Sophie Kinsella; (top/bottom right)/Peter Ackroyd • Samsung Electronics: pages **120** (left), **121** • Simon & Schuster, Inc.: page **3** (top centre, top left)/Joan Brady • © Stockbyte 2002: page **183** (bottom right) • Time Inc.: page **114**/©2006/All rights reserved, reprinted from Time Magazine Syndication ® with permission • Tourism Australia: page **134**/From www.australia.com/home • Warner Bros.: page **57** (right) • World Vision: page **179**/Courtesy of World Vision 2006

Text

• Adrian Mackinder: pages **65–6**/Future Movies • Age Syndications: pages **185**/'Adversarial captain needs deeds to back his words', by Peter Roebuck, published in *The Age* 3/6/2006; **186**/'Honouring our greatest achievers', *The Age* 26/1/06; **228**/'Frustrating the fight to cut the road toll', Age Editorial Opinion, 6/1/2006, taken from *The Age* online • Prof. Alan Hedge: pages **158–9**/Cornell University • Andy Kissane: pages **39–40** • Ann Elmo Agency: page **19–21**/Reprinted by permission of GRM Associates, Inc., agents for the Ann Elmo Agency. From 'Playboy Magazine of 1958', © 1958 by Henry Slesar • CEDA Committee for Economic Development of Australia: pages **126–7**/David Walker/*The Age* • Childnet international: pages **130–1**/

From www.childnet-int.org • CNN: pages 59–60/Online review by Paul Clinton, taken from *CNN* online, www.cnn.com/2005/SHOWBIZ/Movies/11/18/review.potter/index.html, posted 21 November 2005 • Commonwealth Copyright: pages 101–2 • © Currency Press NSW: pages 23–6/Extracts from 'Stolen' by Jane Harrison, pages 6–7, 13–14, 28–9, ISBN 0 86819 680 0 • David Higham & Associates: page 35/Langston Hughes • Dr Edward Spence: pages 201–2 • Faber and Faber U.K: pages 34/13 lines of 'Preludes' from *Collected Poems 1909–1962* by T S Eliot; 102–3/Extract of 920 words of poem 'Memoir' by John McGahern • Gabriella Coslovich: pages 233–4 • Garry Barker: pages 80–2/*The Age* • Guardian Newspapers Ltd: pages 123–4/'Texting "is no bar to literacy"' by Lucy Ward, *Guardian* online, posted 23/12/2004 • HarperCollins Australia: page 36/Nancy Cato • Reprinted by permission of Henry Holt and Company LLC: pages 38–9/'The Road Not Taken' from *The Poetry of Robert Frost*, edited by Edward Connery Lathem, © 1916, 1969 by Henry Holt and Company, © 1944 by Robert Frost • *Herald Weekly Times*: pages 184; 190–1/*Herald Sun*/Kerry Cue; 192/*Herald Sun Online*; 193/*Herald Sun*/Robyn Riley; 206/*Herald Sun* • Hugh Mackay: pages 177–8, 181–2/*The Age* • Translated by Jack David Zipes: pages 12–13/© Irmela Brender extracted from 'I always felt sorry for Rumpelstiltskin' • Jillian & Gary Craven: page 194/*Sunday Herald Sun* • Joanne Dwyer: pages 198–200 • Joel Garreau: pages 234–6/Article adapted by Joel Garreau from his book, *'Radical Evolution: The Promise and Peril of Enhancing Our Minds, Our bodies, and What it Means to be Human'*, Doubleday 2006 • Julio Noboa: pages 35–6 • Kath Walker: page 115 • Katrina Fong: page 99 • Kenley Arndt: pages 155–6 • Reprinted with permission from Little, Brown & Co.: pages 37–8/Extract from poem 'Caged Bird' by Maya Angelou from 'Shaker, why don't you sing?' in *Seven Ages—an Anthology of Writing* (an audio book © Sean Murphy productions) • *New Zealand Herald*: page 232/Gail Bailey • Orion Publishing Group: pages 160–2/Frederick Pohl and CM Kornbluth • Paul Keating: pages 108–10 /'The Redfern Park' speech by Hon. PJ Keating • Penguin Books Ltd UK: pages 16–18/ Extract from 'Everything Bad is Good for You', by Steven Johnson, Allen Lane Penguin Press 2005, pp. 42–7 • Peter Saunders: pages 105–8 • PFD: page 37/Poem 'Sundeath/Greeneaters' (© Roger McGough 1969) is reproduced by permission of PFD (www.pfd.co.uk) on behalf of Roger McGough • Reprinted by permission of The Random House Group Ltd: pages 4–7/*The Accidental Tourist*, by Anne Tyler (published by Chatto & Windus); 10–11/*All Quiet on the Western Front*, by Erich Maria Remarque (published by Vintage); 88–90/from *So Long, See You Tomorrow*, by William Maxwell (published by Harvill) • Richard Yaxley: pages 83–7; 239–43 • Robyn Rowland: page 34/Poem 'Silence' from *The Best Australian Poems 2005*, edited by Les Murray Black Inc. (© Schwartz Publishing), also found in the book *Silence and its tongues* • Roger Bohn: pages 196–8/University of California • Siv Cedering: page 79/Poem 'Twins', © 1975 Siv Cedering Fox, from *Mother Is*, Rowman & Littlefield Publishers, Inc. • Reprinted by permission of Susan Bergholz Literary Sevices, New York: pages 87–8/© Sandra Cisneros 1984, from *The House on Mango Street*, published by Vintage Books, a division of Random House, Inc., also published in hardcover by Alfred A Knopf in 1994 • The Eleven Group: pages 111–13/Richard McEncroe/*The Age* • Ty Burr: pages 60–2/*The Boston Globe* • Victorian WorkCover Authority: pages 148–152/From 'Incidence of Workplace Bullying in Victoria', the VWA website (www.workcover.vic.gov.au) should be accessed for more information and future updates on the references used • Wikipedia: pages 70–1/ From http://en.wikipedia.org/wiki/Big_Brother_Australia is licensed under the 'http://www.gnu.org/copyleft/fdl.html'

Every effort has been made to trace the ownership of copyright material. Information that will enable the publisher to rectify any error or omission in subsequent reprints will be welcome. In such cases, please contact the Permissions Section at John Wiley & Sons, who will arrange for the payment of the usual fee.

reading and responding

VCE UNITS 1 & 2

CHAPTER 1

Print and non-print texts

When writing or talking about the texts that we read or view we must be able to describe how these texts have been put together, or constructed. It is not sufficient just to say that we like them or dislike them. We need to be able to:

- identify and use appropriate **metalanguage** or terminology to describe how the author has constructed the text
- provide our own interpretation of the text, supported by evidence from the text
- show that we understand how others might interpret a text differently from ourselves
- show that we understand how different values and ideas are evident in a variety of texts.

In this chapter we will look at examples of a variety of print and non-print texts, including speeches, extracts from novels, short stories, poetry and **non-fiction**, in order to identify their particular structures and features.

Novels

The **genre** to which a novel belongs is one of the key factors which influences us when we select a novel to read (or teach).

Novels belonging to a particular genre (a French word that means 'kind' or 'type') share certain characteristics in common. As readers, once we identify a novel as belonging to a particular genre (for example, romance, horror, adventure, crime, historical fiction or realistic fiction) we have certain expectations of it.

How do we know what genre a novel belongs to? An examination of the cover — the title of the novel, the font in which the title is written, the cover photograph or design, the blurb on the back cover — will provide us with several clues.

Learning activity **1.1**

Examine each of the following covers to answer these questions:

1. What genre does the novel seem to belong to?
2. What are the clues on the cover that indicate the novel's genre? Refer to both visual and written clues.

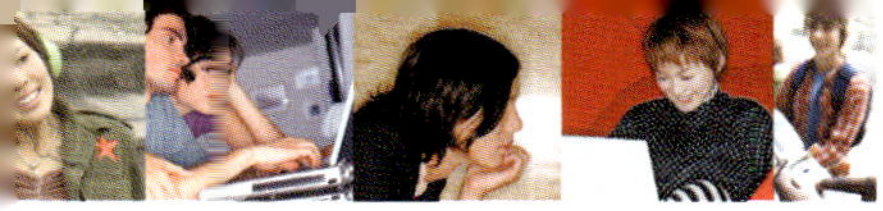

3. Explain what you would expect to find in this novel in terms of plot and characters. Why would you expect to find these features?

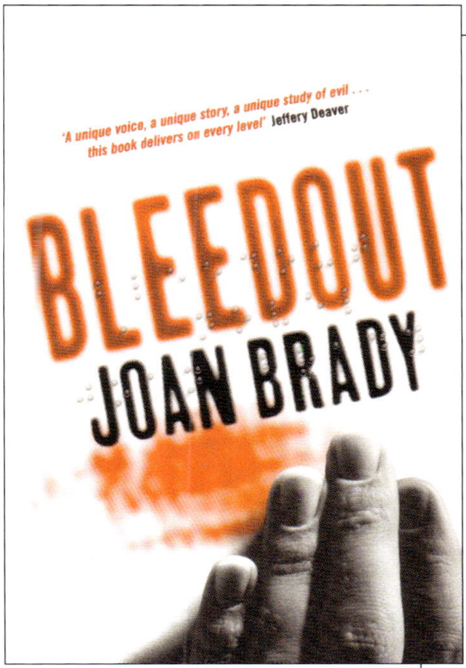

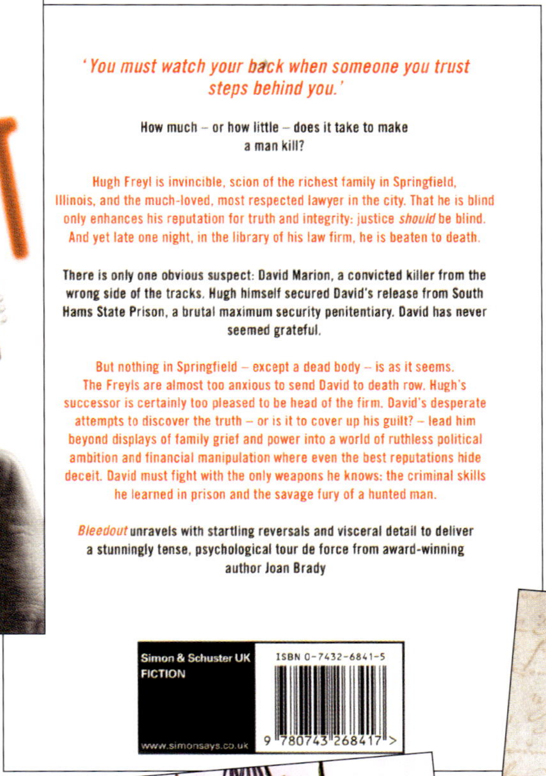

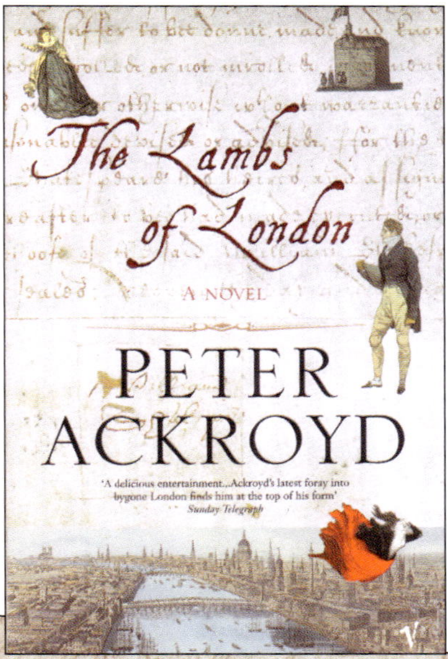

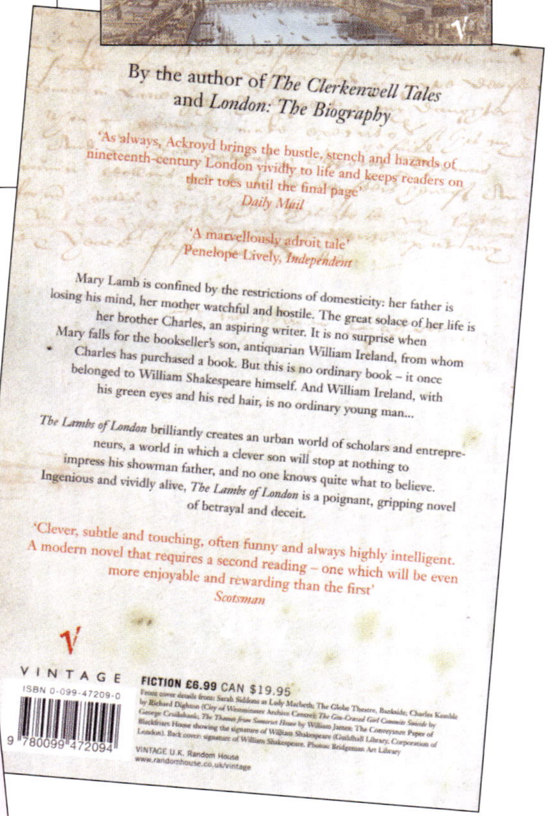

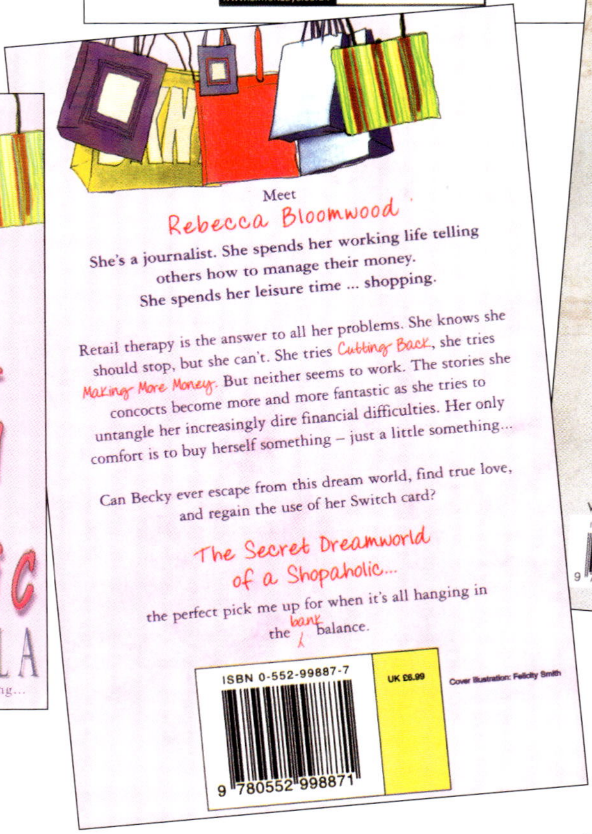

Studying a novel

To study a novel you need to be able to identify and discuss its structure and language features. The following sections will explain what this means and provide you with some of the metalanguage necessary for you to be able to do this.

Strategies | Before you begin to read

- Write down three very specific questions about the title.
- Read the blurb and note the information that it provides about the plot, the setting and the main character/s.
- Are there chapter headings? What clues do they give you about the contents of the novel?

Exposition

The opening pages of a novel usually establish several things for us. The setting is revealed, characters are introduced, we gain insight into their particular qualities or concerns and we perhaps get a glimpse of the central issue, theme or conflict that the novel is going to explore. The writing style and the perspective (or point of view) adopted by the writer are also evident. This process of initiating the reader into the world of the novel is referred to as the exposition.

Learning activity **1.2**

What follows is the beginning of the novel *The Accidental Tourist* by American writer Anne Tyler. Read the extract and then answer these questions.

1. From whose point of view or perspective is the extract written? What implications does this have for you as the reader?
2. Who are the characters that are introduced in this extract? What do you learn about each of them? How do you learn this? (Consider comments made by the author as well as what the author has the characters say and do.)
3. What seems to be the central issue, conflict or theme that is established in this extract?
4. What do you think the rest of the novel will be about? Why do you think this?
5. Based on your reading of this extract, do you think you would enjoy reading this novel? Explain your answer.

The Accidental Tourist

They were supposed to stay at the beach a week, but neither of them had the heart for it and they decided to come back early. Macon drove. Sarah sat next to him, leaning her head against the side window. Chips of cloudy sky showed through her tangled brown curls.

Macon wore a formal summer suit, his traveling suit — much more logical for traveling than jeans, he always said. Jeans had those stiff, hard seams and those rivets. Sarah wore a strapless terry beach dress. They might have been returning from two entirely different trips. Sarah had a tan but Macon didn't. He was a tall, pale, gray-eyed man, with straight fair hair cut close to his head, and his skin was that thin kind that easily burns. He'd kept away from the sun during the middle part of every day.

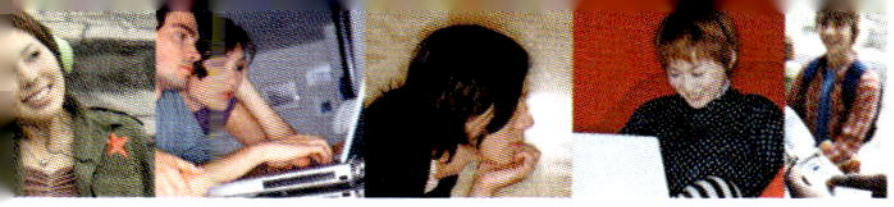

Just past the start of the divided highway, the sky grew almost black and several enormous drops spattered the windshield. Sarah sat up straight. 'Let's hope it doesn't rain,' she said.

'I don't mind a little rain,' Macon said.

Sarah sat back again, but she kept her eyes on the road.

It was a Thursday morning. There wasn't much traffic. They passed a pickup truck, then a van all covered with stickers from a hundred scenic attractions. The drops on the windshield grew closer together. Macon switched his wipers on. Tick-*swoosh*, they went — a lulling sound; and there was a gentle patter on the roof. Every now and then a gust of wind blew up. Rain flattened the long, pale grass at the sides of the road. It slanted across the boat lots, lumberyards, and discount furniture outlets, which already had a darkened look as if here it might have been raining for some time.

'Can you see all right?' Sarah asked.

'Of course,' Macon said. 'This is nothing.'

They arrived behind a trailer truck whose rear wheels sent out arcs of spray. Macon swung to the left and passed. There was a moment of watery blindness till the truck had dropped behind. Sarah gripped the dashboard with one hand.

'I don't know how you can see to drive,' she said.

'Maybe you should put on your glasses.'

'Putting on my glasses would help you to see?'

'Not me; you,' Macon said. 'You're focused on the windshield instead of the road.'

Sarah continued to grip the dashboard. She had a broad, smooth face that gave an impression of calm, but if you looked closely you'd notice the tension at the corners of her eyes.

The car drew in around them like a room. Their breaths fogged the windows. Earlier the air conditioner had been running and now some artificial chill remained, quickly turning dank, carrying with it the smell of mildew. They shot through an underpass. The rain stopped completely for one blank, startling second. Sarah gave a little gasp of relief, but even before it was uttered, the hammering on the roof resumed. She turned and gazed back longingly at the underpass. Macon sped ahead, with his hands relaxed on the wheel.

'Did you notice that boy with the motorcycle?' Sarah asked. She had to raise her voice; a steady, insistent roaring sound engulfed them.

'What boy?'

'He was parked beneath the underpass.'

'It's crazy to ride a motorcycle on a day like today,' Macon said. 'Crazy to ride one any day. You're so exposed to the elements.'

'We could do that,' Sarah said. 'Stop and wait it out.'

'Sarah, if I felt we were in the slightest danger I'd have pulled over long ago.'

'Well, I don't know that you would have,' Sarah said.

They passed a field where the rain seemed to fall in sheets, layers and layers of rain beating down the cornstalks, flooding the rutted soil. Great lashings of water flung themselves at the windshield. Macon switched his wiper blades to high.

'I don't know that you really care that much,' Sarah said. 'Do you?'

Macon said, 'Care?'

'I said to you the other day, I said, "Macon, now that Ethan's dead I sometimes wonder if there's any point to life." Do you remember what you answered?'

'Well, not offhand,' Macon said.

'You said, "Honey, to tell the truth, it never seemed to me there was all that much point to begin with." Those were your exact words.'

'Um …'

'And you don't even know what was wrong with that.'

'No, I guess I don't,' Macon said.

He passed a line of cars that had parked at the side of the road, their windows opaque, their gleaming surfaces bouncing back the rain in shallow explosions. One car was slightly tipped, as if about to fall into the muddy torrent that churned and raced in the gully. Macon kept a steady speed.

'You're not a comfort, Macon,' Sarah said.

'Honey, I'm trying to be.'

'You just go on your same old way like before. Your little routines and rituals, depressing habits, day after day. No comfort at all.'

'Shouldn't I need comfort too?' Macon asked. 'You're not the only one, Sarah. I don't know why you feel it's your loss alone.'

'Well, I just do, sometimes,' Sarah said.

They were quiet a moment. A wide lake, it seemed, in the center of the highway crashed against the underside of the car and slammed it to the right. Macon pumped his brakes and drove on.

'This rain, for instance,' Sarah said. 'You know it makes me nervous. What harm would it do to wait it out? You'd be showing some concern. You'd be telling me we're in this together.'

Macon peered through the windshield, which was streaming so that it seemed marbled. He said, 'I've got a system, Sarah. You know I drive according to a system.'

'You and your systems!'

'Also,' he said, 'if you don't see any point to life, I can't figure why a rainstorm would make you nervous.'

Sarah slumped in her seat.

'Will you look at that!' he said. 'A mobile home's washed clear across that trailer park.'

'Macon, I want a divorce,' Sarah told him.

Macon braked and glanced over at her. 'What?' he said. The car swerved. He had to face forward again. 'What did I say?' he asked. 'What did it mean?'

'I just can't live with you anymore,' Sarah said.

Macon went on watching the road, but his nose seemed sharper and whiter, as if the skin of his face had been pulled tight. He cleared his throat. He said, 'Honey. Listen. It's been a hard year. We've had a hard time. People who lose a child often feel this way; everybody says so; everybody says it's a terrible strain on a marriage—'

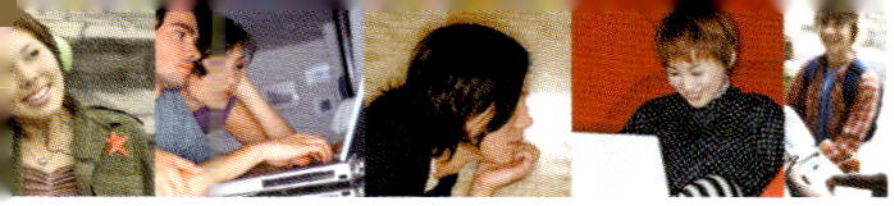

'I'd like to find a place of my own as soon as we get back,' Sarah told him.

'Place of your own,' Macon echoed, but he spoke so softly, and the rain beat so loudly on the roof, it looked as if he were only moving his lips. 'Well,' he said. 'All right. If that's what you really want.'

'You can keep the house,' Sarah said. 'You never did like moving.'

For some reason, it was this that made her finally break down. She turned away sharply. Macon switched his right blinker on. He pulled into a Texaco station, parked beneath the overhang, and cut off the engine. Then he started rubbing his knees with his palms. Sarah huddled in her corner. The only sound was the drumming of rain on the overhang far above them.

Extract from *The Accidental Tourist* by Anne Tyler

Complication

See how characters are created by authors on pages 9–10

The complication in a novel refers to the development of the central conflict. The conflict might exist:

- within a character who is trying to come to terms with who he or she is
- between characters who are in opposition for some reason
- between a character and the social or physical environment in which he or she lives.

The complication forms the main part of the narrative.

See page 100 for an example of a concept map.

Learning activity **1.3**

Select a novel that you are studying and create a concept map to show the nature of the conflict the novel is exploring. Include reference to the major events in which the conflict is evident.

Resolution

In modern novels, the resolution comes after the climax or the central event of the novel. The climax brings the conflict to a head, after which the problems in the narrative are resolved in some way.

The resolution might be negative:

- the central character might be unable to come to terms with her situation
- the conflict between characters might only be brought to an end by having one character die or leave
- the character in conflict with his social environment might lose the battle
- the character in conflict with her physical environment might die.

On the other hand, the resolution could be a positive one:

- the central character might learn from her experiences and be seen to grow into a mature functioning being
- the characters in conflict might be reconciled with each other
- the character in conflict with her physical environment might succeed in surviving
- the character in conflict with his social environment might succeed in having his point of view accepted.

Learning activity **1.4**

1. Identify the climax of a novel that you are studying. Why do you think this is the climax?
2. Explain your reaction to the resolution. Did you find it a satisfactory way of ending the novel?
3. What other resolution might have been possible?

In *Great Expectations*, for example, the author Charles Dickens originally resolved the novel with the central character, Pip, alone at the end. Apparently a friend pleaded with him to unite Pip with Estella, the girl he had loved throughout but who had rejected him. And so he gave the novel another resolution, in which Pip finishes up with Estella. Critics have said, however, that this revised ending is not consistent with the rest of the novel.

Strategies | While you read

Good readers are active readers. The following activities will help you to read actively and increase your understanding.

- Read with a pen or pencil in your hand.
- Ask questions or mark with a question mark if you don't understand or wonder why a character is behaving in a particular way.
- Write comments to help you remember your reactions.
- Mark passages that relate to the theme/s of the novel.
- Write a sentence at the top of the page to indicate the main ideas or events. This will help you locate key passages later when you want to write a response.
- If there are no chapter headings, then write your own. Make sure the chapter heading sums up the key aspect of the chapter.
- Note connections between your life and experience and what is happening in the novel.
- Note passages in the novel that remind you of other novels or films.
- Challenge the text. Ask yourself, for example, whether a particular incident would be different if told from the point of view of another character?

Plot

When you have finished the novel you should be able to explain the plot. The plot is the story of what happens in the novel and why.

Some novels, such as *The Hunter* by Julia Leigh, have **linear plots**: that is, one event leads to another. Other novels, however, have non-linear plots: that is, events are not shown to lead to other events, but the writer provides the reader with a series of 'slices' and it is the reader's task to put these together in order to form the whole. The plot of *Monster* by Walter Dean Myers, for example, is revealed through a series of diary entries and excerpts from a film script. Other novels, especially crime novels, have a plot and a sub-plot, each dealing with two separate sets of characters who are linked in some way.

Learning activity **1.5**

1. Examine the plot of a novel that you are studying. Does it have a linear or a non-linear plot?

2. If it has a linear plot, write down the events in the order in which they occur, and show how events have particular causes and effects.

As an example, here is the beginning of a summary of the plot of *The Wife of Martin Guerre* by Janet Lewis.

- January 1539. In the village of Artigues, Bertrande de Rols marries Martin Guerre. Both are eleven years of age. When she is fourteen, Bertrande goes to live with the Guerre family.
- A year later, Martin goes bear-hunting without his father's permission and is punished as a result. A bond forms between Bertrande and Martin after this incident: 'They were two, a camp within a camp.'
- A couple of years later, after the birth of their son, Martin announces to Bertrande that he is going away for about eight days because he has taken wheat seed without asking his father. He thinks that if he goes away this will allow time for his father's anger to abate.
- It is not until eight years later — after both his father and mother have died — that Martin returns, suddenly and without explanation.
- The estate is prospering, Bertrande is pregnant again, and the returned Martin is 'noble', 'generous' and 'gracious'. But Bertrande begins to doubt that he is in fact the real Martin and demands proof of his identity.

Structure

The structure of a novel refers to the way in which the plot is organised by the author. Some authors adopt a **chronological** approach; others start in the present and provide flashbacks to the past, while others move backwards and forwards between the past and present. For example, *The Sorrow of War* by Bao Ninh is structured as a series of reminiscences, and jumps backwards and forwards in time.

Setting

The setting refers to where and when the novel is set and includes the social and physical environment. A novel's setting may be confined to a single house or town at a particular point in time, or it may encompass a whole country or a longer period of time. As well as providing a background or **context** that helps to clarify the events, it can also provide the reader with insights into the nature of the society depicted in the novel. Depending on the way the writer depicts that society, the reader is positioned to see it in a favourable or unfavourable light.

Learning activity **1.6**

1. What is the setting of a novel that you are studying?
2. What sort of society is depicted in the novel?
3. Does the writer approve or disapprove of that society? How can you tell?

Characters and characterisation

Authors create characters and reveal them to readers in various ways, including the following:

- through what they cause the characters to say, think and do
- through what they have other characters say and think about them

- by making direct or implicit comment on the characters' behaviour or appearance.

There are two ways of looking at the characters in a novel. One way is to think of them as 'real' people, to examine their motivations and behaviour in the light of our own experience, our own attitudes and values, and to judge them accordingly. If we read a novel like this, then we may apply the same set of values to everyone, and it could be argued that this is a narrow way of reading a novel.

The other way in which we can look at the characters in a novel is not to see them as real people, but as creations designed to embody certain values. We can then ask these sorts of questions about individual characters:

- What values and beliefs does this character endorse?
- Does the writer portray this character sympathetically or unsympathetically?
- How does the writer do this (through speech, thoughts, actions and so on)?
- What sort of reader is likely to be sympathetic to this character?

Learning activity **1.7**

The following extract comes from *All Quiet on the Western Front* by Erich Maria Remarque. Set during World War I, the story is told from the point of view of a young German soldier who has come straight to war from school.

Read the extract and then answer the questions listed in the dot points above.

All Quiet on the Western Front

Kantorek had been our schoolmaster, a stern little man in a grey tail-coat, with a face like a shrew mouse. He was about the same size as Corporal Himmelstoss, the 'terror of Klosterberg'. It is very queer that the unhappiness of the world is so often brought on by small men. They are so much more energetic and uncompromising than the big fellows. I have always taken good care to keep out of sections with small company commanders. They are mostly confounded little martinets.

During drill-time Kantorek gave us long lectures until the whole of our class went, under his shepherding, to the District Commandant and volunteered. I can see him now, as he used to glare at us through his spectacles and say in a moving voice: 'Won't you join up, Comrades?'

These teachers always carry their feelings ready in their waistcoat pockets, and trot them out by the hour. But we didn't think of that then.

There was, indeed, one of us who hesitated and did not want to fall into line. That was Joseph Behm, a plump, homely fellow. But he did allow himself to be persuaded, otherwise he would have been ostracized. And perhaps more of us thought as he did, but no one could very well stand out, because at that time even one's parents were ready with the word 'coward'; no one had the vaguest idea what we were in for. The wisest were just the poor and simple people. They knew the war to be a misfortune, whereas those who were better off, and should have been able to see more clearly what the consequences would be, were beside themselves with joy.

Katczinsky said that was a result of their up-bringing. It made them stupid. And what Kat said, he had thought about.

Strange to say, Behm was one of the first to fall. He got hit in the eye during an attack, and we left him lying for dead. We couldn't bring him with us, because we had to come back helter-skelter. In the afternoon

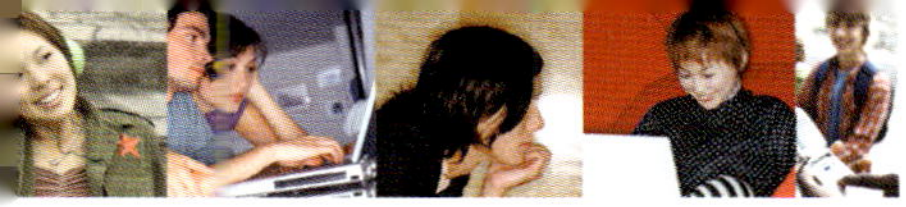

suddenly we heard him call, and saw him crawling about in no man's land. He had only been knocked unconscious. Because he could not see, and was mad with pain, he failed to keep under cover, and so was shot down before anyone could go and fetch him in.

Naturally we couldn't blame Kantorek for this. Where would the world be if one brought every man to book? There were thousands of Kantoreks, all of whom were convinced that they were acting for the best — in a way that cost them nothing.

And that is why they let us down so badly.

For us lads of eighteen they ought to have been mediators and guides to the world of maturity, the world of work, of duty, of culture, of progress — to the future. We often made fun of them and played jokes on them, but in our hearts we trusted them. The idea of authority, which they represented, was associated in our minds with a greater insight and a more humane wisdom. But the first death we saw shattered this belief. We had to recognize that our generation was more to be trusted than theirs. They surpassed us only in phrases and in cleverness. The first bombardment showed us our mistake, and under it the world as they had taught it to us broke in pieces.

While they continued to write and talk, we saw the wounded and dying. While they taught that duty to one's country is the greatest thing, we already knew that death-throes are stronger. But for all that we were no mutineers, no deserters, no cowards — they were very free with all these expressions. We loved our country as much as they; we went courageously into every action; but also we distinguished the false from true, we had suddenly learned to see. And we saw that there was nothing of their world left. We were all at once terribly alone; and alone we must see it through.

Extract from *All Quiet on the Western Front* by Erich Maria Remarque

Theme

Theme refers to the central ideas or issues explored in a text such as a novel. Concepts such as social injustice, personal integrity or the importance of families can be explored through characters, their actions, settings and plot. In some novels, certain themes are made very clear, even by their titles: think of *War and Peace* or *Pride and Prejudice*. However, when we read a novel we tend to pay more attention to certain aspects, according to our own beliefs, values and experience. The theme (or themes) of a novel can therefore be highlighted or ignored according to the particular reading that has taken place. Nevertheless, this does not mean that all readings or interpretations are equally valid, because it is still necessary to find evidence in the text to support the reading or interpretation that you prefer.

Learning activity **1.8**

1. What are the dominant themes in a novel you are studying?
2. If this same novel were read by someone else, what other themes might emerge? Imagine the interpretations that might be made by one or more of the following:
   - a psychologist

- an immigrant
- a policeman
- a feminist
- a conservative male politician.

3. What are the values or beliefs that you think might influence their interpretations of the same novel?

Readings of a text

The last couple of activities will have made it clear to you that when we read a text, the way we read it and the meaning we give it are affected by who we are — by our age, class, culture, position, gender, political beliefs and so on. These differences between groups of readers are said to produce different readings or interpretations of a text. It is important to realise, therefore, that a reading does not come from a text; it is a meaning given to the text by a reader.

Here is an alternative reading of the fairy tale *Rumpelstiltskin* that demonstrates how it is possible to read or interpret a narrative in a way that is entirely different from the dominant reading. The dominant reading views Rumpelstiltskin as a wicked person, intent on depriving the beautiful queen of her child. (You might like to re-read the original fairy tale before you read this interpretation.)

The Use and Abuse of Folk and Fairy Tales with Children

In fairy tales, so people say, good always triumphs over evil, and in the end everything turns out well. But you don't have to believe what people say. You've got to think about things for yourself. For instance, about Rumpelstiltskin. I always felt sorry for him.

Just think about what happened to him. He helped the miller's daughter who was locked up in a room filled with straw and was supposed to spin the straw into gold only because her father was a liar and claimed that she could do this. Actually she couldn't do anything except cry and complain and give Rumpelstiltskin first a necklace and then a ring to thank him for having spun the straw into gold. Can you imagine — Rumpelstiltskin spins a whole room filled with straw into gold, and for this he receives a tiny ring. He could have spun himself a ring in ten minutes without any trouble!

And when the miller's daughter had nothing more to give away and still wanted Rumpelstiltskin to continue working for her because she wanted to become queen, she promised him her first child. A promise is a promise and almost as good as a gift — isn't that true? Well, not for a miller's daughter who then becomes queen. When the time came, she wanted to break the promise, and the nice Rumpelstiltskin even gave her a chance — she was supposed to guess his name. Then she could keep the child. Yet, the former miller's daughter and present queen didn't even make an honest effort to do this. She didn't go to a library and look up various names, nor did she even ask around — she sent out messengers who were supposed to find out Rumpelstiltskin's name. And this worked too — but it had nothing to do with justice. She asked rather insidiously: 'Can your name be Rumpelstiltskin?' and the pegged Rumpelstiltskin became so furious that he ripped himself in two.

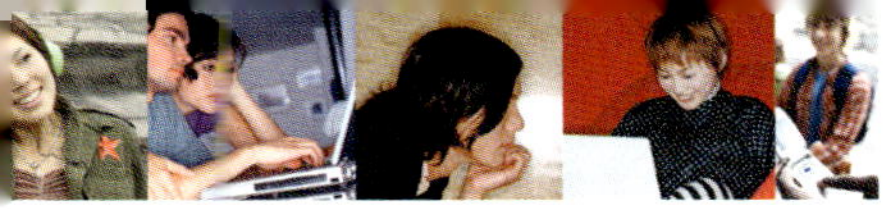

It is easy to imagine that all of this could have ended in a much better and much fairer way. This Rumpelstiltskin was a lonely wretch — the fairy tale refers to him as a 'ridiculous little man'; but when he spun gold, he wasn't ridiculous. For he was needed. What this little man accomplished in his work was worth a kingdom, and one can assume that Rumpelstiltskin knew that. But he wasn't happy because of this. He wanted to have something living, a friend, a human being, who laughed with him and was sad with him, who wished him a hearty appetite before each meal and asked him afterwards whether he enjoyed the meal. This is why Rumpelstiltskin wanted the royal child — so that he would not have to be alone.

Naturally no mother wants to give away her child. In this regard the queen's actions were understandable. But, if she had been a bit more sensible, a bit more just, and a bit more considerate to those who deserved this, then she would have said: 'I can't give you my child, for he belongs only to himself. But why don't you come live with us — with my child, with me and the king? We could do a lot of things together. You'll see how much fun we can have.' Then Rumpelstiltskin would have first turned pale and then blushed for joy. He would have climbed on a chair and would have given the queen a kiss on her cheek and the king a kiss on the crown — honour those who deserve to be honoured — and he would have sung a lullaby for the royal child to help him fall asleep, and a song to rouse him in the morning. And they would have been happy with each other until the end of their days.

But as the fairy tale now stands, that is not what I call justice.

by Irmela Brender

Extract from *I always felt sorry for Rumpelstiltskin*, translated by Jack Zipes

Responding to a novel

As part of your coursework in English, you will be asked to respond to a novel; that is, to show your understanding of the novel and your interpretation of the character and themes.

Strategies | Written analytical responses

In a written analytical response you are usually writing an essay in response to a topic set by your teacher. You might be asked a direct question about a character or theme in the novel, or you might be given a quotation about or from the novel and asked to discuss it or to give your opinion about an aspect of it.

Here is an effective approach to writing such a response:

- Read the topic carefully and underline the key terms that you will need to address in your response. Make sure you use your dictionary to check on the meaning of terms with which you are unfamiliar.
- Rewrite the topic in your own words to make sure you have understood it.
- Brainstorm ideas about the topic, jotting down, in point form, evidence from the text that can be used to illustrate it.
- Group together ideas that have something in common. These groups will become your paragraphs.
- Give each paragraph a topic sentence; that is, a sentence saying what the paragraph will be about. List the evidence from the book that you will use to support your point of view.
- Write your introduction. Make sure that it includes reference to the topic (in your own words, not the exact words of the topic) and an indication of your point of view.

- Organise the paragraphs so that they proceed logically, making certain that each paragraph relates directly to the topic.
- Write your response.
- Read it over when you have finished. Edit and proofread. Editing should include improving your vocabulary, increasing fluency and making sure that you have analysed the topic and presented a view on it. Remember that just retelling the story is not an analysis.

Not all responses to a novel need to be either written or analytical. There are many different ways of responding, all of which can show your understanding of the text. The following assessment tasks offer a broad range of options from which to choose.

Don't forget to edit and proofread your response. See pages 97–8 for guidelines.

Assessment tasks | Responding creatively to a novel in writing

1. Write about an event in the novel from the point of view of a character whose feelings and thoughts have not been disclosed or highlighted.
2. Write another chapter or passage to fill a gap in the narrative. For example, a particular event or conversation may not have been described by the writer, but simply reported as having happened 'offstage'.
3. Write a letter that could have been written by a particular character at a significant point in the novel.
4. Write another chapter to go at the end of the novel.
5. Write a **feature article** about one of the novel's themes or characters.
6. Write a play or film script adaptation of a particular scene from the novel.

See page 44 for the criteria for assessment.

Responding to a novel in oral form

1. Roleplay an interview with a character in the novel. One person plays the role of the interviewer and asks a series of questions about motivation and behaviour; the other assumes the role of the character.
2. In pairs or groups, roleplay a scene from the novel.
3. In pairs, roleplay a **dialogue** between two characters from the novel who do not actually meet during the course of the novel.
4. As a group, conduct a trial of a character who has been guilty of a crime or of blameworthy behaviour.
5. Conduct a guided, small-group discussion on the suitability of the novel as a set text for study by secondary school students.
6. Conduct a guided, small-group discussion on a key scene in the novel, a character or a theme.
7. Use PowerPoint, or a similar program, to present a short talk on an aspect of the novel: setting, characters, theme or symbolism.
8. Perform a **dramatic monologue** in which a central character explains or justifies his or her actions.
9. In pairs, roleplay a dialogue between a character from another novel that deals with similar themes or ideas and a character in the novel you are currently studying.

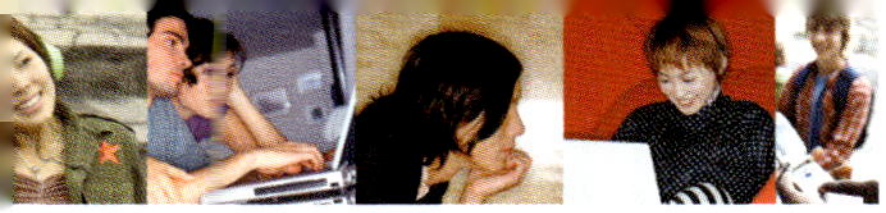

10. Show a scene from the film version of the novel, and discuss how effective or otherwise you find it and why.
11. Use a novel as the focus for a promotional website. Design a website which includes, at least, appropriate photographs and/or diagrams, links to information about the author, a synopsis of the book and reviews. Present your website to the class, explaining how your design choices (font, colours, the 'feel' of the site) are an effective reflection of the novel and its concerns.

See page 44 for the criteria for assessment.

Strategies | Making oral responses

Remember to:

- pronounce words clearly, distinctly and accurately
- vary the pitch and volume of your voice
- avoid ums and ahs
- speak at a moderate pace
- use body language (facial expression, gestures, body position, eye movements) as part of your presentation.

Non-fiction texts

The category of non-fiction text is a broad one. It not only includes **biographies** and **autobiographies**, but also essays and books, such as *Longitude* by Dava Sobel, which explore the development of an idea. (*Longitude* tells the story of the invention of a timepiece which would measure longitude accurately.)

It is easy to describe the features of fictional texts, but not so easy to be explicit about the features of non-fiction. Such features might include a table of contents, an index, a glossary, an introduction, and graphics such as diagrams, sketches and photographs. (This textbook is an example of a non-fiction text which includes many of these features.) The presence of any or all of these features is very helpful to the reader in terms of fostering understanding.

But is it the case that a non-fiction text is 'true'?

We sometimes speak of non-fiction as 'factual' and it is true that non-fiction usually deals in facts. But as readers we have to remember that these are facts that have been selected by the author, keeping in mind his or her purpose and audience. There may be other 'facts', other viewpoints that have not been presented to us. Biographies and autobiographies are particularly interesting from this point of view. When famous people write their autobiographies — or have biographies written about them — there are often claims of bias or omission.

See pages 102–3 for an extract from an autobiography by John McGahern, titled *Memoir*. An autobiography necessarily depends on one point of view only. Read the extract from *Memoir* and decide whether there is another point of view which might give a different version of the described event.

Many non-fiction texts, though, are written in order to provide information or to present an argument. What follows is an extract from a non-fiction book titled *Everything Bad is Good for You* by Steven Johnson. In this extract, Johnson argues in favour of video games — the 'bad' video games, he believes, are in fact 'good' for you.

Learning activity 1.9

Before you read the extract, answer these questions:

1. Why do some people think video games are 'bad' for those who play them?
2. What kind of people do you think are likely to share this opinion?
3. What is your opinion?

Now read the extract and answer the next set of questions.

1. Draw on the information in the extract to create a **Venn diagram** which shows differences and similarities between video games and traditional games.
2. Complete this sentence: According to this extract, whether or not you succeed at a game often depends on your ability to work out what the rules are, rather than your ....
3. James Paul Gee has identified a process that players need to use in order to be successful. Explain the process in your own words.
4. From your own experience, do you think that the process described by Gee is equally relevant to all video games? Or is it applicable only to certain kinds of video games?
5. Johnson says: 'When gamers interact with these environments, they are learning the basic procedure of the scientific method.' How is this claim an important part of his argument that video games are 'good' for you?
6. In this extract, Johnson makes use of comparisons, reference to experts and examples in order to get his point across. Draw up a table as follows and identify the occasions on which he uses each of these strategies.

Strategy	Examples
Comparison	
Expert opinion	
Examples	

7. What point is Johnson making when he refers to the PacMan game?
8. Do you think that this extract would convince people who have a negative opinion of computer games to change their minds? Why?/Why not?

Everything Bad is Good for You

Most video games differ from traditional games like chess or Monopoly in the way they withhold information about the underlying rules of the system. When you play chess at anything beyond a beginner's level, the rules of the game contain no ambiguity: you know exactly the moves allowed for each piece, the procedures that allow one piece to capture another. The question that confronts you sitting down at the chessboard is not: What are the rules here? The question is: What kind of strategy can I concoct that will best exploit those rules to my advantage?

In the video game world, on the other hand, the rules are rarely established in their entirety before you sit down to play. You're given a few basic instructions about how to manipulate objects or characters on the screen, and a sense of some kind of immediate objective. But many of the rules — the identity of your ultimate goal and the techniques available for reaching that goal — become apparent only through exploring the world. You literally learn by playing. This is one reason video games can

be frustrating to the non-initiated. You sit down at the computer and say, 'What am I supposed to do?' The regular gamers in the room have to explain: 'You're supposed to figure out what you're supposed to do.' You have to probe the depths of the game's logic to make sense of it, and like most probing expeditions, you get results by trial and error, by stumbling across things, by following hunches. In almost every other endeavor that we describe using the language of games — poker, baseball, backgammon, capture the flag — any ambiguity in the rules and objectives of the game would be a fatal flaw. In video games, on the other hand, it's a core part of the experience. Many game narratives contain mysteries of sorts modeled after Hollywood plotlines — Who murdered my brother? Who stole the plutonium? — but the ultimate mystery that drives players deeper into the gameworld is a more self-referential one: how is this game played? Non-gamers usually imagine that mastering a game is largely a matter of learning to push buttons faster, which no doubt accounts for all the 'hand-eye coordination' clichés. But for many popular games, the ultimate key to success lies in deciphering the rules, and not manipulating joysticks…

The games scholar James Paul Gee breaks probing down into a four-part process, which he calls the 'probe, hypothesize, reprobe, rethink' cycle:

1. The player must *probe* the virtual world (which involves looking around the current environment, clicking on something, or engaging in a certain action).
2. Based on reflection while probing and afterward, the player must form a *hypothesis* about what something (a text, object, artifact, event, or action) might mean in a usefully situated way.
3. The player *reprobes* the world with that hypothesis in mind, seeing what effect he or she gets.
4. The player treats this effect as feedback from the world and accepts or *rethinks* his or her original hypothesis.

Put another way: When gamers interact with these environments, they are learning the basic procedure of the scientific method.

Probing often takes the form of seeking out the limits of the simulation, the points at which the illusion of reality breaks down, and you can sense that's all just a bunch of algorithms behind the curtain. The first celebrated instance of this arrived in the early eighties with the hugely popular arcade game *PacMan*. The game had its rules, which were so simple you could express them in three sentences: gobble all the dots to finish a level; avoid the monsters unless you've eaten one of the large dots, at which point you can eat the monsters; eat the prizes for extra points. But experienced *PacMan* players soon discovered that the monsters roamed the maze in predictable ways, and if you followed a certain course — literally called a 'pattern' — you'd complete the level without losing a man every time you played. Patterns weren't built into the official rules of the game; they were a legacy effect of the limited computational power of those arcade machines, and the predictable way in which the monsters' behavior had been programmed. To detect those limitations, you had to probe the *PacMan* game by playing it hundreds of times, experimenting with different strategies until one sequence revealed itself.

Probing the limits of the game physics is another oft-ignored facet of gaming culture. I suspect most hard-core gamers would acknowledge that part of the pleasure of their immersions comes from this kind of pursuit, searching out the points where the system shows its flaws — partially because those flaws can be exploited, as in *PacMan*'s patterns, but also because there's something strangely satisfying about defining the edges of a simulation, learning what it's capable of and where it breaks down. Some people find this kind of exploration appealing in ordinary life: they're the sort that actually enjoys looking under the hood of the car, or memorizing UNIX commands. But video games *force* you to speculate about what's going on under the hood. If you don't think about the underlying mechanics of the simulation — even if that thinking happens in a semiconscious way — you won't last very long in the game. You have to probe to progress.

Extract from *Everything Bad is Good for You* by Steven Johnson

Don't forget to edit and proofread your response. See pages 97–8 for guidelines.

Assessment tasks | Responding to non-fiction

1. Prepare an informational datashow presentation on a non-fiction text for a specified audience. The presentation should include a synopsis or summary of the content, background and expertise of the author/s, reviews which have appeared in the media and your own analysis of the impact and interest level of the text.
2. Use a non-fiction text as the focus for a promotional website. Design a website which includes, at least, appropriate photographs and diagrams, links to information about the author/s, a synopsis of the book and reviews. Present your website to the class, explaining your design choices.
3. Compare the print version of the non-fiction text with its film version.
4. Compare two different biographical accounts of the same person's life. Choose two or three key events in or aspects of the subject's life and compare the way in which each biography deals with them.
5. Transpose the description of a key event in the non-fiction text into a short story or playscript.
6. Write an analytical response to a topic set by your teacher.

See page 44 for the criteria for assessment.

Short stories

Because of the limitations of length, the writer of short stories cannot hope to develop a plot or explore theme, character or setting as thoroughly as the novelist or dramatist. Instead, he or she has to decide which of these aspects will be given prominence in the story. There is less room for exposition, for setting up a situation and establishing character and the nature of the conflict. Economy is necessary, and the reader is usually presented with a limited and self-contained world that is being explored from a particular perspective and for a particular purpose: it may be the examination of an idea, theme or setting, the portrayal of a character, a reflection on the significance of a certain event or events, or the telling of a story. In many modern stories there is little or no plot, or the plot is of very minor significance and there may be no narrative closure or resolution.

Learning activity **1.10**

Following is a story called 'Examination Day' by Henry Slesar. Read the story and answer the questions:

Examination Day

The Jordans never spoke of the exam, not until their son, Dickie, was twelve years old. It was on his birthday that Mrs. Jordan first mentioned the subject in his presence, and the anxious manner of her speech caused her husband to answer sharply.

'Forget about it,' he said. 'He'll do all right.'

They were at the breakfast table, and the boy looked up from his plate curiously. He was an alert-eyed youngster, with flat blond hair and a quick, nervous manner. He didn't understand what the sudden trouble was about, but he did know that today was his birthday, and he wanted a happy day above all. Somewhere in the little apartment there were wrapped packages waiting to be opened, and in the tiny wall-kitchen, something warm and sweet was being prepared in the automatic stove. He wanted the day to be happy, and the moistness of his mother's eyes, the scowl on his father's face, spoiled the good mood with which he had greeted the morning.

'What exam?' he asked.

His mother looked at the tablecloth. 'It's just a sort of Government intelligence test they give children at the age of twelve. You'll be getting it next week. It's nothing to worry about.'

'You mean a test like in school?'

'Something like that,' his father said, getting up from the table. 'Go read your comic books, Dickie.'

The boy rose and wandered toward that part of the living room which had always been 'his' corner. He fingered the topmost comic of the stack, but seemed uninterested in the colorful squares of fast-paced action. He wandered toward the window, and peered gloomily at the mist outside the glass.

'Why did it have to rain *today?*' he said. 'Why couldn't it rain tomorrow?'

His father, now slumped into an armchair with the Government newspaper, rattled the sheets suddenly. 'Because it just did, that's all. Rain makes the grass grow.'

'Why, Dad?'

'Because it does, that's all.'

Dickie wrinkled up his brow. 'What makes it green, though? The grass?'

'Nobody knows,' his father snapped, then immediately regretted the tone of his voice.

Later in the day, it was birthday time again. His mother beamed as she handed over the gaily-colored packages, and even his father managed a grin and a rumple-of-the-hair. He kissed his mother and shook hands with his father. Then the birthday cake was brought forth, and the ceremonies ended.

An hour later, seated by the window, he watched the sun force its way between the clouds.

'Dad,' he said, 'how far away is the sun?'

'Five thousand miles,' his father said.

Dick sat at the breakfast table and again saw moisture in his mother's eyes. He didn't connect her tears with the exam until his father suddenly brought the subject to light again.

'Well, Dickie,' he said, with a manly frown, 'you've got an appointment today.'

'I know, Dad, I hope —'

'Now it's nothing to worry about. Thousands of children take this test every day. The Government wants to know how smart you are, Dickie. That's all there is to it.'

'I get good marks in school,' he said.

'This is different. This is a — special kind of test. They give you this stuff to drink, you see, and then you go into a room where there's a sort of machine —'

'What stuff to drink?' Dickie said.

'It's nothing. It tastes like peppermint. It's just to make sure you answer the questions truthfully. Not that the Government thinks you won't tell the truth, but this stuff makes *sure*.'

Dickie's face showed puzzlement, and a touch of fright. He looked at his mother, and she arranged her face into a misty smile.

'Everything will be all right,' she said.

'Of course it will,' his father agreed. 'You're a good boy, Dickie; you'll make out fine. Then we'll come home and celebrate. All right?'

'Yes, sir,' Dickie said.

They entered the Government Educational Building fifteen minutes before the appointed hour. They crossed the marble floors of the great lobby, passed beneath an archway and entered an automatic elevator that brought them to the fourth floor.

There was a young man wearing a uniform, seated at a polished desk in front of Room 404. He held a clipboard in his hand, and he checked the list down to the Js and permitted the Jordans to enter.

The room was as cold and official as a courtroom, with long benches and metal tables. There were several fathers and sons already there, and a thin-lipped woman with short black hair was passing out sheets of paper.

Mr. Jordan filled out the form, and returned it to the clerk. Then he told Dickie: 'It won't be long now. When they call your name, you just go through the doorway at that end of the room.' He indicated the door with his finger.

A loudspeaker crackled and called off the first name. Dickie saw a boy leave his father's side and walk slowly toward the door.

At five minutes of eleven they called the name of Jordan.

'Good luck, son,' his father said, without looking at him. 'I'll call for you when the test is over.'

Dickie walked to the door and turned the knob. The room inside was dim, and he could barely make out the features of the uniformed attendant who greeted him.

'Sit down,' the man said softly. He indicated a high stool beside his desk. 'Your name's Richard Jordan?'

'Yes, sir.'

'Your classification number is 600–115. Drink this, Richard.'

He lifted a plastic cup from the desk and handed it to the boy. The liquid inside had the consistency of buttermilk, tasted only vaguely of the promised peppermint. Dickie downed it, and handed the man the empty cup.

He sat in silence, feeling a little sleepy, while the man wrote busily on a sheet of paper. Then the attendant looked at his watch, and rose to stand only inches from Dickie's face. He unclipped a pen-like object from his pocket, and flashed a tiny light into the boy's eyes.

'All right,' he said. 'Come with me, Richard.'

He led Dickie to the end of the room, where a single wooden armchair faced a multi-dialed computing machine. There was a microphone on the left arm of the chair, and when the boy sat down, he found its pinpoint head conveniently at his mouth.

'Now just relax, Richard. You'll be asked some questions, and you think them over carefully. Then give your answers into the microphone. The machine will take care of the rest.'

'Yes, sir.'

'I'll leave you alone now. Whenever you want to start, just say "ready" into the microphone.'

'Yes, sir.'

The man squeezed his shoulder, and left.

Dickie said, 'Ready.'

Lights appeared on the machine, and something inside whirred. A voice said:

'Complete this sequence. One, four, seven, ten …'

Mr. and Mrs. Jordan were in the living room, not speaking, not even speculating.

It was almost four o'clock when the telephone rang. The woman tried to reach it first, but her husband was quicker.

'Mr. Jordan?'

The voice was cool; a brisk, official voice.

'Yes, speaking.'

'This is the Government Educational Service. Your son, Richard M. Jordan, Classification 600–115, has completed the Government examination. We regret to inform you that his intelligence quotient is higher than the Government regulation, according to Rule 84, Section 5, of the New Code.'

Across the room, the woman cried out, knowing nothing except the emotion she read on her husband's face.

'You may tell us by telephone,' the voice went on, 'whether you wish his body buried by the Government or would you prefer a private burial place? The fee for Government burial is ten dollars.'

Henry Slesar

1. What genre does this short story belong to? Refer to page 2 if you are unsure what is meant by a 'genre'. Explain your answer.
2. In your opinion, is the focus of this short story on plot, character, theme or setting? Explain your answer.

3. List the four words and **phrases** that reveal that Mr and Mrs Jordan are anxious about the examination and the results.
4. Dickie was reading comic books and Mr Jordan was reading the Government newspaper. By the end of the story we understand the significance of their choice of reading matter. Explain.
5. Dickie asks his father several questions to which his father does not know the answers. How is this significant?
6. Suggest some reasons why the Government might want to make sure that children taking the test answered the questions truthfully?
7. List the five words and phrases used by the author to describe the Government Education Building. What kind of environment is he seeking to create by using these words and phrases?
8. How does the author slow down the action once Dickie is called into the examination? Why do you think he does this?
9. How would you describe the language used by the government official who telephones the Jordans with the results? Why do you think the author chose to have the official speak like this?
10. What effect is created by the sentence 'The fee for Government burial is ten dollars.'?
11. Complete this sentence. In this short story, the Government kills those students who have an IQ higher than that allowed by Government regulations because ....

See pages 13–14 for guidance on how to construct a written analytical response.

Assessment tasks | Responding to short stories

Choose one of the following suggestions and use it to respond, either orally or in writing, to a short story or stories that you have studied.

1. Write an analytical response to a topic set by your teacher.
2. Analyse the use of symbolism in the story.
3. Retell the events of the story from another point of view.
4. Retell the events in the story in another form (for example, poem, film script, news report).
5. Use the events of the story to create a **storyboard** for a film.
6. Analyse the ways in which the writer creates character in the short story.
7. Discuss the ways in which the writer explores a specific theme in his/her short story.
8. Decide what the dominant reading of the short story is and discuss whether other readings are possible.
9. Analyse the ways in which certain aspects (themes, **imagery**, types of character) recur in the stories of a particular writer.

See page 44 for the criteria for assessment.

See page 15 for advice about oral responses.

Don't forget to edit and proofread your response. See pages 97–8 for guidelines.

Drama

Some of the terminology used to discuss and analyse plays is the same as that used when discussing novels. Like novels, plays have characters, settings and themes. But when we refer to what happens in the play, we call this the *action*, and what is actually said by the characters is the *dialogue*.

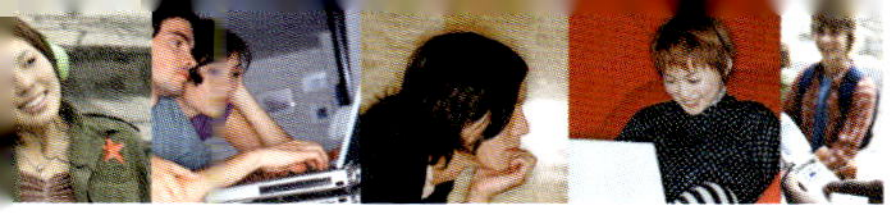

Characters in plays are revealed by what they say and how they say it. However, playwrights do not usually offer much in the way of stage directions to indicate how lines should be delivered or what the actor should be doing as he or she speaks. This interpretation is left to the actor and the director.

Strategies | Before you begin to read a playscript

- Scan the playscript to see whether there is an introduction. Read this before you start reading the play.
- Examine the list of characters. The list will often provide you with information about who the characters are and their relationships with each other.
- Skim through the playscript to ascertain the structure of the play. How many scenes are there? How many settings? (Read the information about the setting that is often provided at the beginning of the scene.) Is the playscript divided into acts?

Learning activity **1.11**

Read the extracts from *Stolen* by Jane Harrison and then answer these questions.

'The Chosen'

In this scene the mother and father have adopted Anne from the Children's Home.

1. How do the names given to the scenes focus attention on their content? (It is unusual to name scenes in a play; usually they have numbers.)
2. In 'The Chosen' scene, the mother and father have no personal names and no real physical presence. How does this influence the way in which you regard the characters and what happens in the scene?
3. The italicised information for this scene tells us that the parents and Anne speak in turn but without hearing what the other is saying. Why do you think the playwright chose to use this particular technique?
4. The mother and father promise each other that they will give Anne 'the best of everything' — a good education, a sense of security and a good upbringing. Discuss what these descriptions reveal about the parents' values and how those values might coincide or conflict with the values of Anne's natural parents.

'Anne's told she's Aboriginal'

5. What does this scene reveal about the parents' attitudes towards indigenous people?
6. How does the dialogue reveal Anne's reaction to the revelation?
7. Imagine the mother later describes this scene to a close friend. What would she say? (Write the speech or act it out.)

'Am I black or white?'

8. What is the purpose of the first speech in this scene?
9. Analyse the appeals made by each group of parents in order to persuade Anne that she belongs with them.
10. What is the effect of the various voices repeating 'Who do you think you are?' and what possible ways can this question be interpreted?

The Chosen

Night lighting with only ANNE *spotlit, sitting on her bed.* ANNE'S WHITE PARENTS *are represented by shadows falling on to a Venetian blind or a white sheet. Her* PARENTS *and* ANNE *speak in turn but do not hear what the other is saying.*

Anne They always said I was special because they chose me. That's what they always said—

Father We didn't have you, Princess, we chose you.
[*To* MOTHER]
Do you think we made a good choice?

Mother [*to* FATHER] Oh yes, she was by far the best.

Anne The day Mum and Dad brought me home they gave me a doll that had white hair. I'd never seen such a doll. And I got my own room.

Mother There's new pyjamas on the bed. They might be a bit big — but I can buy more tomorrow. Now, Anne, just tell us if you need anything. Do you need another blanket? Did you want more to eat?

Anne I mustn't have been in that children's home long, cos I can't remember it at all.

Father It's time to go to beddy-byes now, Anne. Say your prayers.

ANNE *starts her prayers.*

[*To* MOTHER] We'll give her the best of everything.

Mother [*to* FATHER] Oh yes, a good education …

Father [*to* MOTHER] My word! A sense of security …

Mother [*to* FATHER] Yes! And a good upbringing …

They nod to each other.

Anne … God bless Mum and Dad. And God bless me.

They all sleep.

Anne's told she's Aboriginal

ANNE'S PARENTS *are anxiously discussing something off to one side of Anne's bed while she is sitting slumped on the bed, filing her nails.*

Father [*to* MOTHER] Do you think it's the right thing?

Mother [*to* FATHER] I think it's for the best.

They agree, then speak to ANNE.

Father Princess, we need to tell you something …

Mother It's not been an easy decision for us …

Father We feel we have no choice and we want you to hear it from us.

Mother We don't want you to hear rumours …

Anne What are you talking about?

Mother We want you to know we'll always stand by you.

Anne What are you talking about …?

Father There's no easy way to tell you … you know we adopted you, Anne. We chose you at the Cranby Children's Home.

Anne So … I knew that …

Mother Anne, there's something else … it's about your mother … she's dying and she wants to see you and … she's an *Aboriginal* lady.

Anne Why haven't you told me that she's—?

Mother [*tentatively*] —Aboriginal?

Anne Alive! And that's she wants to see me?

Mother Oh.

MOTHER *starts to weep.*

Father We thought it was for the best. You know we love you like our own daughter.

Mother We love you and want the best for you.

Father Anne, there's no reason why anything should change. You only have to see her … once.

Mother No one need ever know.

Anne *I* know. And I want to know why you didn't tell me about this before.

Mother [*sobbing*] The shame …

Anne [*angrily*] You *should* be ashamed—

ANNE'S FATHER *draws himself upright and puts his arm around* MOTHER.

Father *We've* nothing to be ashamed of. We've always acted in your best interests! Look what you've done to your mother!

They walk away, talking amongst themselves. Alone, ANNE *is so confused.*

Anne Mum … Dad! Mum! Dad! Why? This is a nightmare!

She breaks down as the lights go down.

Am I black or white?

Anne [*a little bitter*] So I finally went to meet my real mother. I thought they'd live in the country or the outback or something. You know — 'at one with the land'. But here they were in a Housing Commission flat, all crowded in. I just thought it would be different, somehow.

The sheet is held up and we see the silhouette of a woman and a man, first the white parents and then black family members.

Father [*off*] You're one of us, Anne — we've brought you up as one of our own.

Mother [*off*] We've given you everything — a home, an education, a future.

Father [*off*] Don't you appreciate all we've done?

She runs over to the other side of the stage.

First Black Voice [*off*] But we're your real family.

Second Black Voice [*off*] Yeah, and you have to come back to us — it's where you belong, girl.

First Black Voice [*off*] We lot have got to stick together, you know.

She runs back to where she began.

Mother [*off*] Are you going to just throw away everything we have taught you?

Father [*off*] If you go back, we won't have you here.

Mother [*off*] How can you do this to us, you're breaking our hearts?

She turns away, holding her head as if in pain.

First Black Voice [*off*] Of course, don't just think you have an automatic right to be here.

Second Black Voice [*off*] You have to earn your place if you wanna be involved in our community.

Third Black Voice [*off*] We wanna know who your family is, where you're from and what you've done.

Voices are crowding in on her.

White Voice [*off*] You know nothing about them.

Black Voice [*off*] You know nothing about being a Koori.

Black Voice [*off*] Maybe ya just wanna jump on the bandwagon.

White Voice [*off*] Maybe ya just wanna get a cheap loan or a handout.

They laugh. She's shaken and confused.

White Voices [*together, off*] Who do you think you are?

Black Voices [*together, off*] Who do you think you are?

The voices continue to murmur 'Who do you think you are?' over and over, quietly and repeatedly. ANNE *pulls the sheet down to reveal the others.*

Jane Harrison, *Stolen*

From page to stage

Although you might study the print form of a play, you should always remember that it is on stage that the play truly belongs. Sometimes you might find the performance of a play disappointing because you have internalised your own interpretation of a character or scene; at other times you will find the originality of the interpretation offered by the director and actors very impressive.

If you are studying a play that has been made into a film — *Death of a Salesman*, for instance, or *A Streetcar Named Desire* — it would be interesting to see the film interpretation as well, and to discuss any changes that have been made. Try to explain why those decisions might have been taken, and discuss how effective you find them.

Learning activity **1.12**

1. Choose a scene from a play that you are studying and explore the different ways in which actors might deliver their lines. Think about the facial expressions, gestures and movements that might accompany the lines. How many different interpretations can you think of?
2. Divide into groups to present different interpretations of a scene from the play to the rest of the class.

Structure

Whereas novels are usually structured in terms of chapters or equivalent sections, plays make use of acts and scenes to divide up the action. An act is divided into a number of scenes, which may or may not be clearly marked in the text. A Shakespearean play, for example, has clear demarcations between acts and between scenes. Many modern plays switch between scenes (and locations) without warning. On the page this can sometimes be confusing, but on the stage other clues (such as clothing, lighting and even the demeanor of the actors) help the audience to distinguish one scene from another.

The structure of a play can be chronological, circular (starting at the end of a sequence of events, backtracking to explain, and ending at the starting point or slightly beyond), or even in reverse chronological order. It may move backwards and forwards between the present and the past. In terms of structure, plays can be much more adventurous than novels because clues such as the set and costuming can make time **transitions** readily accessible to the audience.

Learning activity **1.13**

Examine the structure of a play that you are studying and draw a diagram that shows the main events of the play, including the climax or most important event.

If the structure is a simple one, you might be able to depict it in a line graph. If it is more complex, you will probably need a series of boxes and arrows. There is no single answer to this, so you can be creative.

Assessment tasks | Responding to drama

See pages 13–14 for guidance on how to construct a written analytical response.

Choose one of the following tasks.

1. Write an analytical response to a topic set by your teacher.
2. Write a new scene portraying an event that occurs offstage in the original play.
3. Write an extra scene that could have occurred at the beginning or end of the play.
4. Transpose a scene to another setting, for example to another era or another place.
5. Act out the extra or transposed scene.
6. Rewrite a key scene in the play, changing, in a plausible way, the event that occurred so that the action of the play from that point would have been quite different.
7. Rewrite a scene from the play, adding detailed director's notes as instructions for the way in which it should be acted.
8. Write a scene (or part of a scene) from the play as a film script and then film it.
9. Write a review of a production of the play.
10. Roleplay an interview with a character in a play. One person plays the role of the interviewer and asks a series of questions about motivation and behaviour; the other assumes the role of the character.
11. Show a scene from a film version of the play to the class and discuss how effective you found it.
12. Choose one of the following tasks and present your response in written or oral form.
    (a) Choose a key scene from the play and discuss its significance to the play as a whole.

Don't forget to edit and proofread your response. See pages 97–8 for guidelines.

(b) Analyse the way in which dialogue reveals character.
(c) Analyse the importance of the setting of the play and its relationship to the theme.
(d) Discuss and analyse the use of symbols in the play.
(e) Examine the ways in which the structure of the play shapes our understanding of characters and theme.

See page 44 for the criteria for assessment.

Shakespearean drama

During his relatively short life (1564–1616), Shakespeare wrote over 30 plays — tragedies, comedies and histories — many of which are still being studied by students, performed by theatre companies and produced as films. Some, like *Romeo and Juliet*, have almost achieved cult status.

Because his themes are ones that have perennial significance — power, betrayal, love, jealousy, revenge, the battle of the sexes, the search for identity, the nature of leadership, war and friendship — many directors are keen to present both traditional performances and modern adaptations. Some of these adaptations are controversial, and their success is debatable, but they are always interesting.

Shakespeare on film

Hamlet
1948 Directed by Laurence Olivier, starring Laurence Olivier
1990 Directed by Franco Zeffirelli, starring Mel Gibson
1997 Directed by Kenneth Branagh, starring Kenneth Branagh

Henry V
1944 Directed by Laurence Olivier, starring Laurence Olivier
1988 Directed by Kenneth Branagh, starring Kenneth Branagh

Julius Caesar
1953 Directed by Joseph Mankiewicz

King Lear
1969 Directed by Peter Brook

Much Ado About Nothing
1993 Directed by Kenneth Branagh

Macbeth
1971 Directed by Roman Polanski

Othello
1952 Directed by Orson Welles
1965 Directed by Stuart Burge, starring Laurence Olivier
1995 Directed by Oliver Parker, starring Laurence Fishburne

Richard III
1955 Directed by Laurence Olivier
1995 Directed by Richard Loncraine, starring Ian McKellen

Romeo and Juliet
1954 Directed by Renato Castellani
1968 Directed by Franco Zeffirelli
1997 Directed by Baz Luhrmann

Twelfth Night
1995 Directed by Trevor Nunn

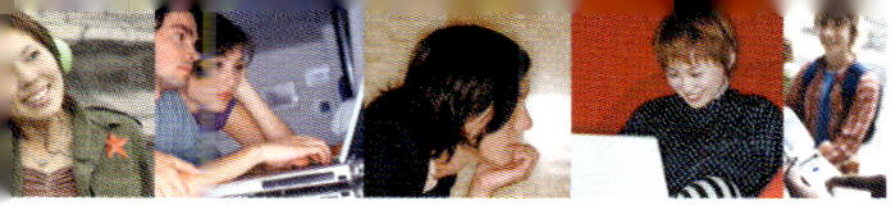

Scene from *Romeo and Juliet*, 1997, directed by Baz Luhrmann

The language of Shakespeare

Shakespeare wrote what is called **verse drama**, most of his plays being written in **blank verse**. That is, they were written in **iambic pentameter** and they did not rhyme. However, many of his plays include scenes that are written entirely in **prose**. Often these are scenes that are comic in intention or feature lesser or lower-class characters. What do you think might have been the reasons why Shakespeare reserved poetry for the main scenes and wrote the others in prose?

See pages 34–8 for more information on imagery, including the use of personification and similes.

Shakespeare's language is rich in imagery, **metaphor** and **simile**. Consider the example below from *Macbeth*, one of Shakespeare's tragedies. In this speech, Macbeth is trying to decide whether or not he should kill his king, Duncan, and concludes that Duncan's virtues are such that, were he to die, the memory of them would arouse pity and horror in everyone. He uses **personification** (the virtues would 'plead' and pity would 'blow the horrid deed in every eye'), simile ('like a naked new-born babe') and the heavenly imagery of 'angels' and 'cherubim'.

Learning activity **1.14**

The following speech is one which is made by Macbeth when he is considering whether or not he should kill the king, Duncan. Read the speech and answer the questions that follow.

Besides, this Duncan
Hath borne his faculties so meek, hath been
So clear in his great office, that his virtues
Will plead like angels, trumpet-tongued against
The deep damnation of his taking-off,
And pity, like a naked new-born babe,
Striding the blast, or heaven's cherubim, horsed
Upon the sightless couriers of the air,
Shall blow the horrid deed in every eye
That tears shall drown the wind.

1. Find an example of personification in this speech and explain how it works.
2. Pity is compared to a 'naked new-born babe'. Do you think that this is an effective simile? Why?/Why not?
3. Macbeth thinks that Duncan has been such a good leader that if he is killed 'his virtues/Will plead like angels trumpet-tongued' against his death. What image do you think Shakespeare wanted to create when he described the angels as 'trumpet-tongued'?
4. 'Deep damnation' is an example of **alliteration**. Do you find it an effective use of alliteration? Why?/Why not?
5. There is a great deal of movement in this speech. List the words that contribute to creating this impression.
6. This speech vividly depicts the power of Macbeth's imagination. Make a sketch of the scene which Macbeth evokes here.
7. Why do you think Shakespeare chose to use heavenly imagery (angels and cherubim)?

Shakespeare's soliloquies

A soliloquy is a speech made by a character, usually when he or she is alone on the stage, in which his or her thoughts are revealed to the audience. Soliloquies reveal the character's inner conflicts, motivations and intentions. The previous speech made by Macbeth is an example of a soliloquy.

Below is a soliloquy from *Othello*, in which Iago, one of Shakespeare's truly evil characters, hatches a plan to take revenge on Cassio, who has been given a position that Iago had expected to be given. He hopes to get Cassio out of the way so that Othello will give him the position instead. He also hates Othello (the Moor), so he will be happy to be able to hurt him in the process.

Learning activity **1.15**

Read the following speech by Iago from *Othello*, Act I, Scene iii, and answer the questions that follow.

… I hate the Moor,
And it is thought abroad that 'twixt my sheets
He has done my office. I know not if't be true,
But I, for mere suspicion in that kind,
Will do as if for surety. He holds me well:
The better shall my purpose work on him.
Cassio's a proper man. Let me see now,
To get his place, and to plume up my will
In double knavery — how, how? Let's see.
After some time to abuse Othello's ears
That he is too familiar with his wife;
He hath a person and a smooth dispose
To be suspected, framed to make women false.
The Moor is of a free and open nature,
That thinks men honest that but seem to be so,

'twixt: between
He has done my office: he has slept with Iago's wife
proper: handsome
To get his place: to get Cassio's job
abuse Othello's ears: tell Othello lies
he: that is, Cassio
dispose: manner
person: appearance
framed to make women false: likely to encourage women to be unfaithful
That thinks men honest that but seem to be so: honest himself, he naively believes others are too just because they seem so

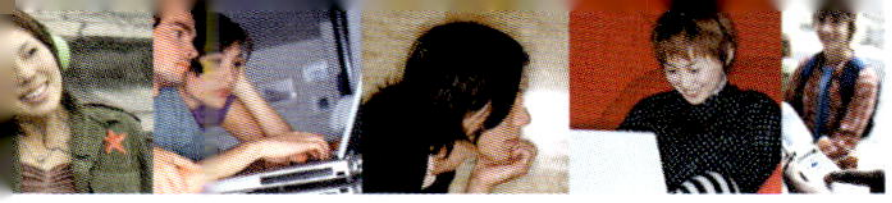

And will as tenderly be led by th' nose
As asses are.
I ha't. It is ingendered. Hell and night
Must bring this monstrous birth to the world's light.

I have it! The Idea has begun or been conceived.

1. Does Iago hate Othello because it is rumoured that Othello has slept with Iago's wife? Explain your answer.
2. What qualities in Cassio does Iago say he will make use of?
3. What qualities in Othello does Iago think he can play on?
4. How does Shakespeare convey the idea of Iago thinking aloud and making up his plan as he goes along?
5. How does Iago show his contempt for Othello?
6. Which phrases indicate that Iago is aware that his plan is an evil one?

The structure of Shakespearean plays

Shakespearean plays are always divided into five acts, each of which represents a section of the action. Each act is subdivided into several scenes, the setting of which can vary considerably. The lines in each scene are numbered for easy reference; for example, III, ii, 56–90 refers to Act III, Scene 2, lines 56 to 90.

The following diagram, referring to *Romeo and Juliet*, shows how a Shakespearean plot develops. Use it as a model to make a diagram of a Shakespearean play that you are studying.

THE STRUCTURE OF A SHAKESPEAREAN PLAY

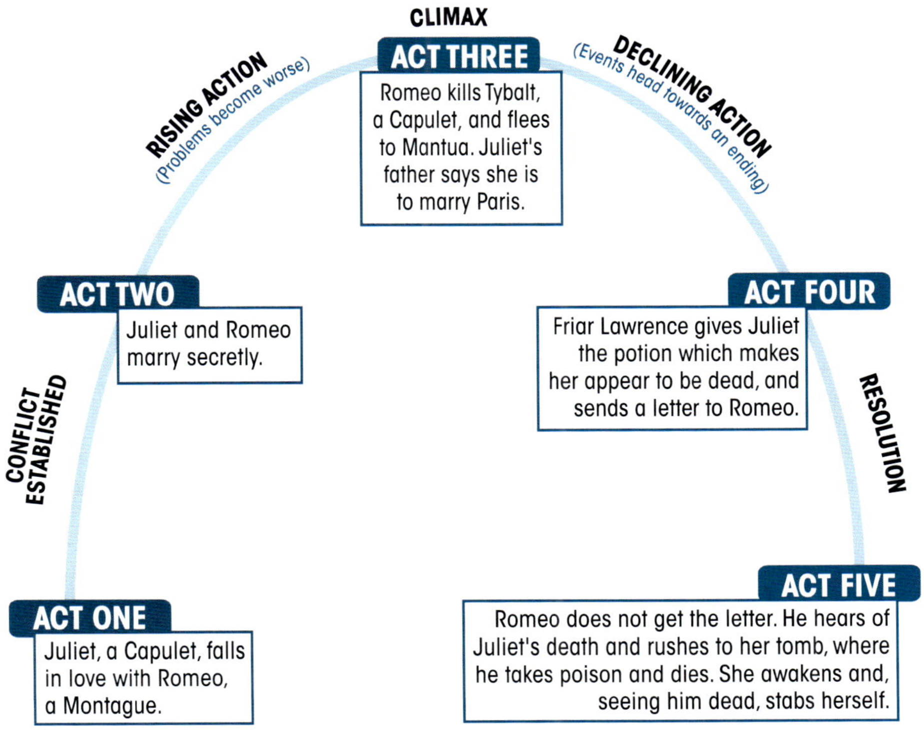

How to quote from a Shakespearean play

- If you are only quoting a word or two, put them in inverted commas and include them in your sentence. For example: the play opens with Verona's 'rebellious subjects' fighting in the streets.
- If you are quoting a couple of lines, you may also include these in the text, but you must mark the line endings with a slash and use ellipses (three full stops) to indicate if you have left anything out. For example: when Paris first asks Capulet if he can marry Juliet, Capulet replies that Juliet '... is yet a stranger in the world/She hath not seen the change of fourteen years'.
- If you are quoting four or more lines you should write or type the lines exactly as they appear in the text, marking them off from your writing by indenting them. For example, Romeo's highly romantic nature is evident in the way in which he speaks of Juliet as he watches her from the garden:

  But soft, what light through yonder window breaks?
  It is the east, and Juliet is the sun.
  Arise, fair sun, and kill the envious moon,
  Who is already sick and pale with grief
  That thou, her maid, art far more fair than she.

Assessment tasks | Responding to Shakespearean plays

1. Choose a scene where a character is present but does not speak. Analyse the events of that scene from this character's point of view.
2. Create character profiles. Work in pairs to produce a list of the play's key quotations that refer to the chosen character. The quotations can include what the character says as well as what is said about the character by others. (These profiles could be presented in writing or as an electronic text incorporating sound and visuals.)
3. Conduct an interview with a character. This can be done in pairs, or the character can occupy a 'hot seat' and be questioned by the class about his or her motives and behaviour.
4. A variation of the above task is to put a character on trial. Witnesses for and against the prosecution can be called, and a judge or jury can present a final summing up.
5. Write a newspaper or magazine feature article on the life and achievements of a central character. Include interviews with other characters who give their opinions.
6. Write an obituary for a character who dies in the course of the play.
7. Choose a scene from the play. Photocopy it onto A3 paper and then write a set of director's notes in the margins, indicating how actors should play the scene. (Alternatively, use the Insert Comments function in Word on the computer to perform the same task.)
8. Prepare a storyboard of a scene to be used as a preliminary to filming.
9. Act out a scene from the play. The setting could either be one consistent with the Shakespearean era or you might like to transpose the scene to a modern setting, with appropriate costuming, set and props.
10. Write an analytical response to a topic set by your teacher.

See pages 13–14 for guidance on how to construct a written analytical response.

See page 44 for the criteria for assessment.

Quotations from the play can be used as evidence to support your point of view, but try to avoid using too many quotations, and make sure the quotations you select are ones that are relevant to the point of view that you are arguing.

Don't forget to edit and proofread your response. See pages 97–8 for guidelines.

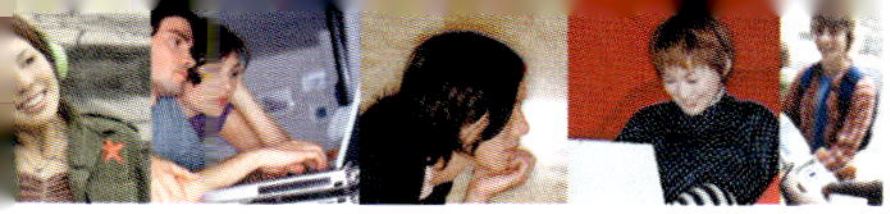

Poetry

There are many different definitions of poetry, some more helpful than others. However, whatever form it happens to take, poetry presents us with ideas and images in a far more concentrated way than prose. There are, perhaps, some subjects that lend themselves more readily to poetry, but in reality anything that can be written about in prose can also be written about in poetry. *Love, Ghosts & Nose Hair* by Steven Herrick is one example of the growing genre of young adolescent novels written in verse.

Ways of approaching a poem

When reading a poem, in order to derive meaning and to appreciate it fully, there are several aspects of which you should be aware. As with every other form of art — painting, music, film — if you know what to look for, then your enjoyment is greatly enhanced.

Strategies | Before you begin to read a poem

- Look at the title. What do you think the poem might be about?
- Scan the poem. What do you notice about its structure? (Is it divided into verses? Does it rhyme? Can you identify a **rhyming pattern**?)
- Scan the poem again. Are there words that you don't know? Highlight them or write them down. Discuss possible meanings with a partner.

While reading the poem

- Remember that the punctuation of the poem helps you to understand it. You won't necessarily stop at the end of each line.
- Reading the poem aloud to a partner can help your understanding.

Purpose

Just as the subject matter of poetry varies, so too does the purpose of the poem. Apart from gaining personal pleasure in his or her manipulation of words and sounds, a poet might write a poem in order to:

- reflect on the meaning of a particular personal experience
- celebrate or describe a person, place or thing
- explore an emotion, such as love
- comment on an aspect of society
- tell a story
- explore a mood
- experiment with language
- condemn (for example, the horrors of war or poverty).

Can you add to this list?

Learning activity **1.16**

Read the following poem. In pairs, discuss its possible purpose. There could, of course, be more than one purpose.

Silence

The blind spins up
snatched by the window frame.
I gaze at this blank day.
Here are the trees so very green
against the blanched sky;
no clouds, no fog
just the back of a mirror,
a pearl in shadow,
a marble sepulchre.
Beneath, grey fences stained with rain,
a pewter water-slick on the concrete drive.
You do not call or write.
Even to one trained for years
in the interpreting of its dialects,
silence is a cold and difficult language.

Robyn Rowland

Imagery

Imagery refers to the 'word pictures' created by the poet. In the following extract from 'Preludes', T.S. Eliot vividly creates a picture of a winter evening in a city early in the twentieth century. Read the poem and then either draw what you can see or describe the scene in your own words. If you are using words, try to capture the mood created by the poet.

Preludes

I

The winter evening settles down
With smells of steaks in passageways.
Six o'clock.
The burnt-out ends of smoky days.
And now a gusty shower wraps
The grimy scraps
Of withered leaves about your feet
And newspapers from vacant lots;
The showers beat
On broken blinds and chimney-pots,
And at the corner of the street
A lonely cab-horse steams and stamps.
And then the lighting of the lamps.

T. S. Eliot

Imagery can be created in various ways. The poet may simply put 'the right words in the right order', or use figures of speech such as similes, metaphors or personification, or make particular appeals to the senses — sight, hearing, touch, smell and taste — in order to prompt a response in the reader.

Similes

A simile is a figure of speech in which one thing is likened to another, usually by using the words 'like' or 'as'. This example of a simile occurs in 'This Place, Here'

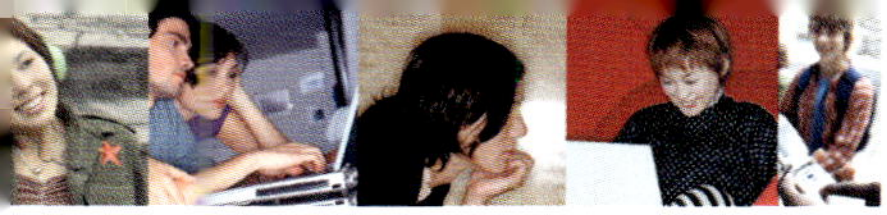

(pages 39–40): 'the white egret sauntering over the mud flats like a teacher on yard duty longing for the end of lunch time'.

Read the following poem in which the similes have been highlighted and comment on how they demonstrate the poet's point of view.

Dream Deferred

What happens to a dream deferred?

Does it dry up
like a raisin in the sun?
Or fester like a sore—
And then run?
Does it stink like rotten meat?
Or crust and sugar over—
like a syrupy sweet?

Maybe it just sags
like a heavy load.

Or does it explode?

Langston Hughes

Metaphors

Metaphors are also figures of speech that liken one thing to another, but they do it not by saying one thing is *like* another, but by implying that it *is* another thing. Sometimes the metaphor is quite clear, as in 'life's but a walking shadow . . .'; other metaphors are less direct: 'The morning melted into nothing'. Read the following extract from 'The Aunts' by Kate Llewellyn. The metaphor is highlighted.

The Aunts

All my aunts are dying
their bones
in the tissue paper
parcels of their hands

Kate Llewellyn

Here the poet is drawing attention to the thinness of the skin that covers the hands of the old ladies. She does not say that the skin is as thin as tissue paper, but instead refers to the skin that contains the bones of the hands as 'tissue paper parcels'.

Learning activity **1.17**

Identify the metaphors in the following poem. How do these metaphors help to emphasise the poem's theme?

Identity

Let them be as flowers
always watered, fed, guarded, admired,
but harnessed to a pot of dirt.

I'd rather be a tall, ugly weed,
clinging on cliffs, like an eagle
wind-wavering above high, jagged rocks.

To have broken through the surface
of stone,
to live, to feel exposed to the madness
of the vast, eternal sky.
To be swayed by the breezes of an
ancient sea,
carrying my soul, my seed, beyond
the mountains of time
or into the abyss of the bizarre.

I'd rather be unseen, and if

then shunned by everyone,
than to be a pleasant-smelling flower,
growing in clusters in the fertile valley,
where they're praised, handled, and
plucked
by greedy human hands.

I'd rather smell of musty, green stench
than of sweet, fragrant lilac.
If I could stand alone, strong and free,
I'd rather be a tall, ugly weed.

Julio Noboa Polanco

Personification

Personification is a type of imagery that attributes human characteristics or behaviour to non-living things. In the following extract from the poem 'The Dead Swagman', fire is personified as a friend, and is seen to be walking across the hill.

The Dead Swagman

He came one winter evening when the tree
Hunched its broad back against the rain, and made
His camp, and slept, and did not wake again.
Now white ants make a home within his skull:
His old friend Fire has walked across the hill
And blackened the old tree and the old man
And buried him half in ashes, where he lay.

Nancy Cato

Learning activity 1.18

Identify and explain the personification in the following poem.

Sundeath/Greeneaters

when you said you loved me
the sun
leapt out from behind st georges hall
and ran around town;
  kissing younggirls' faces
  exposing fatmen's braces
  freeing birds & chasing flies
  pulling hats down over eyes
  making bobbies get undressed
  barrowladies look their best
  wayside winos sit and dream
  hotdogmen to sell ice-cream

but when you said goodbye
i heard that the sun
had been runover
somewhere in castle street
by a busload of lovers
whom you have yet to meet

Roger McGough

Symbolism

Poets commonly make use of symbols to represent particular qualities, emotions or attitudes. In the following poem by Maya Angelou, a famous Black American writer, the free bird and the caged bird are powerful symbols. Read the poem and then, in pairs, discuss what these symbols might represent.

Caged Bird

A free bird leaps
on the back of the wind
and floats downstream
till the current ends
and dips his wing
in the orange sun rays
and dares to claim the sky.

But a bird that stalks
down his narrow cage
can seldom see through
his bars of rage
his wings are clipped and
his feet are tied
so he opens his throat to sing.

The caged bird sings
with a fearful trill
of things unknown
but longed for still
and his tune is heard
on the distant hill
for the caged bird
sings of freedom.

The free bird thinks of another breeze
and the trade winds soft through the sighing trees
and the fat worms waiting on the dawn-bright lawn
and he names the sky his own.

But a caged bird stands on the grave of dreams
his shadow shouts on a nightmare scream
his wings are clipped and his feet are tied
so he opens his throat to sing.

The caged bird sings
with a fearful trill
of things unknown
but longed for still
and his tune is heard
on the distant hill
for the caged bird
sings of freedom.

Maya Angelou

One poem, different interpretations

Sometimes poems can seem daunting to read, so it can be helpful to remember that there is no one specific 'meaning' which you must get right in order to respond appropriately. The poet might or might not have intended the poem to be read in a particular way, but readers draw on their own experiences of life and other poetry when they read a poem. The important thing is to be able to cite the poetic devices (the imagery, rhyme, **rhythm** etc. that we have been discussing in this chapter) in order to support your interpretation.

Learning activity **1.19**

Following each of these poems there is a number of statements indicating possible ways in which the poem might be interpreted. For each poem, choose the interpretation/s that you prefer and justify your choice by referring closely to the poem itself.

The Road Not Taken

Two roads diverged in a yellow wood,
And sorry I could not travel both
And be one traveller, long I stood
And looked down one as far as I could
To where it bent in the undergrowth;

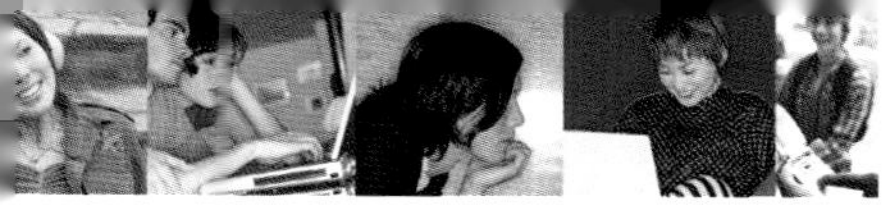

Then took the other, as just as fair,
And having perhaps the better claim,
Because it was grassy and wanted wear;
Though as for that the passing there
Had worn them really about the same,

And both that morning equally lay
In leaves no step had trodden black.
Oh, I kept the first for another day!
Yet knowing how way leads on to way,
I doubted if I should ever come back.

I shall be telling this with a sigh
Somewhere ages and ages hence:
Two roads diverged in a wood, and I —
I took the one less travelled by,
And that has made all the difference.

Robert Frost

Possible interpretations

- The poem is a warning not to procrastinate or put off fulfilling one's dreams.
- The poem is a send-up of someone who could never make up his mind.
- The poem comments on the difficulties of a modern life that is so full of choices.
- The poem is a comment on modern man's tendency never to be satisfied with his life.

This Place, Here

Always moving through the valley, always moving.
In cars, in buses and trains, sometimes on foot with the dog
leading. Or best of all on a bicycle, enjoying the track
that surges, loops and winds from Homebush Bay
to Botany Bay. Once you're in the seat and flowing
you don't have to think about pushing the pedals
and even gear changes take only a half-thought,
the thigh muscles registering a different pressure
as the bike rolls on. Past green fields that are mown
and watered for the crop of the small white ball
that is never harvested, the numbered flags
flapping in the Autumn breeze. Past the place
of the circus tent where elephants graze once a year
under electric power poles, just waiting for Jeffrey Smart
to notice them and put them in a painting.
Past the bloodwoods, ironbarks and swamp gums
planted by the Men of the Trees where the water
occasionally falls from the racecourse sprinklers
and the Sprite bottles bob and float downstream
like teal ducks. That place where shopping trolleys rust
in the mud, where burnt-out cars pause on the banks
like reluctant swimmers, where hopeful fishermen
cast and stand, showing not the slightest scrap of concern
for the chemical residues lying in the belly of the mullet.

On you go, nervously, through the dog-off-the-leash place,
and the swinging toward sky place. Cup and Saucer Creek
trickles around the Greek retirement home to greet you,
and then suddenly you see the old boat harbour, the cormorants
gathered on the grassy headland like they're going to school,
the principal a wise old pelican, the white egret sauntering
over the mud flats like a teacher on yard duty longing
for the end of lunch time. Beneath the bridge where pigeons
line up on the wire fence and on to the rubbish bins
patrolled and pecked over by grey ibis. Around the bend
where you waterplaned once, losing your glasses in the puddles
beneath the paperbarks, hopelessly searching for fifteen minutes
until some kind man found them, your own eyes useless,
your face caked with blood and mud. Ah, the river, the river,
never the blue of those real estate photos, but sometimes
a swamp green, there below the shop of the caramel cone,
the macadamia cluster, the wattleseed truffle. Rats live
under this bridge, but you leave them behind, pedalling on
to the park named after the stately prime minister who told us
to maintain the rage, the park where the Arabs gather each year
for a festival, the women cooking flat bread and marinated meat
on barbeques, the children bouncing, falling and bouncing again
in a castle made out of air. Here they dammed the river once,
then diverted it, but the old swamps are market gardens now.
This place where time seems to have stopped, where it's hard
to know what century you're in, where a Chinese man in a conical hat
pushes a wheelbarrow through the raised beds and a woman
kneels to pull out onion weed as the boats lull and drift in the canal.
The planes scoot in over the home of the Dragons, so low
that if you bounced off the handlebars, you might touch
a wheel or a wingtip. All of a sudden you remember
your smallness, how you are just one person cycling beside a river,
how thousands of years ago this bank lay beneath the sea.
You pass the old middens and the stencilled white feet
hidden by concrete, this place of kangaroo grass and lily bulbs,
all these places of the people who gave Gumbramorra Swamp
its name — the Gwiyagal people, who were here first and are still
here, who fished and lived and moved in this place, here.

Andy Kissane

Possible interpretations

- The poem is a description of a bike ride and all of the things that the cyclist sees along the way.
- The poem condemns the way in which civilisation has destroyed the natural environment.
- The poem celebrates a particular place in all its variety.
- The poem is a tribute to the people who originally settled in this place.

See pages 13–14 for guidance on how to construct a written analytical response.

Assessment tasks | Responding to poems

Select one of the following tasks.

1. Choose one of the poems featured in this chapter and write a response to it. In your response, include reference to these questions and quote from the poem to support your interpretation:
   - What appears to be the main purpose of the poem?
   - What broader theme or themes could it be said to be exploring?
   - How do the poetic techniques used by the poet contribute to its meaning?
2. Prepare and present a reading of a poem. Choose music and a series of images to accompany and add meaning to your reading. You could use a software program such as PowerPoint or create a series of **hyperlinks**.
3. Imagine that you have been asked to select poetry for an anthology. Choose a theme such as love, war, women's lives, Australia or city or country life. Use the resources of your school library to choose six poems on your theme. Write a short introduction to each poem explaining why you chose it, and include a piece of writing that compares and contrasts the various approaches the poets take towards the chosen theme.
4. Select a poem to perform. A **ballad** could be an appropriate choice, or a dramatic monologue or a rap.
5. Write an analytical response to a topic set by your teacher.

See page 44 for the criteria for assessment.

Don't forget to edit and proofread your response. See pages 97–8 for guidelines.

Speeches

A speech is a formal oral presentation which takes place on a particular occasion. It has usually been prepared, although not always. It could be the case that someone is called on to make a speech without warning, but this is unlikely to happen on a formal occasion where the speeches would have been carefully planned.

Do a class brainstorm to establish:

- the kinds of occasions on which formal speeches are made
- the purposes of these speeches.

Features of a speech

There are two main features of a speech: what is said and how it is said. 'What is said' not only includes the content of the speech, but also certain oratorical or speechmaking devices such as

- repetition of words and/or phrases

- **figurative language** such as metaphors and similes
- analogies or comparisons
- the direct addressing of the audience (use of 'you')
- the use of inclusive language ('we').

Features related to the delivery of the speech include:

- the use of emphasis
- pitch and variation of pitch
- pace and variation of pace
- use of pauses
- eye contact with audience
- body language/facial expression.

Strategies | Strategies for active listening

- Always face the speaker.
- Pay attention to what the speaker is saying and watch what the speaker is doing.
- Attempt to understand what the speaker is saying and try to see the speaker's point of view. If you start thinking, 'This is rubbish. He doesn't know what he's talking about,' then you will stop listening actively and will instead simply be waiting for further evidence to support your own point of view.
- Take notes, if appropriate, and jot down questions you can ask if given the opportunity.
- Be aware of **tone**, pitch, emphasis and **register** and how they affect the way you respond to the speaker.

Martin Luther King's 'I Have a Dream' speech was delivered by him on 28 August 1963 before more than 200 000 people in front of the Lincoln Memorial in Washington DC as part of the March on Washington for Jobs and Freedom. In this speech, Martin Luther King urges his people, other Black Americans, to fight for the civil rights which were promised to them after the abolition of slavery, and to share his dream that the day would come when they would achieve freedom and justice.

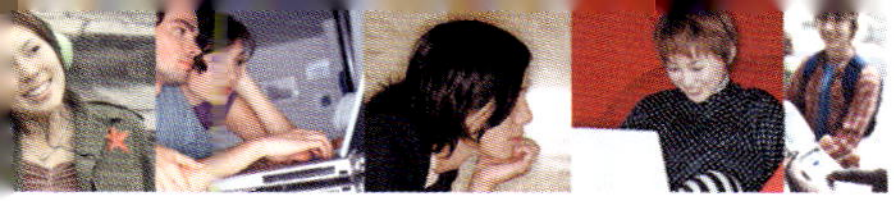

Learning activity 1.20

Visit the website for this book and click on the 'I have a dream' speech weblink for this chapter (see 'Weblinks', page 252). Read through the speech carefully.

1. Are there any references that you don't understand? Make a note of these to be shared in a class or group discussion.
2. Work in pairs to annotate the speech with examples of each of the following:
   - an allusion to the Gettysburg Address, made by Abraham Lincoln during the Civil War, which begins 'Four score and seven years ago … '
   - a reference to history — to Abraham Lincoln and the end of slavery in the US, in 1863
   - use of repetition
   - use of metaphor
   - use of analogy
   - an example of **hyperbole** (that is, overstatement in order to achieve a dramatic effect)
   - a biblical quote
   - addressing the crowd of marchers directly
   - appealing for inclusiveness, for everyone to work together for the same goal.
3. Visit the website for this book and click on the 'I have a dream' speech audio weblink for this chapter (see 'Weblinks', page 252). Listen to the speech to identify the use of pitch, pace, emphasis and pauses. Mark on your annotated copy when the changes in pitch and pace occur, where the speaker pauses and when he uses emphasis.

Don't forget to edit and proofread your response. See pages 97–8 for guidelines.

Assessment tasks | Responding to a speech

Choose one of the following tasks.

1. Choose another speech from the internet and write an analysis, responding to both the content of the speech and the oratorical or speechmaking devices used by the speaker.
2. Examine the features of one of the following genres of speeches and prepare and present an example to the class or group:
   - the eulogy
   - the best man's toast at a wedding reception
   - the 'roast'
   - the 'after dinner' speech
   - a speech at a book launch
   - the speech made by a winner in a particular context.
3. Prepare and present a speech for a specific audience and context.

See page 44 for the criteria for assessment.

Criteria for assessment

Your assessment task will be assessed according to the following criteria. Read them carefully before you begin your task; while working on your task, check your progress against the criteria and then review your completed task against the criteria before submitting it to your teacher.

Knowledge and understanding of content. This includes, where relevant:

- the components of the plot/action
- the setting
- the theme and how it is explored in the text
- aspects of character and characterisation
- ideas or arguments proposed by the author
- views and values expressed or implied in the text.

Understanding of structures and features used by the author in constructing the text. This includes, where relevant:

- the structure of the set text
- the point of view
- the use of symbolism
- the style adopted by the author, including visual style
- the tone.

Ability to construct a personal response to the text using the features and structures of the chosen form. This includes, where relevant:

- relevance of response to a set topic
- use of appropriate metalanguage to discuss the relevant structures and features
- clear and coherent point of view supported by evidence from the text
- control of spelling, punctuation and syntax
- control of aspects of oral presentation including pronunciation, pace, pitch, volume and body language
- coherent organisation, including control of paragraphing
- reviewing, editing and proofreading.

CHAPTER 2

Multimodal texts

Multimodal texts are those that combine, for example, print, visuals, text, sound and spoken word as in film or computer presentation media. In this chapter we will examine the structures and features of the following multimodal texts:

- narrative films
- **documentary** films
- 'reality' TV shows
- hypertexts
- picture books
- websites.

Narrative films

A narrative film tells some kind of story and is the result of a creative process that involves many people, including the producer, the director, the actors, the scriptwriter/s, the editor and the **cinematographer**. Like a print text, it has social, political, cultural and economic aspects. In reading and analysing a narrative film, it is often possible to draw on the approaches you adopted for analysing a print text, but it is also necessary to learn to read in a different way because as well as reading **verbal language**, you are also reading the **non-verbal** and **visual language.** Also, when writing about film there are special terms (**metalanguage**) used to describe what you have viewed.

Casting

The choice of a particular actor for a role can help determine how we, the audience, will react to the character, because our pre-existing knowledge of the actor comes into play. For example, if an actor who is well known for comic roles is cast in a dramatic role, the audience may not find the film plausible. In contrast, an actor who has been associated with a romantic role would be an appropriate choice for another film of the same kind. The physical appearance of the actor is also an important aspect here. If an actor is too old, too young, too fat, too thin, too good-looking or not good-looking enough, the sympathy of the audience will be affected.

Toby Maguire as Spiderman

Learning activity 2.1

1. Who are the actors in a film you are studying? Do they have an association with films of a particular type? Is that association relevant in this case? If so, how does it affect audience response?
2. Is the appearance of the actors appropriate for the roles they are playing? Explain your answer. (If you are analysing the film of a book you have read, this becomes an important factor because you will have already imagined what the particular character should look like. Sometimes you can be disappointed with the casting.)

Acting

The way in which the actor performs his or her role is another factor that helps determine how the audience will react to a character. Acting includes the way in which the lines are spoken or delivered, facial expressions, body language and movement. Some actors are the same in every role they play; some transform themselves completely for each new role. With some actors, we are acutely aware of their techniques and mannerisms, while others appear natural — as if they're not really acting. Terms such as wooden, animated, frenetic, laid-back, controlled, polished, mannered, smooth and studied are some of the expressions used to describe actors' performances. Sometimes, however, the judgement is 'all in the eye of the beholder', and it is possible to find two film critics who comment on an actor's performance in very different ways.

Scene from *Great Expectations*

Scene from *The Accidental Tourist*

Scene from *Girl with a Pearl Earring*

Learning activity 2.2

Select a film with which you are familiar and do an internet search for two reviews of that film. How are the actors' performances described? (Make a list of the words and **phrases** used by the reviewers.) Do the reviewers agree in their assessments of the performances of individual actors?

Characterisation

Characterisation — the creation and depiction of characters — is an element common to both print and non-print narrative texts, but the method of creation is, of course, different. In a narrative film, characters are created through:

- acting
- **dialogue** (what they say)

- behaviour (what they actually do)
- props (for example, flashy car, cute dog, large desk or battered suitcase)
- the sets in which they are placed (for example, the house that denotes power and wealth, the bar that denotes sophistication, the slum that denotes poverty, the darkened street that denotes evil and danger)
- the music or sound effects that might accompany their actions (for example, light and cheerful music, heavy, ponderous music, exciting, thrilling music, loud noises associated with cities and action, soft, gentle noises associated with nature and serenity)
- their appearance, including costuming (for example, neat and pressed, modern, old-fashioned, down-at-heel, casual, formal, loud, subdued) (See image at left.)
- their movements (for example, comic, subdued, large and expansive, tight and controlled, fidgety, confident)
- the lighting (for example, dim and moody, bright and airy, dark and foreboding) (See the images below left and right.)

The way this woman is dressed provides information about her.

The bright lighting here reflects the mood of the subjects.

The lighting here adds a sense of menace.

- the use of particular camera shots (for example, low angle to convey a sense of strength or power, high angle to suggest vulnerability or weakness; close-ups to suggest the importance of a character's reactions or behaviour in a particular scene)
- the way in which the character is positioned in the frame (for example, strong characters occupy the centre of the frame, while weaker or less important characters appear behind or to the side)
- the length of the shot (for example, a long, lingering close-up on the character's face suggesting deeply felt emotions) (See image below right.)
- their relationships with other characters.

A low angle shot looking up makes the subject appear large, strong and powerful.

A high angle shot looking down makes the subject appear small, weak and vulnerable.

A close-up shot on a character's face shows emotion.

Learning activity 2.3

In groups, use the following graphic organiser to analyse one of the characters in a film you are studying.

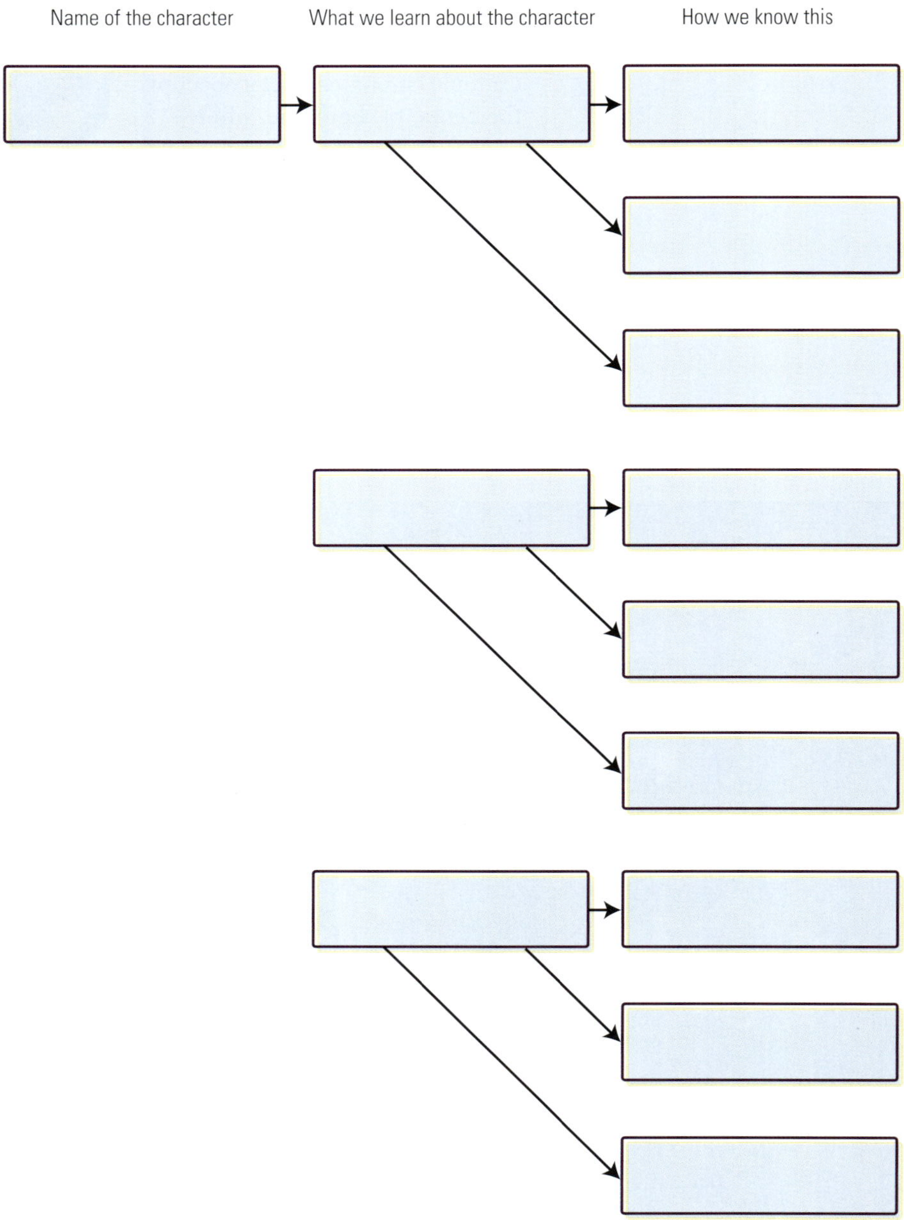

Structure

The narrative structure of a film can be linear/sequential in nature — that is, one event leads to another — or the narrative can be told in the form of a flashback or series of flashbacks. Sometimes more than one story is being told — there is a plot and a sub-plot — and these might occur concurrently (that is, at the same time). The order in which the events occur has an effect on the way in which the

audience perceives the narrative. If we already know 'what happens', the interest lies in discovering why it happens. If we don't know what is going to happen, then naturally there is a certain amount of suspense and interest in the outcome or resolution, and flashbacks can be a way of enhancing audience knowledge and interpretation of events that are supposed to be occurring in the present.

Learning activity **2.4**

1. List the key events in a film you are studying and analyse the sequence of cause and effect. Do this in a diagrammatic form.
2. How are the events in the story presented? Are they sequential or non-sequential? How does the way in which they are presented affect the audience's appreciation of the narrative?

Genre

Genre refers to broad categories of films that share certain features, including:

- character types
- settings
- themes
- resolutions
- motifs or symbols.

Examples of film genres include:

- western
- detective drama
- rite of passage (films in which young people undergo an experience or experiences which initiate them from childhood into adulthood)
- horror
- *film noir* (a French term literally meaning 'black film', used to describe films that are sometimes shot in black and white, have seedy settings and main characters who are not heroic)
- science fiction
- disaster
- road
- romance
- comedy
- romantic comedy.

Many films, however, draw on more than one genre. *The Third Man*, for example, has features of the western, detective, *film noir* and romance genres. (See pages 62–3.) Other films play around with the conventional features of a genre and so are said to subvert it. Wes Craven's *Scream*, for example, alters the conventions of the horror film and turns the film into a horror-comedy.

Learning activity **2.5**

1. Divide into groups. Choose a film genre, provide examples of films that fit the genre and describe the characteristics of the genre in relation to:
   - character types
   - settings

- themes
- resolutions
- motifs or symbols.

2. Look at the following scenes from a number of different films. Is it possible to tell, just by looking at the scene, what genre the film belongs to? If so, what are the clues that reveal the genre?

Style

Style refers to the distinguishing characteristics of the text. Style is what allows us to read a piece of writing that we may not have seen before, and yet recognise who wrote it or where it came from, or classify its genre immediately. Most people would recognise where the following extract is from: 'And it came to pass, that when Jeremiah had made an end of speaking to the people … '. This is clearly from the Bible. In the same way that most writing has a distinctive style, so too do films — they have a visual style, which may be that of the director or of the genre. The elements of visual style are listed below.

Lighting

Some films are very brightly lit, others are dimly lit. The decision about lighting is often associated with the genre of the film. *Noir* films, such as *The Third Man*, for example, are shot in black and white and make much use of stark contrast in lighting. Sometimes individual scenes within a film are lit in different ways: a change in lighting from one scene to another can indicate a change in mood.

Learning activity **2.6**

In pairs, choose a scene in a film you are studying and examine the lighting. How would you describe it? Why do you think it is lit in this way? What kind of mood does the lighting help to create? The table below might be of assistance to you. Share your findings with another pair.

Key lighting	This is the main source of light on the subject. Usually it comes from about 45 degrees above and to the left or the right of where the camera is situated.
Fill lighting	This is soft lighting and fills in the shadows caused by the main light.
Back lighting	This comes from behind the subject and makes it stand out against the background.
Flat lighting	Light is distributed within the image so that bright and dark tones are not in sharp contrast.
High-key lighting	Light is distributed so that bright tones are dominant.

Symbolism

Symbols are all around us. Signs such as crosses, hearts and arrows are very basic symbols that we unconsciously interpret every day. But we can also see many functional objects as symbols of other things: our hairstyles, clothes, the houses we live in and the contents of our rooms can be interpreted as symbols because they also represent our personalities, our values, even our status in society and the sub-groups to which we belong. The actual meaning of these symbols depends to a large extent on who is doing the 'reading' and on the values and attitudes of that person.

Symbols are a shorthand way of conveying ideas. If you have already studied some poetry or a novel you will be aware of the way in which writers use symbols to represent ideas, themes or qualities. Film-makers do the same thing. In the film *Bladerunner*, for instance, images of the eye feature as a recurring symbol or motif. This symbol can be interpreted as a device to draw our attention to how things are 'seen' and to cause us to question what is 'true'. What symbols can you identify in a film that you are studying?

Camera shots

What role does the camera play? Sometimes, as viewers, we are aware of the camera, yet in other films we are not. It can remain stationary or it can move with the action. It can provide interpretations for the viewer by zooming in on a significant object or facial expression. In television, the wobbly, hand-held camera is often used, but this is less common in films for the wide screen.

Aerial shot

Tracking shots

Long-distance shot

Middle-distance shot

Wide shot

Directors can use a variety of shots in a film: tracking shots, aerial shots, close-ups, long-distance shots, middle-distance shots, wide shots and shots from various angles. In a film you are studying, you may notice that one type of shot predominates.

Learning activity **2.7**

Choose a short scene in a film you are studying and examine the role played by the camera. What kind of shots and angles are used? What effect is created by these choices? Use the following table to help you.

Effects created by various camera shots and angles	
Camera angle or shot	**Effect created**
Extreme long distance	Usually used to establish the scene. Orients the viewer. Can provide an idea of scale. For example, 'This is a 'big' city . . . ' or 'This desert goes on and on and on . . . '
Long distance	Usually shows a full-length view of a character and some of the surroundings. Provides an immediate **context** so we know where the subject is — for example, in a room.
Medium distance	Usually shows a character from about the knees or waist up. Used in scenes where a dialogue takes place. Allows us to see gestures and body movements as well as facial expressions.
Close up	This shot shows very little background and focuses on the face of a character or an aspect of the mise-en-scene (see page 58). Can be used to draw the viewer into the emotion of a particular character, or to draw attention to, for example, a facial expression that indicates the character's response to something. A close-up shot might also focus on some aspect of the mise-en-scene which is of significance to the action.
Aerial shot	The camera looks down on a scene, usually from a long way up. Can make people look insignificant. If the camera is following (for example, in a car chase) this kind of shot can make the viewer feel that s/he is part of the action.
High angle	Camera is above the action, but not as high as an aerial shot. High angles make the object photographed seem smaller, and less powerful or frightening.
Low angle	This shot increases the height of a character or object and can cause the viewer to see what is being photographed as threatening and dominant. Sometimes the angle suggests that the camera is looking at the object or character through the eyes of another character, and so the viewer is able to experience how that less powerful or frightened character feels.
Tracking	The camera moves towards and away from a character or object. Can draw the viewer into a closer relationship with the character. Rapid tracking (especially tracking in) adds to the excitement of a scene, while tracking back causes interest to relax.

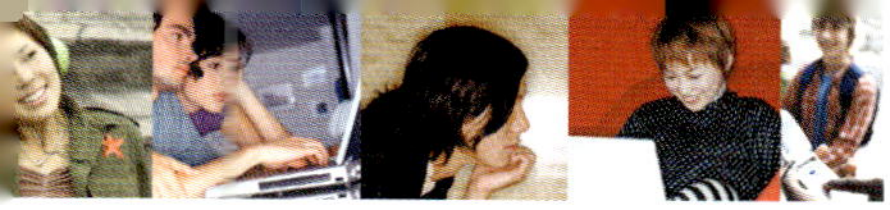

Framing

Characters can be framed in many ways: they may be in the foreground or background; they may be shown in shots with other people or alone. The film-maker can use framing to make implications about the characters themselves and their relations with others.

Learning activity 2.8

Consider the following scene from the film *Citizen Kane,* directed by Orson Welles. From the way in which the characters are framed, what conclusions can you draw about the relationship of the three subjects to each other?

Scene from *Heat* showing blue filter

Colour

Films can be shot in black and white or colour; a particular colour may predominate; they can be shot through a colour filter in order to achieve a specific effect. You may have seen films in which colour is used to evoke a mood or an era. A blue filter is sometimes used to create a cold or lonely mood, while sepia tones are used to suggest early decades in the twentieth century.

Sound

The use of silence on the soundtrack of a film can be very powerful, but usually a soundtrack is packed with a variety of noises. The most common sound, and the one that the audience expects to hear, is that of dialogue — what the characters say and, more importantly, how they say it. In addition to dialogue there is a variety of sound effects. Many of these are natural sounds — sounds that are there because they should be. But others are sounds deliberately used to create a particular mood. A howling wind, for instance, might forewarn the appearance of something frightening in a horror film. Music is a particular aspect of the soundtrack and is used to create or reinforce a particular mood.

Learning activity **2.9**

Choose a scene from a film you are studying and analyse the use of sound. Use the following table.

Scene	Dialogue — what is said and how it is said	Natural sounds	Sounds designed to create a particular mood	Music

'Mise-en-scene' is a term used to describe everything that goes to make up a particular scene. It includes:

- sets, props and costumes
- lighting
- colour
- the actors' performances and movements
- the framing
- sound such as the dialogue or sound effects which are a 'natural' part of what is happening on the screen

Transitions:

Cut (a shift straight from one scene to the next)

Wipe (a gradual replacement of one scene with another)

Fade (Fade-in: an image gradually appears out of a black screen. Fade-out: the image gradually disappears into a black screen.)

Dissolve (the new image appears over the old image)

Special effects

Special effects created by computer technology, evident in films such as those in the Harry Potter series, enhance audience appreciation both of the plot and characterisation. They also enable the creation of films that would otherwise be too difficult and costly to produce.

Editing

In the post-production period, decisions are made about, for example, where to cut or intercut scenes and how to **transition** from one scene to the next. These editing decisions are extremely important in terms of the finished film and contribute to audience understanding.

Learning activity **2.10**

Take note of editing when watching a film, and try to analyse the effect of transitions and juxtaposition (the placing of two scenes next to one another).

Film reviews

Reviewing films is big business and a very important part of the promotion of a film. Reviews are to be found in newspapers, magazines and on websites and they vary considerably in quality and length. They target specific audiences and this is reflected in the sophistication of the analysis and the language that is used. Compare the following two reviews of the same film. What comments can you make about the likely audience in each case?

Review: New 'Potter' tries to do too much

Latest in the series lacks sparkle of earlier works

BY PAUL CLINTON
FOR CNN.COM

(CNN) — I have enjoyed the magical charms of the Harry Potter franchise since the highly anticipated (and highly hyped) first film, *Harry Potter and the Sorcerer's Stone*, cast its spell upon the big screen in November, 2001.

My love affair with the residents of the Hogwarts School of Witchcraft and Wizardry continued with *Harry Potter and the Chamber of Secrets*, in 2002, and was sustained with *Harry Potter and the Prisoner of Azkaban* in 2004. I not only loved the films; I read the books too.

Now, in the spirit of full disclosure, I did not read *Harry Potter and the Goblet of Fire* (life, somehow, just got in the way), the fourth in the series. Perhaps that is one reason that the new film based on the book didn't work its wizardry on this reviewer. Frankly, the entire film felt like the cinematic version of Hamburger Helper — too little meat trying to do too much.

I'm sure that the movie is true to J.K. Rowling's book — she (or her fans) would allow nothing less. And I am aware that *Goblet of Fire* was darker and more sinister than the previous wildly successful books — this is the first 'Potter' film with a PG-13 rating — but, still, I was a bit underwhelmed.

I'm not saying the magic is gone, but I've lost that loving feeling. Director Mike Newell and screenwriter Steve Kloves have attempted to make a movie that is part thriller, part action flick and part budding love story. None of the themes mesh together very well. The result feels somewhat clunky and disjointed.

Goblet's basic plot involves a competition between the three largest European schools of wizardry: Hogwarts, Durmstrang and Beauxbatons. The contest, called the Triwizard Tournament, is being hosted at Hogwarts; the prize is the highly coveted Triwizard Cup.

The boys from Durmstrang all look like throwbacks from a Hitler youth group and the girls from Beauxbatons, devoid of expression, float around like butterflies trying to escape a net.

At the outset, the *Goblet of Fire* selects one student from each school to compete in three life-threatening tasks; all candidates must be 17 years or older. But after one name from each school is picked, the Goblet spits out one more nomination: that of 14-year-old Harry.

Against his will — and better judgment — he resigns himself to playing the game, thereby risking his life. Not even Hogwarts's headmaster, the beloved Albus Dumbledore (Michael Gambon) can save him from taking part.

Love and Death Eaters

But Harry has other problems: working up the nerve to ask his beautiful classmate Cho Chang (Katie Leung) to the annual Yule Ball. Yep, the kids are growing up and the hormones are kicking in. Adolescent romance is in the air — and so is adolescent clumsiness. Ron Weasley is totally oblivious to the growing feelings of Hermione (Emma Watson) as she tries in vain to get him to ask her to the social event of the year.

Even Hagrid is not immune to the love bug as he falls under the spell of the flamboyant Madame Maxime (Frances De La Tour), the Headmistress of Beauxbatons. I don't want to be nasty and say his character is amazingly unattractive, let's just say she's perfect for Hagrid.

Hovering over all these events is the return of Lord Voldemort (Ralph Fiennes), who after 13 years is once again appearing in public and has unleashed his followers, the Death Eaters, to do his dirty work.

The cast of Hogwarts instructors has mostly stayed the same, but there's one new — and really interesting character — in the mix. That would be Mad-Eye Moody, played by the excellent Irish character actor Brendan Gleeson (*Gangs of New York*, *Cold Mountain*). He's asked by Dumbledore to keep his bright blue eye on Harry and help in any way he can during the tournament.

But Mad-Eye is one of the rare sparks in *Goblet of Fire*. Indeed, I guess my biggest beef with the film is that many of the other characters we have grown to love and hate — Draco Malfoy (Tom Felton), his evil father Lucius (Jason Isaacs), Professor Severus Snape (Alan Rickman), Professor Minerva McGonagall (Dame Maggie Smith) and Hogwarts Academy itself (which has become a character just as much as the human cast) — are all given short shrift. Even the interaction between Harry, Ron and Hermione has been trimmed down to almost nothing.

Newell, best known for directing *Four Weddings and a Funeral* and *Pushing Tin*, is not necessarily the go-to guy for projects with computer-generated images, but he proves here that he's a fast learner and does a commendable job of pulling off all the action needed to make a 'Potter' film work. It's just that it would have been nice to give him more to work with.

So I'm less than thrilled. No matter. Seeing a 'Potter' film is generally worth it. There's much to appreciate here, and there will be many people to appreciate it.

And now, there's always that fifth film to look forward to.

Review: Harry Potter and the Goblet of Fire

Harry Potter and the Goblet of Fire is filled with dark enchantment

BY TY BURR
BOSTON GLOBE
PUBLISHED: 11/17/2005

Starts by focusing on what he thinks is the most striking aspect of the film

There's a darkness on the edge of Hogwarts, and its name is adolescence.

Origin of the movie

Cast

Harry Potter and the Goblet of Fire, the latest big-screen installment of the unstoppable popculture juggernaut, marks a sea change. Just as J.K. Rowling's fourth novel — a 734-page anvil that stood as the white-hot apex of the Potter fad — poured a bucket of teen hormones into the Gryffindor stew, so the new film finds Harry (Daniel Radcliffe), Hermione (Emma Watson), and Ron (Rupert Grint) casting 14-year-old puppy eyes in various directions.

Friendships are torn asunder by jealousy and suspicion. There's a school dance to which Hermione actually wears a gown. Ron takes one look at her and mutters, 'They're scary when they're grown up, aren't they?'

Brief reference to the plot

More to the point, *Goblet of Fire* is the entry in which Rowling finally took off the gloves — a much-liked character dies, Lord Voldemort returns from exile with powers strengthened — and the movie rigorously follows suit. Entire plotlines and characters have been sliced off to fit the confines of a two-and-a-half-hour running time (Winky the Elf, we hardly knew ye), but the sense of impending doom remains.

Evaluation

Is this the best of the series? It's beside the point. Long as it is — and the movie verges on overlong — *Goblet of Fire* is the first that plays for keeps.

Director

The director this time is not Chris Columbus, the proficient journeyman of the first two films, nor Alfonso Cuaron, who gave the third installment a dose of needed magic (which, ironically pleased everyone except hard-core Potterheads), but Mike Newell, the British director of *Four Weddings and a Funeral* and *Donnie Brasco* (and *Mona Lisa Smile*, but we'll let that slide, although Hogwarts *could* possibly pass for Wellesley College on a lousy day). Newell specializes in relationships rather than special effects, and, fittingly, *Goblet* is most interested in the curses and enchantments of adolescent behavior.

Plot

So while the movie starts off with a Quidditch World Cup bang, the sequence feels rushed and secondary, like a highlight reel of the book's opening chapters. Soon enough, Newell assembles the relevant troops: the students of two rival academies of magic convene at Hogwarts for a grand Triwizard Tournament, with one student from each school chosen by the Goblet of Fire to take part in an enchantment triathlon.

Cast

From Durmstrang comes Viktor Krum (Stanislav Ianevski), Quidditch star and glowering Slavic jock. From Madame Maxime's Beauxbatons comes Fleur Delacour (Clemence Poesy) — think Ludwig Bemelman's Madeline all grown up and with a wicked knack for casting spells. And from Hogwarts comes Cedric Diggory (Robert Pattinson), upperclassman, dreamboat, all-around good chap.

Plot

Then the Goblet has the effrontery to belch out one more name for the contest: Harry Potter. Because everyone assumes that Harry has engineered this development, all of Hogwarts turns against him in a fickle rage. Now *this* is adolescence: humiliation, isolation, an inflamed sense of social persecution that may or may not be deserved. Suddenly Harry is no longer the hero of the tale but its goat. All that's missing is acne.

Special effects

The tournament's three contests provide the excuse for the expected state-of-the-art CGI whizzbangery, and they are visual marvels. A Hungarian Horntail dragon perched angrily atop Hogwarts's highest spire, a seaweedy underwater world of beastly mermaids, a maze of perversely mobile hedges — these are images with staying power, like Arthur Rackham illustrations sprung to life. They don't feel multiplex-trendy but organic to the series' darkening tone.

Plot

The main order of business in *Goblet*, though, is the sorting out of unwelcome new loves and lusts. Harry stammers whenever he sees classmate Cho Chang (underwhelming newcomer Katie Leung), while Krum sets his shako (again, not quite believably) for Hermione. Ron just sulks; the scene in which he and Harry double-team the Patil twins (Shefali Chowdhury and Afshan Azad) at the Yule Ball is a nice study in young male doltishness. Any sparks between Ron and Hermione, by the way, will apparently have to wait until the next movie.

Evaluation

Strip away the special effects and you could be watching an episode of *Degrassi Junior High*, and is that such a bad thing? At times the movie squirms: Harry's encounter with ghostly Moaning Myrtle (Shirley Henderson) in a fifth-floor bathtub flirts along the line between comedy of embarrassment and full-on kink. (That the 39-year-old Henderson has 23 years on Radcliffe makes the scene even more interestingly bent.) *Goblet* knows, though, that where some teenagers flounder others find their legs, and Harry's roommate Neville Longbottom (Matthew Lewis) makes a touching entry into adulthood here.

As for the adults, Michael Gambon's Dumbledore has a greater presence in this film, but Professors McGonagall (Maggie Smith) and Snape (Alan Rickman) are forced to the back of the line. Hagrid (Robbie Coltrane) indulges in a queasy romance with Madame Maxime (Frances de la Tour), who resembles nothing so much as a transvestite on stilts.

Acting

With any new 'Potter' entry, the newcomers hog the stage, and luckily *Goblet* has two prize hams: Brendan Gleeson as Dark Arts professor Alastor 'Mad-Eye' Moody — mad eye swinging like a marble in a shot glass — and Miranda Richardson as Rita Skeeter, the perky tabloid journalist of any young wizard's nightmares.

Acting

And, of course, there's Voldemort, who rises from the depths of this film's climax like the devil himself. I'm not sure whose idea it was to cast Ralph Fiennes as the devil, but it's an inspired choice: bald, elegantly muscular, eerily noseless, and very, very unpleasant, this Voldemort provides a jolt that promises to last the entire series, wherever that may lead.

Recommendation

Is the movie for kids? Even with a PG-13 rating, *Goblet of Fire* is oddly less scary in some ways than last year's *Prisoner of Azkaban* — less predicated on computer-generated ghoulies and funhouse shocks. The dread here cuts deeper, though. When we hear the wail of a grieving father toward the end of the movie, it's the first genuinely human moment in a Harry Potter film, and it is awful.

'Soon we must all face the choice between what is right and what is easy,' Dumbledore tells his rattled charges, and with those words the franchise becomes no longer a corporate toy but a metaphor for growing up in a world where magic spells are never quite enough 'Everything's going to change now, isn't it?' asks Hermione. Yes, dear, it is.

Learning activity **2.11**

One of the reviews already has annotations to indicate the various aspects of a review. Use this as a model to help you make similar annotations on the other review.

The Third Man

The Third Man (directed by Carol Reed, screenplay by Graham Greene, 1949) is a classic example of *film noir*, where there is no traditional hero or a happy ending. There is, however, a strong narrative and complex characterisation, and the film deals with significant themes.

Learning activity **2.12**

You will probably need to view the film more than once before you answer the following questions.

Scenes from *The Third Man*

1. What was the significance of the title?
2. Whose is the voice-over that is narrating the film? To whom do you think he is speaking?
3. This film is noted for its distinctive music, created by a musical instrument called the zither. Select a couple of key scenes and describe how the music is used to comment on the action. Note, also, the music that is associated with Harry Lime himself.
4. How do the opening scenes establish the mood of the film and provide the viewer with necessary information about the situation in Vienna at this time?
5. What do you notice about the use of camera angles in this film? Choose a scene and analyse the variety of angles used and the effect created.
6. A significant feature of the film is the use of lighting: there is a great deal of emphasis on light and shadows, sometimes accompanied by water, and many scenes take place at night. What effect is achieved as a result? Refer to a particular scene or scenes in your response.
7. Examine the use of symbolism in the film, for example: Holly walking under the ladder as he goes to Harry Lime's apartment for the first time
   - the frequent framing of characters in windows and doorways
   - the title of Holly's talk at the Cultural Re-education Centre: 'The Crisis of Faith'
   - steps and stairs, particularly circular staircases
   - the parrot that bites Holly
   - Holly's injuries
   - the use of bars, as in barred windows and gates
8. Explain the features of the film that draw on the western genre. (Consider, for example, the titles of Holly's books, the roles of both Holly and Anna, particular quotes from Holly, the final scene in the sewers and the last scene in the film.)
9. The film also draws on the detective genre and the romance genre. Explain how it does this.
10. Use a diagram to explain the nature of the fraud in which Harry was involved.
11. How does the film convey the fact that although post-war Vienna was largely impoverished, there were still some people who lived well? Who were these people and what conclusions is the viewer asked to make?
12. Explore the significance of naming and names. (Holly calls Callaway 'Callahan', Anna calls Holly 'Harry', Holly mispronounces Dr Winkler's name, and Holly's final comment to Major Calloway was: 'I haven't got a sensible name.')
13. What kind of person was Harry? Note Holly's descriptions of him at school, what Anna has to say about him and the way in which she sacrifices her freedom for him, and what Harry himself has to say in the scene at the Prater Wheel. Is it possible to explain why both Holly and Anna find him so attractive?

Assessment tasks | Responding to film as text

Choose one of the following:

1. Write an analytical essay in which you examine one of the key themes explored in *The Third Man*.
    - innocence and experience
    - betrayal and loyalty
    - decadence and corruption

    In your response, identify associated characters, dialogue, scenes and events. Are there any particular 'messages' associated with the theme? Explain.
2. Write an essay in which you examine how the various elements of the sewer scene in *The Third Man* contribute to an atmosphere of confusion and deception.
3. View two films by the same film-maker (for example Lasse Hallstrom, Zhang Yimou, Woody Allen, Ang Lee, Robert Altman, Kenneth Branagh or Gillian Armstrong) or by the same production team (for example, Merchant Ivory) or in the same genre (for example, *film noir* or romantic comedy). Analyse the common elements of visual style. What other aspects of the films made them characteristic of the director/producer/genre? Present your findings orally, in writing or in multimodal form.
4. Write your own review of a film or compare two reviews of the same film.
5. Respond to a review of a film with which you disagree, putting forward your own point of view. (You could do this orally or in writing.)
6. Examine the use of symbols in a film that you have studied and provide an interpretation. (You could do this orally or in writing.)
7. You're on TV. In pairs, play the roles of presenters on a television show that discusses films. Present a prepared discussion of a selected film for the class.

See page 76 for the criteria for assessment.

See pages 13–14 for information on how to write an analytical response

See pages 59–62 for examples of film reviews.

Don't forget to edit your response. See pages 97–8 for assistance with editing.

Documentary films

We are familiar with documentary films as a **source** of information, but it is important to remember that, just like narrative films, they are a constructed product, the result of a series of decisions made by people who have particular viewpoints on a subject and a particular purpose in mind when creating a film. The documentary film, therefore, should not be regarded as 'factual', but should be analysed in order to determine the views and values that it promotes. They also have a particular audience in mind, perhaps even more so than narrative films.

Like narrative films, documentaries make use of filmic techniques, such as:

- camera shots
- framing
- lighting
- sound effects.

Therefore, some of the questions you applied in order to analyse narrative films are also relevant if you are analysing documentaries. However, documentaries may have some of the following features, which narrative films do not necessarily have:

- a narrator who is also involved in producing the film
- an interviewer, who may be seen or not seen, and heard or not heard
- a narrator who is an actor or 'personality' and is not involved in production
- people who are willing subjects in the film

Examples of documentaries:
Bowling for Columbine
To Be and To Have
Touching the Void
The Corporation
Mad Hot Ballroom
Land Mines — A Love Story
Super Size Me
Seven Up (series)
McLibel
Born into Brothels

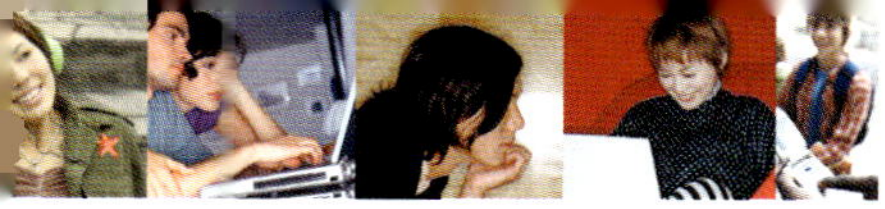

- people who are unwilling subjects in the film
- wildlife
- unforeseen situations, including dangerous ones
- historic film footage or photographs
- statistics and data
- a lengthy intrusion into a person's, family's or organisation's daily life (sometimes over many years).

See pages 218–19 for learning activities associated with the documentary *Bowling for Columbine*.

Assessment tasks | Responding to documentary films

Choose one of the following:

1. Write an analytical response to a topic set by your teacher.
2. Prepare and present an oral or written evaluation of *Bowling for Columbine* as a documentary. Include an evaluation of both the content and the techniques used by Moore to present that content. Refer to some of the criticisms of the documentary and provide your response to these.
3. Here is a review of the documentary *Spellbound*. Use it as a model to write a review of another documentary that you have seen or studied.

Spellbound review

Ok, so it may not sound the most riveting of premises on which to make a documentary: the journey of eight young American kids from very disparate backgrounds as they compete in the National Spelling Bee — a bizarre competition where children are tested on their ability to spell words such as 'cephalagia' or 'monotonous' before a panel of judges. Yet, Blitz has managed to create a satisfying, engrossing and often hilarious piece of pure Americana.

The key to the success of this film lies in the gifted storytelling skills of Blitz, combined with the quirkiness of his eight subjects. In particular, Angela, whose father came over from Mexico to Texas where he became a cattle-rancher yet still does not speak a single word of English; Neil, an East Indian boy with a meticulous routine of studying hundreds of words a day under the supervision of his kind but disciplined parents and Harry, a hyperactive ball of energy with a repertoire of bad jokes and who is quite clearly an absolute lunatic.

In his low-key documentary, Blitz has succeeded in creating drama out of everyday life that is highly absorbing, despite its lightweight subject matter. By focusing on just eight entrants from the hundreds who take part each year, we are invited to spend considerable time in their homes and lives as they struggle to overcome what is to them something very arduous and important, and in seeing their level of commitment to each round of the Spelling Bee, you empathise with them to the point of becoming utterly gripped in the proceedings. And when the actual final competition takes place with its sudden death, one-mistake-and-you're-out format, it's exhilaratingly tense as you watch them fall one by one, wondering who is going to be next to make that critical mistake.

Underneath the drama, however, lies a rich study of modern American life. Within each of the eight case studies we get an insight into the mentality of those living in diverse parts of the US, from the Washington DC projects to the posh San Clemente coastline via a Missouri trailer park. All these kids and their families are united by the common goal to win what is essentially nothing more than self-validation and a grand sense of achievement; there is no enormous prize money at stake, nor do the winners of the Bee go on to gain celebrity status.

But what is perhaps most remarkable and indeed refreshing about *Spellbound* is its uplifting tone. It could have been very easy for Blitz to portray this from a more condemnatory angle, as a study of overbearing parents making up for their thwarted ambition by pushing their reluctant children to extremes for their own gain. Instead, we are presented with eight, determined children who want to take part in this event voluntarily. In one instance we see how bemused the parents are that their child is so intelligent when all they want him to do is join the army.

Spellbound was nominated for Best Documentary Feature at the 2002 Academy Awards and it is interesting to compare this with another recent documentary — the Academy Award winning *Bowling for Columbine* by Michael Moore. Both present us with a vignette of how things are in the US right now but while Moore's film is a blistering statement about everything that is wrong with America, *Spellbound* is more interested in showing you what the US has managed to get right, and while it is undoubtedly important to be reminded about the burning issues still needing to be addressed within American society, it is refreshing to be served up a slice of American Pie that, with its themes of equality and struggling against all odds, captures the essence of precisely what that country set out to be.

This is not the most obvious choice of film to see at the cinema but it is definitely worth a look, if nothing else merely because it has as much drama, comedy and pathos as the best Hollywood can offer and it leaves you feeling uplifted and utterly satisfied. And you might learn one or two ridiculously long words on the way.

Review by Adrian Mackinder

4. In groups, plan a short documentary. Perhaps your subject could be your school, your suburb, a person or an activity. Include a diagram showing the structure, reference to the various techniques you will use and the features you will include (visuals, interviews, a narrator, expert commentary etc.), the use of various camera shots and the soundtrack. Also try to predict the problems you may encounter (weather, access to information, unwilling subjects etc.). What will be your purpose and what image of your subject will you be trying to convey?

Present your plan in multimodal form — sketches, writing, photographs, speech, music and so on.

See page 76 for the criteria for assessment.

'Reality' TV

'Reality' TV is a fairly recent phenomenon on our television screens, but it has been a form of programming that has proved to be very successful.

What exactly is this phenomenon called 'reality' TV? Do you agree with any of the following descriptions?

- Just a cheap way of producing television programs.
- The equivalent of stopping on the side of a road to look at an accident.
- There is no such thing as 'reality' TV — just the fact that the cameras are there makes it 'unreal', not to mention the editing and so on.
- 'Reality' TV is exactly what people want. It appeals because it is so ordinary. It features ordinary people competing for a prize and sometimes there is the opportunity for more ordinary people (the audience) to participate.

Learning activity **2.13**

Work in pairs to decide whether you agree with any of the above descriptions. If you don't agree with any of the above, suggest your own description.

The phenomenon of 'reality' TV began with the production of shows such as the American series *Cops*, in which a camera followed policemen as they went about their daily work and recorded the kinds of incidents that they were involved in. Since then, there have been many changes. Some 'reality' TV shows still focus on the 'real', but many others have constructed environments. Some involve participants completing tasks, which could be regarded as positive because they develop real and worthwhile skills, while others create an artificially competitive environment.

Scene from *Australian Idol*

Scene from *Backyard Blitz*

Scene from *Big Brother*

Learning activity **2.14**

1. Do a paired or group brainstorm to draw up a list of all of the 'reality' TV shows that you can think of and then group them into categories according to the kind of 'reality' TV show that they represent. (There is more than one way to group the shows.) Share your findings with the class.
2. Choose one of the categories and make a list of the kinds of things that programs in this category have in common. (Consider such features as the format, the participants, the setting and the purpose.)
3. Choose one of the following questions for a group discussion. Following your discussion present a summary of your findings to the class.
   - How 'real' are 'reality' TV shows?
   - Does 'reality' TV reflect the culture of Australian youth?
   - What values are promoted by 'reality' TV?
   - How exclusive is 'reality' TV? (Which groups in society are not represented?)

Focus on *Big Brother*

One of the more successful 'reality' TV programs has been the one called *Big Brother*. On Australian television *Big Brother* can occupy up to 16 hours of programming time in a single week.

Although the show itself is far from literary, it owes its title to *Nineteen Eighty-Four*, a novel by George Orwell. In this novel, set in 1948, Orwell imagines that in 1984 the world will be governed by three great powers. One of these, Oceania, is a totalitarian nation where surveillance of the population occurs even in their own homes. Here is an extract from the novel:

> It was a bright cold day in April, and the clocks were striking thirteen. Winston Smith, his chin nuzzled into his breast in an effort to escape the vile wind, slipped quickly through the glass doors of Victory Mansions, though not quickly enough to prevent a swirl of gritty dust from entering along with him.
>
> Winston made for the stairs. It was no use trying the lift. Even at the best of times it was seldom working, and at present the electric current was cut off during daylight hours. It was part of the economy drive in preparation for Hate Week.

On each landing, opposite the lift shaft, the poster with the enormous face gazed from the wall. It was one of those pictures which are so contrived that the eyes follow you about when you move. BIG BROTHER IS WATCHING YOU, the caption beneath it ran.

Outside, the black-moustachio'd face gazed down from every commanding corner. There was one on the house-front immediately opposite. BIG BROTHER IS WATCHING YOU, the caption said, while the dark eyes looked deep into Winston's own. In the far distance a helicopter skimmed down between the roofs, hovered for an instant like a bluebottle, and darted away again with a curving flight. It was the police patrol, snooping into people's windows. The patrols did not matter, however. Only the Thought Police mattered.

Behind Winston's back the voice from the telescreen was still babbling away about pig-iron and the overfulfilment of the Ninth Three-Year Plan. The telescreen received and transmitted simultaneously. Any sound that Winston made, above the level of a very low whisper, would be picked up by it; moreover, so long as he remained within the field of vision which the metal plaque commanded, he could be seen as well as heard. There was of course no way of knowing whether you were being watched at any given moment.

Winston kept his back turned to the telescreen. It was safer; though, as he well knew, even a back can be revealing. A kilometre away the Ministry of Truth, his place of work, towered vast and white above the grimy landscape.

From where Winston stood it was just possible to read, picked out on its white face in elegant lettering, the three slogans of the Party:

WAR IS PEACE
FREEDOM IS SLAVERY
IGNORANCE IS STRENGTH

The Ministry of Truth contained, it was said, three thousand rooms above ground level, and corresponding ramifications below. Scattered about London there were just three other buildings of similar appearance and size. So completely did they dwarf the surrounding architecture that from the roof of Victory Mansions you could see all four of them simultaneously. They were the homes of the four Ministries between which the entire apparatus of government was divided. The Ministry of Truth, which concerned itself with news, entertainment, education and the fine arts. The Ministry of Peace, which concerned itself with war. The Ministry of Love, which maintained law and order. And the Ministry of Plenty, which was responsible for economic affairs. Their names, in Newspeak: Minitrue, Minipax, Miniluv and Miniplenty.

The Ministry of Love was the really frightening one. There were no windows in it at all. Winston had never been inside the Ministry of Love, nor within half a kilometre of it. It was a place impossible to enter except on official business, and then only by penetrating through a maze of barbed-wire entanglements, steel doors and hidden machine-gun nests. Even the streets leading up to its outer barriers were roamed by gorilla-faced guards in black uniforms, armed with jointed truncheons.

Learning activity **2.15**

The world of 1984 has been referred to as a dystopia — that is, an imaginary place or state in which the condition of life is extremely bad. The people suffer from deprivation or oppression. Read the extract again to identify the words and phrases that create the dystopia.

The opposite of a dystopia is a utopia — a world in which everything is perfect — especially from a social, political and moral point of view.

Issues raised by *Big Brother*

Any analysis of the show *Big Brother* needs to look further than what actually happens on the show itself, to include other issues raised by the way in which it is structured. Below are some of the issues that could be considered. Perhaps you can think of others?

Contestants' rights

Should contestants give up all their civil rights when they enter the House?

Consider the case of housemate Merlin Luck who staged a protest when he was evicted live on TV. He carried a sign which asked for the refugees to be freed and having taped up his mouth, refused to speak. The next night he apologised to the host, Gretel Killen, for his actions. Although he attracted a large viewing audience on the second night, there was a great deal of popular disapproval of his action.

Why do you think people might have disapproved? Did he have a right to do what he did? Should he have apologised?

Sponsorship

How does the marketing associated with the program fit with its primary purpose of entertaining? Do you think that it is unethical to disguise marketing as part of entertainment?

Consider this information found at http://en.wikipedia.org/wiki/Big_Brother_Australia

What is wikipedia? Is this a reputable source of information?

Sponsorship

The show attracts major sponsorship from large Australian telecommunication companies hoping to gain promotion from the many telecommunication tie-ins during the series. Sponsorship deals have also included the naming rights to the bigbrother website domain name. Past websites have been located at bigbrother.optus.com.au, bigbrother.3mobile.com.au, and bigbrother.iprimus.com.au.

Other major sponsorship comes in the form of advertising space and product placement. During the 2005 series almost all food products in the house came from a food company with commercial agreements with the show production company. Any food that did not have a sponsorship agreement had its label removed.

Big Brother also receives substantial grants from the Tourism Queensland Board.

Criticisms

Many criticisms are aimed at the program including:

- Obvious product placement, examples being
  - In 2001, a preview of *The Secret Life of Us* that was shown to the housemates late in the first series. *The Secret Life of Us*, another Channel Ten program, was preparing to make its premiere immediately after that *Big Brother* season ended. The housemates' seemingly ingenuine positive reaction to the new show was aired during the prime time daily update show.
  - During the 2003 season, housemates were given a task to count a large bowl of M&M's, a sponsor for the season.
  - During the 2004 season, the entire backyard of the house was filled with snow, to tie in with a special viewing of the film *The Day After Tomorrow*.
  - During the 2005 season, the housemates were required to take Tango dancing lessons and were treated to a special viewing of the film *Mr. & Mrs.*

Smith. Other 20th Century Fox tie-ins included a 'favourite fantastic four' housemates competition, linked to the Fantastic Four movie. In one episode, approximately ten minutes of the Up-Late show focused solely on the use of a mobile phone which had been provided by one of the show's major sponsors.

- Home viewer competitions not being open to all residents of Australia (WA, NT & SA) due to the time zone difference. However this has been rectified with a new competition in the 2005 series called *Hammer Down* which enables all residents of Australia to enter.
- Telephony costs associated with housemate evictions.
- The content of its Uncut shows, which during the 2005 series was said by some commentators to border on pornography. These criticisms were even made by Federal Government Parliamentarians led by Trish Draper.
- The advertisement content of the Up-Late shows, particularly during the 2005 series. The show featured increasing numbers of premium charge SMS and telephone competitions. On some nights less than half the show was footage from the house.

Learning activity **2.16**

Watch a couple of other television programs to compare the extent of product placement in them with the extent of product placement in *Big Brother*, as described above. What conclusions can you draw?

'Reality' TV and privacy

Learning activity 2.17

In pairs, decide whether you agree with the point of view put forward by the cartoonist (see page 71). Is this why people agree to be contestants in 'reality' TV programs?

Assessment tasks | Responding to 'Reality' TV programs

1. Write an analytical response to a topic set by your teacher.
2. How does 'reality' TV draw on a variety of other genres such as the adventure/action film. (Select one or more 'reality' TV shows to be the basis of an essay or oral presentation. Refer to the 'plot' of the TV shows, the roles played by the participants, the language they use and the implied values.)
3. Select a 'reality' TV show and examine the way in which it makes use of the following elements: a particular setting, interviews with participants, games, and conflict. Present your analysis in writing or orally.
4. Why are 'reality' TV programs so popular? Prepare an oral presentation that analyses this question. (Your conclusions should be based on research — either your own or others'.)
5. What is your idea for a 'reality' TV program? Prepare a 'pitch' for a television studio. Include reference to the concept, participants, location and 'rules'. Present your 'pitch' as a datashow presentation.
6. Respond, either orally or in writing, to the idea that some 'reality' TV programs are more worthwhile and acceptable than others? Justify your response.

See page 76 for the criteria for assessment.

See page 15 for advice on oral responses.

See pages 97–8 for guidelines on proofreading and editing.

Hypertext

Most hypertexts are essentially language-based narratives which make use of the technology of the internet to link objects such as text, pictures and sound. Just as users of the internet are able to choose which information they want to access, so the readers of a hypertext are able to choose the links in the story that they wish to follow. For example, you might follow a text from beginning to end without deviating to a **hyperlink** or, alternatively, you might click on the first hyperlink in a story, which might lead to another, and another again. The way you read and understand the narrative may be entirely different as a consequence of taking these different pathways.

Nine Vicious Little Hypertexts

Nine Vicious Little Hypertexts is a series of hypertexts written by Deena Larsen who has constructed her hypertexts as a series of squares or samplers.

Each square or sampler shows a different non-linear way to organise a narrative. For example, the sampler on page 73 leads to the narrative titled 'Crossed Ends'.

Each arm of the cross tells the story from a different point of view, and each bar of colour on the arms of the cross leads to a different part of a single narrative. You can click on any of these, in any order you want, to read the narrative. (A left-hand mouse click takes you forward to the next screen; a right-hand mouse click takes you backwards.)

A sampler is 'a piece of cloth embroidered with various patterns, which is intended to show the skill of the person who made it.' Collins English Dictionary

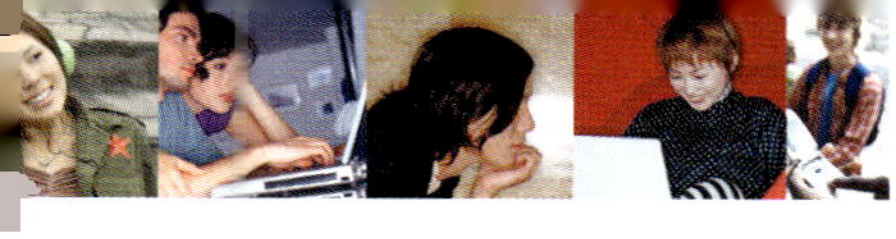

Sampler from *Nine Vicious Little Hypertexts*

Learning activity **2.18**

1. Use a datashow projector to read 'Crossed Ends' as a class. For the first reading, choose an arm of the cross and individual bands of colour at random. Then go back and work your way through each of the arms, in each case starting with the colour band closest to the centre.
   (a) Is there one single narrative here or several narratives? Are you able to provide a summary of what happened?
   (b) Describe your first impressions of reading this hypertext. How did it make you feel? (A bit lost? Intrigued? Interested?)
   (c) Explain the title.
2. In pairs, experiment with the other Samplers. Select a Sampler of your choice. First, follow the links through sequentially, reading the 'story' from beginning to end. Next go back and read the story again, this time following a 'hyperlink' each time it arises. How does your perception of the story change? Keep a record of your choices as a reminder.
3. After reading some of the Samplers, complete the following table which draws attention to the differences between a print narrative and a hypertext.

Print narrative	Hypertext
Contained between the covers of a book.	
There is only one order in which the text can be read.	
There is a definite beginning to the text.	There may be multiple beginnings, and the reader chooses which one to start with.
The beginning of a text usually establishes setting, character etc.	
There is usually, but not always, an ending that is a resolution.	There may be no endings or multiple endings.
There is no interaction between the reader and the text, beyond turning the pages.	
The reader can see the extent of the text before starting to read.	

Assessment tasks | Responding to a hypertext

Choose one of the following tasks.

1. Do you think the term 'vicious' can be applied to all of the Samplers? In writing or orally, explore the degree to which you think two or three of the Samplers are 'vicious'.
2. Keep a journal of your reading experience. Choose a Sampler and click on the links that interest you as you follow the story. Record the links that you follow and a brief reason for selecting that particular link. How satisfactory was your reading experience?
3. In 'Seed Voices' we hear two voices. Analyse the characteristics of each of the voices (the language used, the concerns expressed, the use of different coloured fonts to differentiate between them). Is there a single narrative here or more than one?

4. Take on the role of a director and create an audio or video recording using different actors or different voices for the different aspects of one Sampler. For example, you may engage the help of three friends to read the different parts in 'Crossed Ends' or 'Caught Out'. Alternatively, you might simply read each of the parts yourself using different character voices. Consider the way the voices you use reflect the ages, personality, feelings and nature of the characters.
5. Write your own hypertext. Think back to a conflict you have observed or experienced in your life. Write about the experience/perception from the perspectives of three people who were involved. (Do about a page for each perspective.) Divide up your descriptions into three or four screens and decide how you would link each of these screens to make a hypertext. Present your hypertext in the form of a series of documents linked by hypertext, as a PowerPoint presentation with hyperlinks or in print form with a diagram showing how the various screens would link.

See page 76 for the criteria for assessment.

Picture books

We normally associate picture books with the early years of childhood, but not all picture books are designed solely for a younger audience. In fact there are many picture books which explore quite complex themes in both text and pictures and encourage multiple interpretations or readings.

The Rabbits, written by John Marsden and illustrated by Shaun Tan, was the winner of the Children's Book Council Children's Picture Book of the Year in 1999 and is an example of a picture book which can be satisfyingly read by an older audience.

Learning activity **2.19**

Read the picture book *The Rabbits* and then answer the following questions:

1. After your first reading, which of the following statements do you agree with and why?
   (a) This book demonstrates how the process of industrialisation ruins the environment.
   (b) This book shows how the importation of rabbits into Australia has had dramatic results for native animals.
   (c) This book is an **allegory** for the colonisation of Australia.
   (d) This book demonstrates how the process of change is not good for everyone.
   (e) This book shows how, in any society, the powerful succeed and the weak fail.
2. Examine the cover illustration. List the images that you can see. Do they have any associations for you? What event seems to be taking place? What comments would you make about the mood suggested by the colours?
3. Look at the illustration which occurs on the inside of the front and back covers (the end papers). Examine the ways in which this contrasts with the cover illustration.
4. Trace the use of colour in the illustrations. How and why does it change throughout the book?
5. Use a **Venn diagram** to compare the way in which the native animals are depicted with the way in which the rabbits are depicted. Note both their appearance and the objects with which they are associated. Describe and interpret the differences.
6. Examine the placement of the text as part of the design on the book. Do you think it is effective?
7. The illustrations are particularly detailed. In pairs, examine each double page spread of illustrations in terms of colour, figures, objects and symbols. Read the accompanying text. What does it all mean? Share your findings with the rest of the class.
8. From whose point of view is the story told? Write the text from the point of view of the rabbits. How would the message change?

Websites

A website is a text whose structure makes use of the hypertext function of the internet and whose features include verbal and visual language. Like a print text, a website is constructed for a particular purpose and audience, and reflects certain values, either directly or implicitly.

The structure and features of websites are dealt with in more detail in Chapter Four, where you can examine an annotated website and work through a series of learning activities. After doing those activities come back to this assessment task.

Assessment tasks | Responding to websites

Prepare a written or oral report which analyses the way the major Australian political parties present themselves via their official websites. In your report refer to, for example:

- the main emphasis of the home page (policies, personalities, the Party) as revealed through the text and graphics
- the links from the home page and the language used to label them

- the relationship between the site and the readers (How are the readers addressed? Is there any interactivity?)
- the use of slogans and images and their purpose
- the design and complexity of the site (Comment on the 'feel' of the site, the use of colour and number of audio and visual texts.)
- how the site shows an awareness of the needs and interests of each of the following groups of Australians
  - women
  - the indigenous
  - the young
  - families
  - the disabled.

See below for the criteria for assessment.

Criteria for assessment

Your assessment task will be assessed according to the following criteria. Read them carefully before you begin your task; while working on your task, check your progress against the criteria and then review your completed task against the criteria before submitting it to your teacher.

Knowledge and understanding of content. This includes, where relevant:

- the components of the plot/action
- the setting
- the theme and how it is explored in the text
- aspects of character and characterisation
- ideas or arguments proposed by the author
- views and values expressed or implied in the text.

Understanding of structures and features used by the author in constructing the text. This includes, where relevant:

- the structure of the set text
- the point of view
- the use of symbolism
- the style adopted by the author, including visual style
- the **tone**.

Ability to construct a personal response to the text using the features and structures of the chosen form. This includes, where relevant:

- relevance of response to a set topic
- use of appropriate metalanguage to discuss the relevant structures and features
- clear and coherent point of view supported by evidence from the text
- control of spelling, punctuation and syntax
- control of aspects of oral presentation including pronunciation, pace, pitch, volume and body language
- coherent organisation, including control of paragraphing
- reviewing, editing and proofreading.

creating and
presenting
VCE UNITS 1 & 2
9004

CHAPTER 3

Exploring and presenting themes or ideas

In this section, the focus is on creating and presenting texts in print, non-print and **multimodal** form. When we create texts, we need to know:

- why we are creating the text (our purpose)
- for whom we are creating the text (our audience)
- the form that the text will take
- the **context** in which the text will be created.

These decisions need to be clear before we can decide what kind of language will be most appropriate to use.

Analysing the texts of others, in order to identify the choices those authors have made, will help us to be aware of the kinds of choices that are available to us, too.

In the next three chapters we will look at texts which reflect three different contexts — a thematic context, the world of technology and communication, and the context of the workplace. (According to the VCE English Study Design, you are only required to study one of these contexts in each Unit.) We will examine the choices made by the authors when they create their texts, and then you will have the opportunity to create your own text in the chosen context.

The theme is the 'big idea' — the central idea or issue which is explored in a text.

In this chapter we will focus on exploring and presenting texts based on a theme. The selected themes will be:

- *Who am I?* (the theme of identity)
- *It's not fair!* (the theme of fairness or justice).

Exploring and presenting: Who am I?

The answer to this question is one that is of great interest to most of us for most of our lives. Who are we? What do we believe in or stand for? What made us the way we are?

These are questions associated with the theme of identity and the following texts all present ideas associated in some way with that theme. Read the annotations to see how the texts explore and present ideas about identity and how they suggest other aspects of the theme for further exploration.

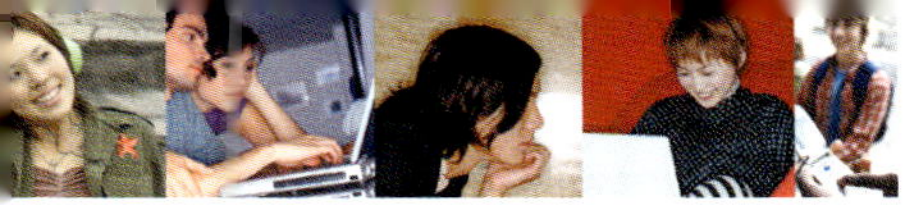

Exploring theme in a poem

Before you begin to read:

- What do you think it would be like to be a twin? (If you are a twin, then you'll definitely be able to answer this question with some authority.)
- Do you think that you would feel that your identity was shared, rather than being an individual one? What would be the advantages and disadvantages of this?

Twins

Purpose: creative/imaginative

We wear the same clothes:
dresses, coats and hats
fill our closet
like animals the ark.
Shoes and gloves come
by four.

'Our' and 'we' constantly repeated in order to emphasise their bond — which at this stage appears to be a positive thing. Later in the poem, we see the bond as something which stifles.

Simile

Our hair is parted on the same
side. We have rings on the same
finger. We play
the piano. We bite
our nails. Our beds
are close to each other.

Further repetition for emphasis

A series of short, **simple sentences**

Sudden change of focus — 'we' becomes 'I', 'me' and 'my'

But her ribbons choke me
in my sleep. I awake
and her smile in my mirror
fractures
my features.

This choice of words reflects the damage one twin does to another.

Complexity of content is reflected in longer sentences.

Metaphor

When she eats my food, tears
my dress and destroys the bird's
nest, I am God's angel.
When she is good, I beat her
in my dreams and pray:
Let her be evil.

Different interpretations possible here. Perhaps when her twin misbehaves she is deliberately 'good'; or perhaps she is referring to the way in which others view her — her 'identity' in their eyes.

As a twin, her identity is so bound up with her sister's that she only seems to have an identity by contrast.

Siv Cedering

Learning activity 3.1

1. Who is speaking in this poem?
2. Why do you think the author has written this poem?
3. The poem raises questions about the struggle for identity within a family, a family's perceptions of one's identity and what one knows about one's own identity. How does it do this?
4. Compare the content of the poem with the content of the article about sibling rivalry on pages 101–2 to identify any similarities and differences.

Use a **Venn diagram** to record similarities and differences.

Exploring theme in a media text

The next text is a **feature article** about identity theft. Before you begin to read:

- What do you understand by the term identity theft?
- Do you know anybody who has been a victim of identity theft?

Headline

Source and date of publication

Pun/play on words

Short, one-sentence paragraphs, typical of this kind of media feature article

Use of statistics to shock readers

Specific example or 'case'

Use of language associated with crime

Local example makes the topic more meaningful to local readers

Purpose: informative

Byline

Identity theft a $100-billion industry

SMH.COM.AU
JULY 7 2003

What's in a good name? A fortune, for those who play your cards wrong. Garry Barker reports.

If, in the days before plastic, online banking and the internet, you saw someone rummaging through a garbage bin, you knew they were a mostly harmless vagrant.

Today, the person burrowing through the dumpster full of discarded documents could be a millionaire criminal looking for more identities to steal.

Identity theft is big business. In Australia alone the proceeds of identity frauds, including dud cheques, still one of the largest sources of fraud, is estimated to be nearly $6 billion a year.

Worldwide, it may be as high as $100 billion.

In the US in 2002, an estimated 700 000 people were victims of identity theft, were stripped of their savings and their credit ratings, thrown into dispute with banks, loan companies, stockbrokers and even governments because their identities had been stolen and put to criminal use.

One of the most celebrated of recent ID thieves, Abraham Abdallah, a 32-year-old former dishwasher, pleaded guilty in a New York court last October to masterminding what investigators said was the largest identity theft so far attempted, a scam aimed at scoring more than $US80 million ($117.5 million).

Abdallah had fraudulently obtained loans from finance companies using the stolen identities of numerous celebrities including Microsoft co-founder Paul Allen and film maker Steven Spielberg. He used computers in public libraries and phone calls to get the credit records of stockbroker and bank accounts belonging to billionaire investor Warren Buffett, George Lucas, Oprah Winfrey, Ross Perot and the mayor of New York, Michael Bloomberg.

The most sobering point is that so many of the organisations hit by the fraud attempt appeared to take Abdallah's approaches at face value and as genuine . . .

In Melbourne last year, a Taiwanese man was arrested and charged with defrauding Victorian merchants of more than $500 000. He was carrying 103 forged credit cards, all with genuine numbers, most probably obtained from documents

stolen from letter boxes or in 'dumpster raids' in Australia and elsewhere…

Computer-based financial crimes are now at a level in Australia and the rest of the world that, according to a report on fraud published in March by the Australian Institute of Criminology and PricewaterhouseCoopers, 'has the capacity to retard legitimate business development…and security risks have slowed the implementation of online business models'.

Cites a reputable source for the quote

The rapid growth in the use of the internet and computers has made the misuse of identity much more common and easier to perpetrate…

Begins to discuss the link between technology and identity theft

Even the holograms that distinguish cards such as driver's licences and Visa credit cards are now relatively easy for criminal gangs to copy and produce quickly in vast numbers.

'The use of computers has made theft of identity much easier for criminals,' says Dr Russell Smith of the Australian Institute of Criminology. 'Most of our systems for identifying people in government and business are based on people submitting documents and computers make it easy to alter or counterfeit documents.

'Even the more secure documents such as passports and driver's licences can be counterfeited or altered by enterprising criminals.'

Millions of dollars are regularly skimmed out of government welfare systems through false identities, some of them produced by highly organised gangs operating nationally and internationally. About 40 per cent of such crimes in Australia are committed by locals. Of the rest, by far the largest group (about 10 per cent of the total) originate in South-East Asia, the institute's figures show.

Australian laws on identity theft vary from state to state, Dr Smith says, 'but they tend not to be used in prosecutions which are more often based on the consequences of the deception, such as obtaining money, or opening a bank account in a false name, rather than on the theft of the identity'.

The crime of identity theft

In the UK, for example, it is not illegal to take someone else's identity, or even manufacture a bogus credit card, but it is illegal to profit from either activity.

'In the US, theft of identity is regarded as a crime but that has not been investigated in Australia,' he said. 'I think we probably have enough laws to cover these cases but often they are very difficult to prosecute.'

Identity theft, such as is the central theme in the movie *Catch Me If You Can*, about the exploits of Frank Abagnale, a notorious fraudster who now works with the FBI and international banks in fighting fraud, is generally done by individuals.

An example of identity theft

Counterfeiting of credit cards or 'skimming' their PIN numbers at automatic teller machines or in shops and restaurants is generally the work of organised gangs.

St George Bank's automatic tellers were hit last year by criminals who inserted electronic skimmers into the card slots of the machines to read card numbers. They then used a video camera with a telephoto lens to record the PIN number being punched in on the machine's keypad. From that information it was easy for them to produce usable cards.

An example of a crime committed by a gang

Australia now has a central high-tech crime centre operating out of the Australian Federal Police complex in Canberra but staffed by specialist detectives and technicians from every state and territory police force. It will target a broad range of cyber crime, ranging from child pornography to card fraud.

Describes future efforts to combat high-tech crime, which includes identity theft

'High-tech crime is no longer the province of science fiction movies,' says Mal Hyde, chief commissioner of the South Australian police, who is chairman of the new centre.

A quote from an 'expert'

The centre has its own investigators and acts as a clearing house for information on online crimes and identify theft in Australia and internationally, co-operating with security agencies in the US and UK.

Establishes the global credentials of the new centre

Learning activity **3.2**

1. Which of the following is the focus of this article?
   - (a) identity theft
   - (b) the fraudulent use of other people's identities
   - (c) high-tech crime

   Explain your answer.
2. The 'identity' referred to in this article is an official identity. List all the elements that make up your official identity. Start with your birth certificate, and then list all the other documents, numbers and passwords that identify you. (You don't need, of course, to reveal the actual passwords and numbers, but the reason for their existence — for example, your bank account.) What do you think your life in this society would be like if you didn't have this official identity?
3. This article draws attention to the way in which the internet has made the misuse of identity much more common. This raises the issue of the virtual identities that

internet users often assume in chat rooms. Do you think that assuming a virtual identity is:

(a) just something you do for fun and quite harmless
(b) deceptive and potentially dangerous
(c) an opportunity to recreate ourselves and to play a role?

Explain your answer.

4. Do you think Australians should have identity cards? Would this help to control identity theft?

Exploring theme in a playscript

Before you read *Snap-Snap!* by Richard Yaxley, consider the following:

- Do you like to read articles and look at photographs about famous people?
- Where do you think that magazines like *Who Weekly* get their information about famous people?
- In your opinion, how accurate is the information in these articles?

Snap-Snap!

Cast list

Purpose: creative/imaginative

(In order of appearance)

Note that unlike the other characters in the play, JT is not given a full name.

JT	A news photographer, member of the 'paparazzi'
Chrissie Carruthers	Famous actress in her late twenties
Mrs Wellbeloved	Ordinary citizen, late fifties; fan of Chrissie

This word has negative **connotations**, shaping our opinion of JT even before we meet him.

Scene 1

Stage directions are printed in italics.

A bare stage, except for a small table with an expensive-looking camera on it. JT enters from the right. He is neatly dressed, shuffling a set of photographs as he crosses to centre stage — from where he sees the audience for the first time.

Addresses the audience directly

JT Oh. Hello. Didn't see you all there. Actually, I was thinking about something else — little job I've got this afternoon. See, I heard on the grapevine that Chrissie Carruthers is planning a little out-and-about around four o'clock. Could be interesting; might get a few candid shots. [*Laughs.*] The best shots are the candid ones. You can name your own price on those. [*Cups a hand to his ear.*] Who's Chrissie Carruthers? You're kidding, aren't you? Only the biggest film star in the world, that's who! Known to her adoring public as the face of Hollywood — the girl who's everything to everyone. It's such a load of you-know-what. Read the magazines if you don't believe me: read all about sweet Chrissie, pure Chrissie, Chrissie who gives money to every charity ever invented, Chrissie this, Chrissie that, blah-blah-blah!

Chrissie's public image

[*He pauses, drops the photos onto the table and picks up the camera.*]

Wanna know the truth about Chrissie Carruthers? Well, follow me … because I'm going to show you, and then I'm going to show the world! That's my job, isn't it? I'm the

Rhetorical question that assumes the answer will be 'yes'

legendary JT, news photographer extraordinaire: hound the stars, snap-snap-snap!

> This choice of language acknowledges his intrusion into her privacy.

[He mimes taking a series of photos.]

Chrissie shopping for toilet paper, snap-snap-snap! Chrissie meeting some bloke in a dark little nightclub, snap-snap-snap! Chrissie sun-baking on a private yacht in Hawaii — put on the zoom lens and snap-snap-snap!

[He laughs again then there is another pause as he lets the camera swing from his shoulder, stares out at the audience as if someone has said something.]

Eh? Hate her? Hate dear, sweet, Chrissie Carruthers? No … no, I don't hate her. Jeez, I love her! Love her … she's my bread and butter, isn't she? She's my new car and my down payment on a flash inner-city apartment. She's my everything; my leather jacket, my cellar full of French champagne. She's my lifestyle, baby … my shot at the big time. Because photos of Chrissie pay … big money. Mega-bucks. Twenty grand for last year's beach shot in California. Forty grand for a stolen kiss … sixty if I can get a bikini shot — because the whisper is she might have anorexia. Hate her? Why would I hate someone like that, someone whose snap-snap-snap pays so much?

> Style of speaking establishes his character — brash, cynical, exploitative

[He checks his watch, nods to himself.]

Nearly four o'clock. I'd better make tracks. Gotta job to do … snap-snap-snap. Try to get there before the others. There'll be forty, maybe fifty of us. All jostling for position, yelling out, trying to get the right angle, the right light, keep any shadows in the right places. Snap-snap-snap! Gotcha Chrissie Carruthers … gotcha *[Points to the camera.]* in here … forever.

> Shows extent of media interest in Chrissie

[He laughs quietly to himself and exits left. From stage right, CHRISSIE CARRUTHERS *enters. She is dressed as if she is 'in hiding' — large dark glasses, a wig, long overcoat. She walks to the table nervously, looking around constantly. When she reaches the table, she places her handbag on it then faces the audience.]*

> Impact of paparazzi on the 'star'

Chrissie Has he gone? Has he? That awful man … has he gone?

[She straightens, obviously relieved, removes the glasses cautiously.]

Good. That's really good. He's one of the worst, you know. One of the most persistent. He's a grub. A worm. Every time I step outside, every time I go somewhere, every time the stupid rumours start — he's there. Along with all of the others, forty or fifty of them. Waiting like rats in the basement — flash-flash-flash! And for me, a life caught in pictures — yet lived alone.

> Language chosen to show her opinion of the paparazzi and JT in particular

[She walks downstage, stretches her hands.]

Did I say rumours before? Ha — that was silly! There are no rumours about my life, just plenty of lies. Wanna know how a lie starts? It's easy. Someone invents an idea which they think is maybe interesting or funny, then they tell someone else and

> Role of rumour in the star's life

that gives it just a shade of truth. Then both of them decide to tell more people — because if lots of people have heard the lie, then it must be worth believing. And it must be true. Must be!

[*She sits cross-legged, still bitter but conversational.*]

Chrissie's **tone** is very different to JT's.

There's never been much truth about me in the media. Remember this one: [*As if she is reciting a headline.*] 'Chrissie Carruthers smooches mystery man in seedy nightclub.' Remember that? It went on for months — he was my Swiss lover, he was the estranged husband of an Argentinean opera-singer, he was the son of a Saudi oil magnate, he was vaguely related to the Kennedys or the Windsors, he was Bill Gates' secret love-child ... on it went. On and on — puerile rumour, speculation and lies — all of it lies.

Childish

[*Pause, while she considers.*]

The great JT took that particular photograph. Within the hour, it had been downloaded to every major news outlet in this country, the world, the rest of the universe and probably even beyond that. Newspapers ran it full-colour front page, magazines quoted sources 'close to the family' who 'confirmed' that I had a new boyfriend, the photo was on TV bulletins, radio updates, over ten thousand websites within a day. Ten thousand!

Refers to the language used by the media to establish authority

[*A beat.*]

Pause

Wanna know the truth? That guy in the photo — he was my half-brother. We hadn't seen each other in years. Dad left when I was a baby, remarried, lived a quiet life in the country, had a son — my half-brother. Used to see him once, maybe twice a year — then the whole movie thing took off and I was always too busy, filming, reading scripts, public appearances, being a 'star' (*She says the word sarcastically.*), too busy to see him — until that night. We met by accident, saw each other, hugged spontaneously — just so the whole world could watch and invent a lie. It's ... disgusting. It disgusts me, makes me feel sick inside. Sick and disappointed, because — against my wishes — I am so much a part of it all.

The way she says this word tells us she doesn't value her 'star' role.

Hints at her own role of encouraging the media

[*She stands, replaces her glasses, moves over and picks up her handbag.*]

Gotta go. If I stay too long in the one place they'll track me down — next thing you know it'll be flash-flash-flash. Today ... today I just felt like a walk. Can't even do that any more, most of the time. Walk too far and it's flash-flash-flash! Gotcha Chrissie Carruthers ... gotcha [*Points to an imaginary camera offstage.*] in there ... forever.

Seeks pity from the audience

Echoes JT's earlier comment

[*She shrugs and exits as* MRS WELLBELOVED *enters from the opposite side. She is a woman in late middle age dressed in her 'going-out' clothes, kindly and dreamy. She carries a magazine that she is preoccupied with reading. when she reaches the table, she puts the magazine down carefully and lets out a huge, romanticised sigh.*]

The fan — stereotypical characteristics?

The media create fans.

Wellbeloved Funny things, dreams. They carry you, stay with you, give you hope. I can still remember from when I was at school, what that English poet said — Keats, I think it was . . .

[*She holds up a finger and recites with exaggerated theatricality.*]

'Ever let the Fancy roam, pleasure never is at home.' Ah, that's lovely that is. Ever let the Fancy roam . . . you know, when I was . . . younger, I dreamed about being a star. In the movies, of course — I'd wear exotic costumes and sing lovely songs, jump and dance — tap-tap-tap! I'd put on different faces — the dashing pirate-girl . . .

The role of fantasy and the yearning for a different identity

[*She jumps onto the table and 'looks to the sea'.*]

Ahoy, yer land-lubbers — sharpen yer cutlasses, we're comin' to town! [*Back in character.*] Or the leading man's love interest . . .

[*She holds herself coquettishly.*]

Oh, Mr O'Grady . . . I couldn't possibly be outside with you . . . alone! What might folks think? [*Back in character.*] Or an evil face, maybe Lady Macbeth . . .

[*She adopts a vicious pose.*]

We, fail? Screw your courage to the sticking place and we'll not fail! [*Back in character.*] Oh . . . those sweet dreams . . . tap-tap-tap.

[*She hops down from the table and holds the magazine tightly to her chest.*]

Course, life doesn't always happen like that. I ended up married to Eddie the plumber's son. He's a good man, reliable. Had three kids, lived in the same house behind the old shopping centre for nearly thirty years now. Did the books for Eddie, kept the place spotless and the kids in school, cooked Eddie's steak or his sausage casserole or his roast lamb every night of the week, half-past six . . . on the dot.

Reality — so much more mundane, conventional and uninteresting

[*She grins at the irony of it all.*]

But I can still dream, can't I? I can still dream that one day I might meet Chrissie Carruthers, the girl who became everything I wanted to be! It's too late for me now — but I can still meet Chrissie.

[*She holds the magazine out, points to it.*]

Look — that's her! Gorgeous, isn't she? And so nice with it — not spoiled, like some of them are. I go to all her movies . . . three or four times, at least. She's so talented and beautiful, and she does so much for people . . . I'd love to meet her. Just for a few seconds . . .

Impressions gained from reading the media articles

[*She hops onto the table and pretends to be shaking hands with* 'CHRISSIE'.]

Oh hello, Ms Carruthers. Yes, Denise Wellbeloved. Why thank you, you're looking lovely too. Coffee at your house? Of course, that would be delightful. Yes, I'm sure you're right — we will become best friends. It was meant to be.

[*Back in character, she sighs again, gets down to the floor.*]

Imagine that! Me and Chrissie Carruthers — best friends.

Wow! Maybe there's still room in my life for some songs, some exotic costumes, some tap-tap-tap. Maybe the dream can come true . . .

[She reflects briefly, rolls up the magazine lovingly and exits . . . curtain.]

End of scene

Leaves the stage

by Richard Yaxley

Learning activity 3.3

1. In pairs or groups, discuss the following issues raised by the playscript:
   - the way in which the media creates public identities for famous people
   - the amount of control a public identity has over the creation of a public image (Consider the roles played by public relations people, the media, the paparazzi.)
   - rumour and its power to create or ruin identity — both for 'stars' and ordinary people
   - our dissatisfaction with our 'ordinary' identities and the way in which 'stars' can fuel our fantasies. Is this harmless or unhealthy?
2. Can you think of any real-life examples of famous people who have a public identity created for them by the media? (Do you know of any 'stars' who have publicly complained about something that has been written about them?) Is it possible for the public to know the 'real' person behind that creation?

Exploring theme in an imaginative text

This text is a chapter from *The House on Mango Street* by Sandra Cisneros. Each chapter is a snapshot of the childhood of a young Latin-American girl.

Purpose: creative/imaginative

My Name

Conversational tone addresses the reader

Simile

Metaphor

In English my name means hope. In Spanish it means too many letters. It means sadness, it means waiting. It is like the number nine. A muddy color. It is the Mexican records my father plays on Sunday mornings when he is shaving, songs like sobbing.

The legacy of the name

It was my great-grandmother's name and now it is mine. She was a horse woman too, born like me in the Chinese year of the horse — which is supposed to be bad luck if you're born female — but I think this is a Chinese lie because the Chinese, like the Mexicans, don't like their women strong.

Focus moves from her name to her great-grandmother

Metaphor

Simile

My great-grandmother. I would've liked to have known her, a wild horse of a woman, so wild she wouldn't marry. Until my great-grandfather threw a sack over her head and carried her off. Just like that, as if she were a fancy chandelier. That's the way he did it.

Metaphor

And the story goes she never forgave him. She looked out the window her whole life, the way so many women sit their sadness on an elbow. I wonder if she made the best with what she got or

was she sorry because she couldn't be all the things she wanted to be. Esperanza. I have inherited her name, but I don't want to inherit her place by the window.

Aspirations for a different, more independent life

Focus moves back to the name

At school they say my name funny as if the syllables were made out of tin and hurt the roof of your mouth. But in Spanish my name is made out of a softer something, like silver, not quite as thick as sister's name — Magdalena — which is uglier than mine. Magdalena who at least can come home and become Nenny. But I am always Esperanza.

Simile

Shortened form of her name — diminutive

I would like to baptize myself under a new name, a name more like the real me, the one nobody sees. Esperanza as Lisandra or Maritza or Zeze the X. Yes. Something like Zeze the X will do.

The link between one's name and one's identity

Learning activity **3.4**

This passage explores the links between names and our identities. In this case, the narrator feels there is a mismatch between what her name seems to say she is and what she believes is the 'real me'.

(a) In 2005, the following names were included in the list of most popular Australian babies' names: Jack, Joshua, Lachlan, Thomas and William; Emily, Chloe, Olivia, Sophie and Jessica. In pairs, select a couple of these names and try to decide what kind of identity parents hope for their child when they select each of those names.

(b) What kind of identity seems to be suggested by 'alternative' names such as Tree, Zahara, Alaisha, Cinnamon, Jovan, Mi'Quel?

(c) Select another culture with which you are familiar or which you can research. What are the most popular baby names in this culture? What do these names suggest about the desired identity of the child?

Exploring theme in a novel

The next text is an extract from the novel *So Long, See You Tomorrow* by American author William Maxwell. When the narrator was a young boy, the father of his friend, Cletus, murdered Lloyd Wilson, who had been having an affair with his wife. The father later drowned himself. To his great shame, the narrator never acknowledged or spoke to his friend again, but deserted him at this terrible period in his life.

In this extract, which occurs towards the end of the novel, the narrator remembers that he had seen Cletus again, some time later, in another town, at another school. Even then, he did not acknowledge him.

So Long, See You Tomorrow

The meeting in the school corridor, a year and a half later, I keep reliving in my mind, as if I were going through a series of reincarnations that end up each time in the same failure. I saw that he

Creates a feeling of repetition

recognized me, and there was no use in my hoping that I would seem not to have recognized him, because I could feel the expression of surprise on my face. He didn't speak. I didn't speak. We just kept on walking.

Short sentences emphasise the drama of the moment, its importance.

I remember thinking afterward, *When enough time has passed he will know that I haven't told anybody* . . . But I still went on worrying for fear he would think that the reason I didn't speak to him was that I didn't want to know him, after what happened. Which is, I'm afraid, what he did think. What else?

Did he go home and tell his mother? And did they then pack up and move to another part of Chicago to get away from me?

If I'd had the presence of mind to say, 'You don't have to worry, I won't tell anybody,' would they have been able to stay where they were? Would his mother have trusted a fifteen-year-old boy to keep such a promise, even if I had made it?

Going back over what might have been, had he behaved differently

He believes that this would have protected the identities of Cletus and his mother.

Sometimes I almost remember passing him in the school corridors afterward. And I think, though I am not at all sure of this, that I can remember being happy that I was keeping his secret. Which must mean that he was there, that we continued to pass each other in the halls, that he didn't move away. But if he had stayed on at that school, sooner or later we would have been in the same classroom, and I know that we weren't.

Perhaps this is something he wants to believe.

More realistic

Five or ten years have gone by without my thinking of Cletus at all, and then something reminds me of him — of how we played together on the scaffolding of that half-finished house. And suddenly there he is, coming towards me in the corridor of that enormous high school, and I wince at the memory of how I didn't speak to him. And try to put it out of my mind.

His behaviour here shows that the impact of what he did does not lessen with time.

One day last winter, plagued by guilt, I brought down from the attic a grocery carton stuffed with old papers, diplomas, newspaper clippings, letters from college friends I haven't seen for thirty or forty years, and so on, and went through it until I found my high-school yearbook. The photographs of the graduating class are arranged in vertical panels, fifteen oval likenesses to a page. Cletus ought to have been between Beulah Grace Smith and Sophie Sopkin and he isn't. If he had been, I would, I think, have been able to put him out of my mind forever. I went through the yearbook carefully from cover to cover looking for him. He isn't in any group picture or on any list of names.

Shows that his image of himself is a negative one

He cannot put the past behind him, even after all these years.

Because he would know that his lack of acknowledgement had made no important difference in Cletus's life

> This sounds as if he is trying, unsuccessfully, to convince himself to 'move on'.

There is a limit, surely, to what one can demand of one's adolescent self. And to go on feeling guilty about something that happened so long ago is hardly reasonable. I do feel guilty, even so. A little. And always will, perhaps, whenever I think about him. But it isn't only my failure that I think about. I also wonder about him, about what happened to him. Whether he was spared the sight of his father's drowned body. Whether after a while he and his mother were able to look at each other without embarrassment. Whether he had as lonely a time as I did when he first moved to Chicago. And whether the series of events that started with the murder of Lloyd Wilson — whether all that finally began to seem less real, more like something he dreamed, so that instead of being stuck there he could go on and by the grace of God lead his own life, undestroyed by what was not his doing.

> Expresses the hope that the events of Cletus's childhood will not mar the rest of his life

Learning activity 3.5

This extract explores how events in childhood can shape our identities.

1. How has the narrator's identity — or view of himself — been shaped by his childhood experience?
2. How might Cletus's identity be shaped by the family tragedy?
3. How might the events in Cletus's childhood affect his identity in the eyes of others?
4. Do you sympathise with the narrator or condemn him?

Exploring theme in a blog

The next text is the first page from a blog. This is an online journal posted by an individual and, as you might expect, it is a reflection of his virtual identity.

Learning activity 3.6

What kind of virtual identity has the blogger created here? Fill in the following table.

Aspect of his identity	How this is revealed in his blog

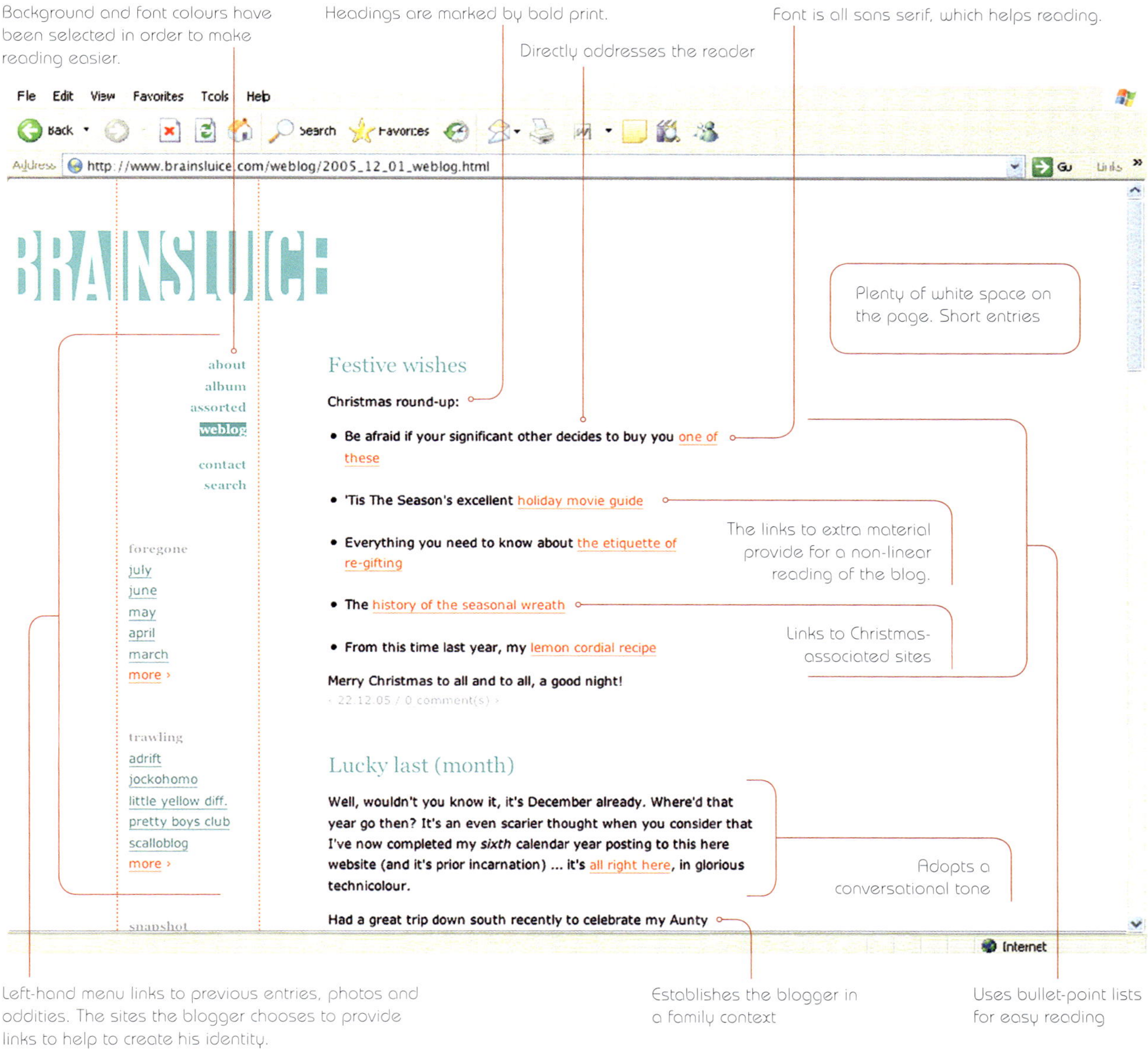

Purpose, audience, context and form

The authors of the previous annotated texts made choices about the form, context, audience and purpose of their writing, which in turn shaped the language they used to create their texts. These same choices will need to be made by you as the author of a text that presents a perspective on your chosen theme. The table below demonstrates what is meant by these terms.

Purposes for creating texts	
to explain	to analyse
to shock	to recount (an incident)
to reflect	to describe
to instruct	to argue

Purposes for creating texts (continued)	
to complain	to report
to examine	to satirise
to discuss	to entertain
to comment on	to inform
to create	to persuade

Audiences for whom we create texts	
oneself	readers of a magazine
peers	young children
family	the school or local community
friends	readers/internet users with a specialised interest in your subject
readers of fiction or a particular **genre**	readers of a particular section of a particular newspaper

Contexts within which we create texts	
academic (e.g. essays, research papers)	media
online	literary
cultural	workplace
personal (e.g. journal, diary)	

Forms	
diary entry	review (book, film)
personal letter	report
short story	poem
web page/blog	feature article
comment/opinion article	photographic essay
speech	hypertext

Learning activity **3.7**

For each of the texts you have read so far in this chapter, identify the form, the context, the audience and the purpose. The annotations will be of assistance to you. In the last column describe the kind of language in which the text is written.

Words and phrases which can be used to describe language:

formal
informal
colloquial

conversational, friendly
simple, clear
complex or sophisticated word choice
elegant
poetic, lyrical, full of **imagery**
short, simple sentences
long, **complex sentences**
technical terms, **jargon**

Text	Form	Context	Audience	Purpose	Language
Twins					
Identity theft a $100-billion industry					
Snap-Snap!					
My Name					
So Long, See You Tomorrow					
www.brainsluice.com					

Other creative choices

Authors make a whole range of creative choices in relation to the language they use in their texts and how they structure those texts. Here are some of the choices that you might consider before you begin.

What will be your point of view, or perspective?

Will you write in the first person, using 'I', to put forward a point of view, or will you write in the second ('you') or third person ('s/he')?

First person: I strongly believe that when I was born my parents were extremely disappointed. I was not what they had been hoping for.

Second person: You feel fairly confident that no-one will pay much attention to you, that you have dressed to blend in and that everyone will be far too preoccupied with their own attempts to be noticed. But what you don't realise is that everyone automatically checks out everyone else.

Third person: He spent a long time deciding what his atavar should be. Something edgy, he thought. Something that would say 'Be careful. Don't mess with me.'

Learning activity **3.8**

In pairs, discuss the following questions:

- What are the advantages and disadvantages of writing in the first person?
- What are the advantages and disadvantages of writing in the third person?

What will be the voice of the text?

For more information on tone see pages 187–8.

If you have trouble with the concept of 'voice', read the picture book *Voices in the Park* by Anthony Browne. This book has four distinct voices and it is useful to analyse how Browne creates each one.

The voice of a text is closely connected to point of view and contributes to the 'personality' or style of the piece of writing. The voice of a text is created by, for example, tone, word choice, sentence length and punctuation.

When creating a text you do not always have to use your own voice, although there is nothing wrong with doing so, especially if your voice is a distinctive one. Writing is generally more effective if it has a distinctive voice, so it is worth experimenting with different voices in order to achieve this.

Consider the voice in the following extract from a novel by Sophie Kinsella. What do you learn about the narrator?

The Secret Dreamworld of a Shopaholic

I don't look bad, I think. I'm wearing my black skirt from French Connection, and a plain white T-shirt from Knickerbox, and a little angora cardigan which I got from M&S but looks like it might be Agnès B. And my new square-toed shoes from Hobbs. And even better, although no-one can see them, I know that underneath I'm wearing my gorgeous new matching knickers and bra with embroidered yellow rosebuds. They're the best bit of my entire outfit. In fact, I almost wish I could be run over so that the world would see them.

Voice can also be evident in **non-fiction** writing, particularly in writing that is argumentative. Consider the following letter to the editor. What sort of voice do you think the writer adopts here?

Hey, what is going on here? I've got my VCE, I'm not too ugly to look at, I can hold my own in a conversation, but no matter how hard I try I can't get a job.

So far I've responded to dozens of advertisements, travelled all over town on the Met knocking on doors — even tried the internet. No luck.

I just don't get it. What do I have to do to be noticed?

In the meantime, of course, I've been down to the local Centrelink office and I'm officially a dole recipient. I don't like it. It makes me feel bad. Not good for the old self-esteem, you know?

OK so there are hundreds of thousands like me. It doesn't really help to know that. What I want to know is, if it's my fault I'm unemployed, what can I do about it? If it's not my fault, what's somebody else doing about it?

Or perhaps I've got it all wrong. Perhaps nobody gives a stuff.

D. McKenzie, Oakleigh

Word choice and sentence structure

Your word choice and sentence structure will, of course, reflect your chosen form, purpose, audience and context, but here are some general tips to consider:

- Use fewer rather than more words.
  A long sentence, using lots of words, is not necessarily an example of good style. Try to make sentences shorter but the words more specific. (See next point.)
- Use specific **verbs** and **nouns** rather than a lot of **adjectives** and **adverbs**.
  'He spoke loudly' can become 'He bellowed.'
  'A large, frightening dog' can become 'a rottweiler'.
  'An imposing, rich-looking house' can become 'a mansion'.
- Avoid **clichés** and jargon.
  Predictable writing relies on clichés and jargon. If you want your writing to be different, you need to use your own language rather than that of others.

Examples of clichés include:
He was dealt a crushing blow.
My grandmother is fiercely independent.
Going to the developing country was a moving experience.

- Consider the use of passive and active voice according to your purpose in writing.
  Passive voice: Ann was killed by her husband.
  Active voice: He killed his wife.
  Formal, bureaucratic writing is often written in passive voice. Livelier writing will make use of the active voice.
- Vary the length and structure of your sentences so that you use simple, complex and **compound sentences**.
  A simple sentence: The celebration was a huge success.
  A compound sentence: The celebration was a huge success and the organisers were very pleased with the result.
  A complex sentence: The celebration was a huge success from the point of view of the guests, but the organisers said that they would choose a larger venue next year.
- Consider using **figurative language** (for example, similes and metaphors) but only where appropriate and don't overdo it.
  Some people never want others to enjoy themselves. They're like teachers on yard duty, always on the lookout for students misbehaving.

Online design

If you are creating for an online environment, you have further options to consider because you will make use of both **visual** and written language. The following advice applies to websites created for a professional purpose.

- Decide what 'feel' you want your site to have. The 'feel' should reflect the purpose and audience of your website.
- A 3-column layout is a convention worth considering.
- Decisions about font:
  Use sans serif for headings and serif for text.
  Don't use too many different fonts.
  Be consistent in your use of fonts across your website.
- Avoid a cluttered look. White space is an important part of design.
- Use graphics and photographs that reflect the content and make them part of the design.
- Use colours that make reading easier rather than more difficult.
- Avoid too many 'tricks'. Remember the purpose of your website. (For instance, if it is mainly intended to provide information, you don't want to distract or annoy your readers.)
- Use font, including size and style, bolding, italics and colour as cues to help your reader understand your site.
- Use a consistent tone across all parts of your site. (Don't, for instance, adopt a formal, objective style in one section and a chatty, conversational style in another.)
- Avoid large chunks of text because this makes reading more difficult. Consider the use of bullet points as a way of conveying information, and keep paragraphs short.
- Avoid the situation where readers have to scroll down long pages of information. Instead, break up the information into a series of pages.
- Instead of writing a lot, provide links to other pages which expand on the basic information.

Learning activity **3.9**

If you intend to create another kind of multimodal text — a photographic essay or an audiovisual presentation, for instance — there will be further stylistic choices for you to consider. Brainstorm these before you begin.

The assessment tasks on the next page list examples of the ways in which you might go about exploring and presenting on the theme of identity. You can choose one of these tasks or design one of your own.

The following table is designed to assist you in planning your thematic exploration. In the left-hand column list the decisions that need to be made before you begin. (Some examples have been listed already.) In the next column you can indicate your choice and in the final column provide a reason for that choice.

After completing the table, seek feedback from someone else about your choices and review them in the light of the advice you receive.

Focus	My choice	Reason for my choice
Purpose		
Audience		
Form		
Context		
Language — first person/second person/third person — tone (See list of possible tones to adopt on pages 187–8.) — **tense** (**present** or **past**?)		
Designing a website — font size and type — colours — graphics		
Creating a video or DVD — **storyboard** — setting		

Strategies | Beginning a piece of writing

If you choose to write a short story or a personal recount, here are some ways in which you might begin:

- by creating a suspenseful situation
- with a particular event
- by setting the scene
- with **dialogue**
- with a one-sentence paragraph
- by introducing a character
- by introducing a problem.

See pages 13–14 for help in planning an analytical response.

Assessment tasks | Exploring and presenting themes or ideas

Choose one or more of the following assessment tasks. Be prepared to explain, either orally or in writing, why you chose to use specific language structures and features.

1. Select an aspect of the theme and develop a piece of writing in which you explore your own ideas on the topic. The following are examples of written forms and possible aspects of the theme which could be explored further.
   - Write an analytical essay on one of the following topics:
     'I am the result of everyone I have met and everything I have seen and heard.' Discuss.
     'Our modern western society, perhaps more than any other society which has been before, allows us to create and re-create our identities as much as we like.' Do you agree?
     Is it true that each of us needs more than one identity? Explain.
   - Write a poem which reflects on your national identity.
   - Write a script in which a dialogue between parent and child demonstrates the theme of identity.
   - Write a short story which explores how an event in childhood can help shape an individual's identity.
   - Write the lyrics for a song which reflects on the complexity of ethnic identities in a multicultural society.
2. Choose an aspect of the theme and develop a multimodal text in which you explore your own ideas on the topic. For example:
   - Create a website which seeks to promote understanding about the identity of an ethnic group in Australia.
   - Create a photographic essay, with accompanying written text, on the way in which clothes can be used to create identity.
   - Create an audiovisual presentation on the conflicting representations of the identity of a well-known person and present it on a CD.
   - Create an anthology of collected poems or short stories on the theme of identity. Design a suitable way of presenting these, with accompanying visuals, and write an introduction in which you explain your choices in terms of their relevance to the theme.
   - Create a blog and your own virtual identity.

See pages 117–18 for the criteria for assessment.

Editing and proofreading

Any text that is intended for a public audience should always be edited and proofread to ensure that it is both accurate and effective.

Editing refers to the process of reviewing your text to ensure that it is consistent and accurate in terms of the chosen form, audience, purpose, language and content.

Proofreading tends to focus more on accuracy of spelling and grammar and consistency of stylistic features such as font size, spacing and so on.

It is useful to have a checklist that you can apply to your text after you have completed the first draft. The following is an example.

Checklist for editing a written text

- Is the language I have used appropriate for my intended audience? (Would your audience expect formal language, colloquial language or a special jargon?)
- Is the form which I have chosen a suitable one for my audience and purpose?
- Have I achieved my intended purpose?
- Is the content interesting and substantial?
- Have I obeyed the conventions of my chosen form? (If you are writing a feature article, for example, have you included elements that are usually found in a feature article?)
- Is the structure of my text coherent and effective? (This refers not only to your overall structure but also to the order in which you present ideas or events. Is there an obvious connection between one paragraph and the next?)
- Have I made use of appropriate paragraphing?
- Have I used accurate and precise vocabulary?
- Is my sentence structure varied? (Do the majority of your sentences start in the same way and have the same structure? You can change these so that some sentences start with a **subject**, others with a **phrase** and others with a **clause**.)
- Are my sentences grammatically correct?
- Have I used correct punctuation?
- Have I used correct spelling?

Learning activity **3.10**

If you are creating a multimodal text, brainstorm your editorial checklist with someone else who is creating a similar kind of text. You can start by identifying the dot points from the above list which will also be relevant for you, and then add other points which will be specific to your kind of text.

How did others respond?

Here are some examples of student work in response to the assessment tasks on page 97. This is part of a poem written by Loretta Nichol:

I've locked up my identity,
and forgot where I left the key.
Now when they turn to judge me,
it's just a clone they'll see:
a vision of modern society,
the media's latest pop dream.
The same as any replica,
the same as any teen.
We march in lines, all looking the same,
And dream our dreams at night.
On the outside we are happy,
On the inside we struggle and fight.

Learning activity **3.11**

What aspects of identity does Loretta refer to in this extract from her poem? What is her view of her own identity and the identity of other teenagers?

This is a page from a blog created by Katrina Fong:

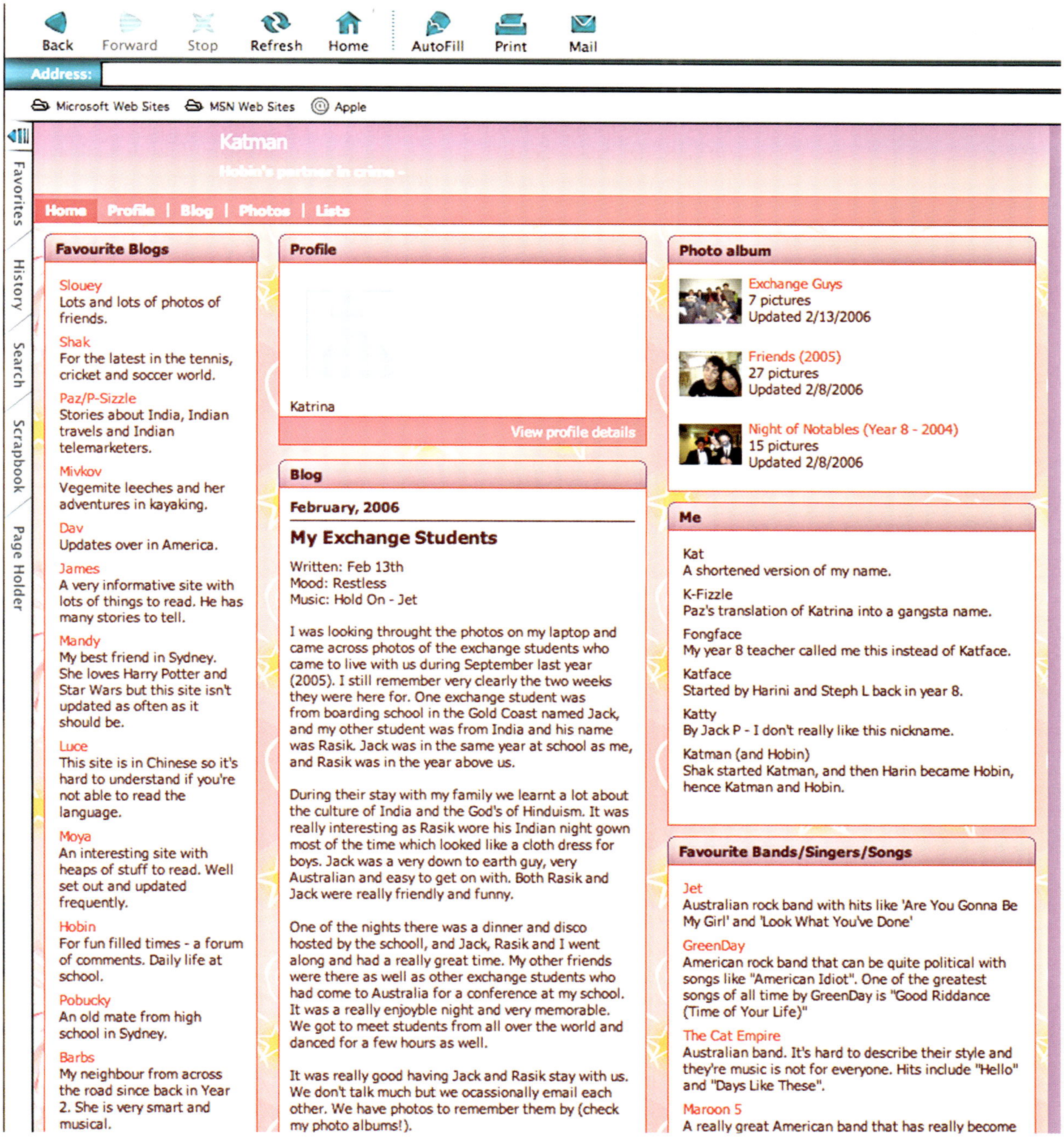

Back Forward Stop Refresh Home AutoFill Print Mail

Address:

Microsoft Web Sites MSN Web Sites Apple

Favorites History Search Scrapbook Page Holder

Katman

Hobin's partner in crime -

Home Profile | Blog | Photos | Lists

Favourite Blogs

Slouey
Lots and lots of photos of friends.

Shak
For the latest in the tennis, cricket and soccer world.

Paz/P-Sizzle
Stories about India, Indian travels and Indian telemarketers.

Mivkov
Vegemite leeches and her adventures in kayaking.

Dav
Updates over in America.

James
A very informative site with lots of things to read. He has many stories to tell.

Mandy
My best friend in Sydney. She loves Harry Potter and Star Wars but this site isn't updated as often as it should be.

Luce
This site is in Chinese so it's hard to understand if you're not able to read the language.

Moya
An interesting site with heaps of stuff to read. Well set out and updated frequently.

Hobin
For fun filled times - a forum of comments. Daily life at school.

Pobucky
An old mate from high school in Sydney.

Barbs
My neighbour from across the road since back in Year 2. She is very smart and musical.

Profile

Katrina

View profile details

Blog

February, 2006

My Exchange Students

Written: Feb 13th
Mood: Restless
Music: Hold On - Jet

I was looking throught the photos on my laptop and came across photos of the exchange students who came to live with us during September last year (2005). I still remember very clearly the two weeks they were here for. One exchange student was from boarding school in the Gold Coast named Jack, and my other student was from India and his name was Rasik. Jack was in the same year at school as me, and Rasik was in the year above us.

During their stay with my family we learnt a lot about the culture of India and the God's of Hinduism. It was really interesting as Rasik wore his Indian night gown most of the time which looked like a cloth dress for boys. Jack was a very down to earth guy, very Australian and easy to get on with. Both Rasik and Jack were really friendly and funny.

One of the nights there was a dinner and disco hosted by the schooll, and Jack, Rasik and I went along and had a really great time. My other friends were there as well as other exchange students who had come to Australia for a conference at my school. It was a really enjoyble night and very memorable. We got to meet students from all over the world and danced for a few hours as well.

It was really good having Jack and Rasik stay with us. We don't talk much but we ocassionally email each other. We have photos to remember them by (check my photo albums!).

Photo album

Exchange Guys
7 pictures
Updated 2/13/2006

Friends (2005)
27 pictures
Updated 2/8/2006

Night of Notables (Year 8 - 2004)
15 pictures
Updated 2/8/2006

Me

Kat
A shortened version of my name.

K-Fizzle
Paz's translation of Katrina into a gangsta name.

Fongface
My year 8 teacher called me this instead of Katface.

Katface
Started by Harini and Steph L back in year 8.

Katty
By Jack P - I don't really like this nickname.

Katman (and Hobin)
Shak started Katman, and then Harin became Hobin, hence Katman and Hobin.

Favourite Bands/Singers/Songs

Jet
Australian rock band with hits like 'Are You Gonna Be My Girl' and 'Look What You've Done'

GreenDay
American rock band that can be quite political with songs like "American Idiot". One of the greatest songs of all time by GreenDay is "Good Riddance (Time of Your Life)"

The Cat Empire
Australian band. It's hard to describe their style and they're music is not for everyone. Hits include "Hello" and "Days Like These".

Maroon 5
A really great American band that has really become

Learning activity **3.12**

What elements of Katrina's virtual identity are established in this blog? Annotate the blog to show where and how she creates this identity.

Exploring and presenting: It's not fair!

Apparently, children say 'it's not fair' about 80 times each day, and it is argued that they have a very finely developed sense of what is fair and what is not. But what is fairness? Is it the same as justice? How important are notions of justice and fairness in our personal lives? Are notions of justice and fairness part of the Australian way of life? Do we hold the same standards of justice and fairness for people of other nationalities as we do for ourselves and other Australians?

The texts that follow explore various aspects of the theme of fairness and justice. You might like to supplement them with other texts in order to expand your exploration of the theme.

If you brainstorm the theme you will be able to see its extent and the possibilities for further exploration. Here is the beginning of a concept map:

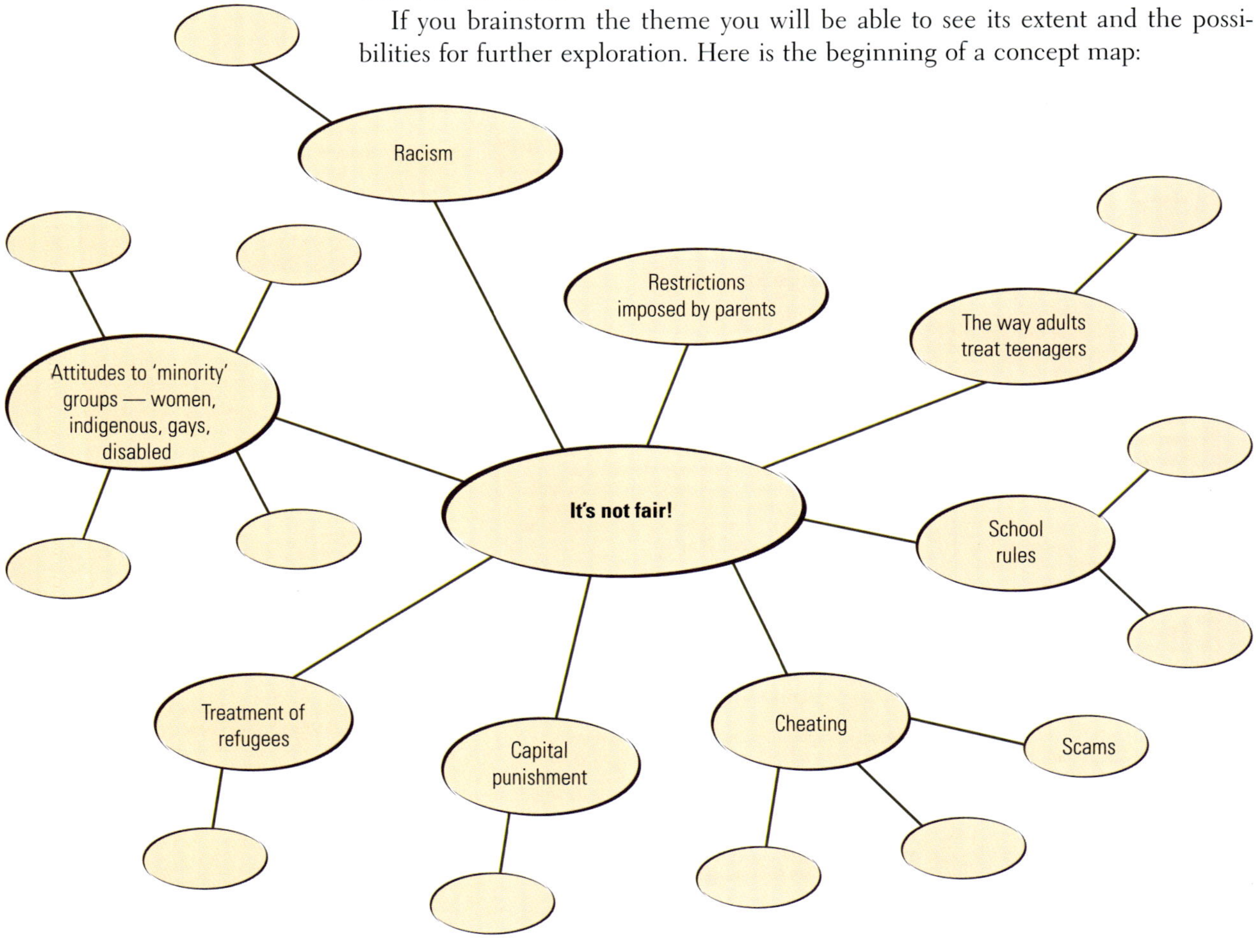

Learning activity 3.13

1. Work in pairs or groups to add to the concept map and then share your results with the class.
2. Do a further brainstorm to identify novels, poems, short stories, media articles, websites and movies that explore the various aspects of the theme that you identified in the concept map.

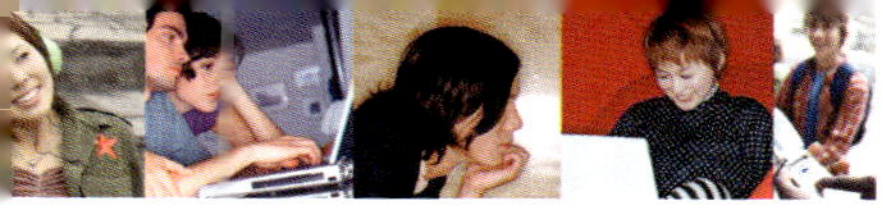

Other suggested texts:
Twelve Angry Men (play)
Mississippi Burning (film)
Dead Heart — Nick Parsons (play and film)
After the First Death — Robert Cormier (novel)
Snow Falling on Cedars — David Guterson (novel)
A Long Time Dying — Ernest Gaines (novel)
Montana 1948 — Larry Watson (novel)
A good Friday was had by all — Bruce Dawe (poem)

Fairness and families

The following texts explore how the concept of fairness operates in some families. Before you read the texts, scan each one briefly to identify the form in which it is written. In pairs, discuss what expectations you will have of the text in terms of language and features.

Sibling Rivalry

Sibling rivalry is used to mean a destructive interaction between children when one tries to beat the other or manipulate a situation to their own advantage. One child can damage another's self-esteem through such behaviour.

Temporary sibling rivalry is nothing to worry about, all kids fight. But a destructive cycle of sibling rivalry often ends with one child winning the contest, and the other becoming discouraged, giving up trying and perhaps developing emotional or behavioural problems.

It is understandable that most parents would like all of their children to be equally successful, so they use the behaviour of one as an example for others. Unfortunately, this often serves to create unpleasant feelings between siblings, because they see the 'example' child as the favourite. Some will accept being one down, but others will fight back, undermining the 'example' child's special role by attracting negative attention.

What parents can do to reduce sibling rivalry and conflict

Recognise each child's strengths and assets. No two children are identical. Encourage differences by stimulating and developing their individual characteristics and interests.

Avoid making too many comparisons. Children who constantly hear their brother or sister held up as a shining example soon come to resent that sibling and deliberately avoid following in their footsteps.

When fights occur, deal out the same consequence to all children involved. You may think that you have collected enough evidence to know who started the fight, but there is always the chance that you may be missing some vital bit of information. No matter who seems to be at fault, see that the consequences for both children are similar. It is safer to rely on this strategy than to risk blaming the wrong child. It will also teach children that no matter who is at fault, both participants are partly responsible.

Let your children know in advance what you call a fight. This enables you to hand out the consequences for fighting early on, when you are in control. If you intervene when the fight is already well underway and you lose your patience, you may be inconsistent and perhaps overreact. Another advantage for early intervention is that it cuts down unpleasant feelings between children. The fewer fights they have, the fewer nasty things they say to each other, and the fewer hurt feelings there are. Useful early warning signs of fights between siblings include:

Loud voices, name calling, swearing, screaming or crying
Pushing, jostling, poking
Hitting, kicking, scratching, biting
Taunting or dobbing

Reward children for co-operating with each other. If the pay-off is better for co-operating than for fighting, children will quickly get the message and fight less. To set up a system of rewards and privileges for not fighting, first record on a calendar the number of fights your children have each day in one week. Then set up consistent consequences for fighting and rewards for days with no fights. Another approach is to negotiate a daily privilege for all children if they co-operate. If all children receive a benefit for some of the children co-operating, there will be less competition between them and they might even help each other so they will earn the joint reward.

Relationships Australia

Learning activity **3.14**

1. Annotate the article above with the answers to the following questions. (Use the annotated *Who am I?* articles as models if you are unsure how to do this.)
   (a) What is the purpose of this article? (Did you have to read the entire article to work this out, or did a particular part of the article reveal the purpose?)
   (b) Who is the audience for this article? How do you know? (Annotate a part of the article that demonstrates your answer.)
   (c) What do you think is the tone of this article? Authoritative? Reassuring? Supportive? Find examples.
   (d) How does the article make use of specific examples to illustrate a point of view? Do you think this is an effective feature of the article?
   (e) How does the article make use of bolded subheadings? Do you think this was a good choice on the part of the author? Explain.

2. Do you think that the content of this article could be reshaped for a different audience? Nominate an audience and say how the content would be changed.

3. Do you think the content of this article could be produced in a different form? Nominate a form and say how the content would need to be altered in order to fit that form. Create the new text that you have nominated.

4. Summarise the points made in the article about fairness in a family situation. You might do this under these headings:
- the behaviour of siblings towards each other
- the effect of parents' behaviour on their children.

5. Did you agree with what the article had to say? Explain your answer.

Memoir

Breedge was apprenticed to a dressmaker, Mrs Daly, who lived in one of the Rockingham gatehouses, a beautiful circular stone house. Mrs Daly's family was reared. She was hard-working and kind. Breedge was well liked by the Dalys and became a skilled clothes-cutter and seamstress. As she was my father's favourite, he might have chosen dressmaking for her because of his own mother's trade; but in the narrow, emerging world of the people who belonged to the lower echelons of the new infant State it was seen as a come-down in the world for the daughter of a teacher and sergeant. I remember a man congratulating him ambiguously, 'People will always need clothes any-how'.

Rosaleen he sent as a trainee assistant to a family drapery in Cootehill in his own county of Cavan. They were a large prosperous family, the elder children away at university, the others at boarding schools. The father and mother ran the successful business, a mixture of fashion and serviceable clothes and footwear for people from the country, and they were both pillars of the church and town. Rosaleen was given her board and a minute weekly wage. She did serve in the shop from time to time, but most of what she did was housework. Except when

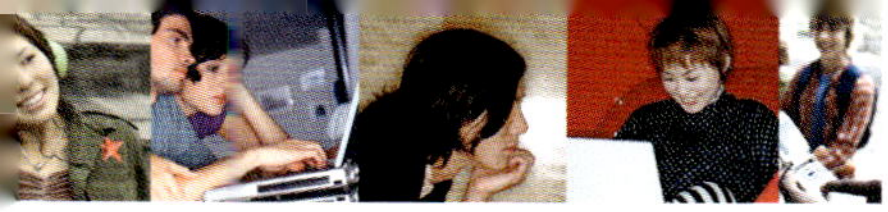

she was in hospital, this was the first time the twins had ever been separated, and Rosaleen was miserable. From the start, the draper made sexual advances. 'He could not keep his hands to himself.' She preferred housework because she was in the comparative safety of the wife's domain. For a long time she suffered in silence. I was closer to Rosaleen than to any of the other girls, and she wrote me at the school in Carrick where the letter couldn't be intercepted. I didn't tell my father, got away for the day with money on some excuse or other, and took the morning bus to Cootehill. I found the shop. She got leave to come out with me for the day, and when she told me all that was happening I saw that we had no choice but to leave together on the evening bus.

'What will he say when we turn up?' was her only fear. 'Will he not go crazy?'

'He'll say nothing,' I reassured her. 'He better not say anything.'

Rosaleen may have had Breedge in mind. Earlier, Breedge had run foul of his blind rage. She had twisted and fallen on her ankle carrying spring water from the priest's well. She managed to limp home, but her foot started to swell quickly. It was a Friday evening in Lent, and we all had to attend the Stations of the Cross in the church. He demanded that she go. She showed him the swollen ankle, spoke of the pain, and showed him that she could no longer get her foot into her shoe; but there was no way of reasoning with him in this mood.

If she could not wear her own shoes, she could go in his boots. She had many admirers and the thought of tramping up the village to the church in her father's boots was more horrifying than the swelling and pain. She refused. He took her upstairs and started to beat her into submission. Hearing his shouts and her cries, Guard Walshe opened the dayroom door, as if he was considering going upstairs, and paced about and rattled the door knob before going back into the dayroom. I was studying at the table in the living room.

'Why don't you go up and see if you can help her?' Monica begged me.

'He'd just beat me up as well. What good would that do her?' I answered. I was inured to such beatings. Hardly a day went by without one or more. I had not yet reached that time when I'd be forced to meet him and take him on.

'Maybe Guard Walshe will go up?'

Guard Walshe came out and rattled the doorknob again, but he did not go upstairs.

He failed to get her to go to church in his boots. Her vanity was stronger than his brutality, but even if she had been willing to wear his boots she would not have been able to walk. It was a bad break. During the night the pain worsened so much that she cried out and continued crying. No one in the house slept. In the morning he took her to Donoghue, the bonesetter in Cloone who set the ankle but botched the setting. In certain weathers the whole leg swelled. Veins had been set into the break. The ankle had to be rebroken, the veins taken out and sewed back together and the bone reset when she went to nurse in England. Donoghue set a number of our bones before he had to leave for America, pursued by litigants, but my father always defended him, blaming the litigants for their greed: Donoghue was cheap.

John McGahern

Learning activity **3.15**

1. This extract is set in the 1940s in Ireland. Are there any words that are unfamiliar to you? (What is a drapery, for instance?) Make a list and, in pairs, check their meaning.

2. In this extract from his **autobiography**, the author describes several examples of his father's brutality towards his family. List two of the examples.
3. In this extract, apart from the father's behaviour towards his family, what other examples are there of individuals not being treated fairly?
4. The author chooses to write in a very simple, matter-of-fact kind of style about content that is quite dramatic. Why do you think he chose this style and do you think it is effective?
5. What if this extract were rewritten from the point of view of the father? What do you think would be his perspective on the events described here?

Strategies | What does this word mean?

- Look for context clues. Sometimes the meaning of a word or phrase is explained immediately following its use, so look at the sentence in which it occurs.
- What do you think it means? Substitute the unfamiliar word with a synonym and re-read the sentence to see if it makes sense.
- Does it look like another word you know? Examine how the word is structured.
- Ask someone who might know.
- Use a dictionary.

Fairness and sport

Do you agree or disagree with each of the following statements?

	Agree	Disagree
1. Playing the game fairly is more important than winning.	☐	☐
2. In life, a person sometimes has to cheat in order to succeed.	☐	☐
3. In sport, people who are prepared to break the rules are more likely to succeed than people who do not.	☐	☐
4. People should play by the rules even if it means they will lose.	☐	☐
5. No sportsperson should take performance-enhancing drugs because they're unhealthy.	☐	☐
6. If a referee makes a mistake that favours you/your team, you should point out the mistake.	☐	☐
7. Taunting an opponent who is losing is just part of the psychological warfare.	☐	☐
8. Deliberately seeking to physically disable an opponent in a body-contact sport is acceptable behaviour.	☐	☐
9. If everybody else is taking performance-enhancing drugs, then it's okay for you to do so, too.	☐	☐
10. Sport is a serious business. It's quite okay to get annoyed with fans who intrude on your time because you need to be focused.	☐	☐

Learning activity **3.16**

1. What do you think is the purpose of this survey? What helps you to draw that conclusion?

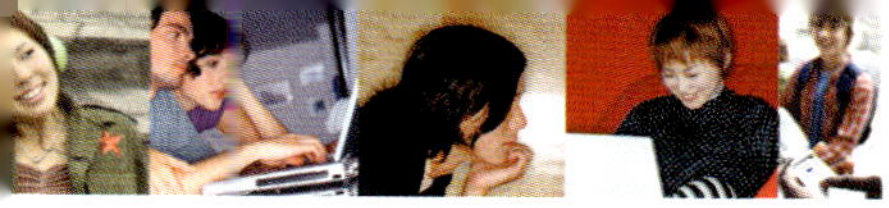

2. Work out a scoring system for this survey. Which answers were 'rewarded' and which ones were 'punished'? Why? Might someone else design a scoring system with a different emphasis? (Compare your scoring system with someone else's to identify similarities and differences.)
3. In a group, discuss these questions: In your opinion, what is fair in sport? What is unfair?
4. Use the model above to design a survey on cheating. To make the survey as broad as possible, include references to a variety of ways of cheating — for example, cheating on your boyfriend, cheating on exams or assignments, cheating on your taxes, cheating when playing games and so on.)

Notions of fairness in Australia

Learning activity **3.17**

1. Check the meaning of these words before you read the following article:
   - hegemony
   - egalitarianism
   - orthodox
   - tenuous
   - meritocracy
   - pragmatic.
2. Scan the article to check for other unfamiliar words. Make sure you know their meaning before you begin to read.

When equal can mean unjust

Australia has always prided itself on its sense of 'fairness'; it is central to the national identity. But what does this widespread commitment to the notion of 'giving people a fair go' really mean?

The hegemony of the Left

The 'Left' assumes that fairness means 'egalitarianism' — the forcible reallocation of money from one group of people to another by use of State power. They think that a 'fair society' is one where the distribution of income and wealth is made more equal through government tax and welfare policies.

In a recent article in the Melbourne *Age* Pamela Bone, its associate editor, described egalitarianism as 'part of the great Australian tradition of the "fair go"' and she took me to task for asserting that egalitarianism belonged to a specifically left-wing political agenda. Seen through her eyes, economic equality is one of those principles we should all unquestioningly accept. Increased equality indicates a move towards a more decent, caring and civilised society, while any move in the opposite direction indicates a decline into barbarism and the dog-eat-dog society of 'social injustice'.

This seems to have become the orthodox position in Australia. Even in the higher reaches of the public service bureaucracy in Canberra, there is now apparently an assumption that egalitarianism is one of those self-evident 'good things' that we no longer need to debate. How else can we explain the recent report from the Australian Bureau of Statistics (*Measuring Australia's Progress*) which sees nothing contentious or political about defining 'social progress' as the achievement of greater income equality?

This is an extraordinary assumption for a statutory body like the ABS to have made, for the idea of 'fairness' is essentially contestable. It need not equate with economic equality, for there are at least two other, equally plausible, interpretations of what 'fairness' and 'social progress' entail. Far from being obvious, the link between fairness and equality is highly tenuous.

Egalitarianism as fairness

The basic assumption of egalitarianism is that everybody is as good as everybody else. I don't have to do anything to prove I am your equal, for Jack is as good as his master, even if Jack stays in bed all day and his master works all hours to build up some assets. It is this belief (which egalitarians suppose to be 'moral' and 'ethical') that lies behind the regular calls from bodies like ACOSS for those who earn higher incomes to pay more tax to help those who are worse off. Egalitarians don't really care whether or not people have worked hard for their success, for their focus is on outcomes, not causes. What matters for egalitarians is the final distribution of rewards. An unequal society is an unfair society, regardless of what factors have led to the inequalities.

Equalisation of incomes and wealth is an article of faith in the western socialist political tradition. For most people on the left, such a policy needs no justification — it is a moral end in itself. Wide disparities between 'rich' and 'poor' are deemed to be 'unjust', and because socialist politics are about rectifying social injustice, it is felt that there is a compelling case of seizing resources from the first group and reallocating them to the second.

But is it fair to expect working people to share their earnings by paying taxes to support people who do not work? Is it fair, for example, forcibly to take money away from hard-working people to hand it over to young unemployed people, or to single parents of teenage children who prefer to stay at home than take employment? If you believe all this is fair (as opposed to being unavoidable), then you are an egalitarian.

Meritocracy as fairness

One alternative interpretation of what the notion of 'a fair go' means is grounded in the principle of meritocracy. This is the idea that people should be properly rewarded for their talent and ability and for the personal effort that they make to improve their situation. Meritocracy is grounded in the ethic of 'equality of opportunity' rather than 'equality of outcome'. Egalitarianism wants us all to cross the finishing line together, whereas meritocracy demands only that we line up on an equal footing at the start of the race.

From the point of view of 'meritocracy', a fair and just society requires only that everybody should have an equal opportunity to succeed (e.g. there should be open access to education and no legal barriers preventing particular groups from practising any trade or profession). Social justice does not require that all individuals end up with the same, for this would reward those who are lazy and would penalise those who work hard, and this is the antithesis of justice and fairness.

Is it fair to reward talent and hard work? Many wealthy individuals were born into humble circumstances, but have blended their inborn talents with a lot of training, dedication and hard work. Is it fair that they should now enjoy such high rewards? Is it fair that the bright kid in your class at school who swotted in the library while you were smoking behind the bike shed has now gone on to become a mega-successful brain surgeon while you are plodding away in a

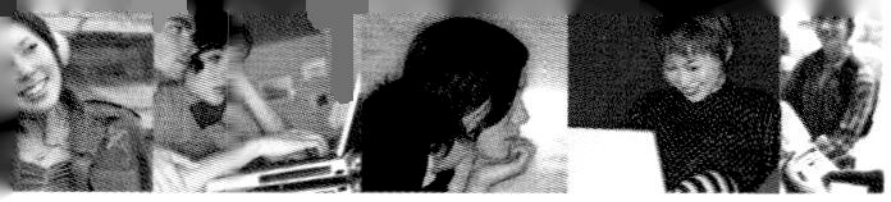

boring office job on one-tenth of their salary? If your answer is 'yes', then you are probably a meritocrat. If it is 'no', then I suggest you inspect your motives very carefully to ensure that your response is (as you probably believe) an 'ethical one'. Are you sure there is no trace of envy?

Liberal freedoms as fairness

Another ideal of the fair society is the liberal or free market ideal, in which fairness has nothing to do with equality, nor with how bright you are or how hard you work. Rather, fairness is the inevitable result of free exchange of goods and services between consenting adults. Provided the exchange does not involve deception or coercion, if someone offers goods or services that people want and someone else chooses to purchase them, then the end result is fair.

In a liberal society, fairness means that those who end up at the top of the heap are those who, by luck or design, have found out what other people want to buy and have provided it. Unlike the meritocrat, the liberal is quite happy to accept that sometimes, stupid and even lazy people can be successful. Equally, bright and hard-working people will struggle if they are not devoting their talents and effort to meeting other people's wants.

Provided people come by resources 'justly' (e.g. they do not steal them), they are morally entitled to keep them, in which case an egalitarian policy will be highly 'unethical' and extremely 'unjust' if it tries to use the power of the State to take away what is rightfully theirs.

Is it fair that people who spot opportunities and take risks should be rewarded when their hunches prove correct? Somebody like Rupert Murdoch is rich and powerful because millions of people worldwide want to buy his television programs and newspapers. Is he entitled to his success, or should we try to stop him producing successful newspapers, or take away his profits? Is it fair that Mel Gibson should be so wealthy simply because he has a handsome face that millions of cinema-goers are willing to pay to see, or that sports stars earn millions of dollars by entertaining millions of fans? If you think all this is fair, then you are probably a liberal. If you don't, you should stop to think why you are so opposed to ordinary people freely choosing to pay money to people who offer a few hours of harmless enjoyment. After all, none of us is compelled to buy Murdoch's newspapers, or to go to see Gibson's movies — but we are compelled to pay taxes.

The clash of ethical principles

Looked at in isolation from each other, all three of these principles of fairness might seem reasonable. The problem, however, is that all three contradict each other. We cannot simultaneously reward people according to their talents and efforts (meritocracy), allow them to keep the rewards accruing to them through market exchanges, irrespective of effort (liberalism), and make sure that they all end up with roughly the same (egalitarianism).

Research I conducted in Britain ten years ago found substantial popular support for all three ideals. Nine out of 10 people favoured the meritocratic ideal, but the other two ideals also each received the endorsement of about half the population. I suspect that this is also true in Australia, although just 2 per cent of respondents in a 2001 Morgan opinion poll mentioned pursuit of greater equality as one of three key issues deserving of the government's attention. This put it equal 18th in the public's list of priorities. The apparent consensus about giving people 'a fair go' may therefore actually disguise deep-seated disagreements over what this entails in practice.

Moral dilemmas

All three definitions of fairness have their problems. The clash between these competing principles represents a real moral dilemma for any thinking person, for none is self-evidently 'correct'. The problem in Australia, however, is that the egalitarians have tended to monopolize the discussion.

Any society needs to be seen as fair and just by its citizens, otherwise people will become disillusioned, alienated and disaffected. But simply insisting that Australia is committed to fairness and social justice is mere rhetoric unless we understand exactly what this means in practice, and why we prefer one notion of fairness over others. If we are going to debate these issues seriously, let us start by admitting that there are different criteria of 'fairness' and 'justice', and the earnest pursuit of one will result in the violation of others just as important.

Peter Saunders
Posted on Online *opinion* — Australia's e-journal of social and political debate
Monday, 15 July 2002

Learning activity **3.18**

1. What question does the article above set out to answer?
2. Complete the dot points. According to the author, there are three ways in which we can examine the issue of fairness:
   -
   -
   -
3. The author finishes each of sections two, three and four by asking a series of questions of the reader. Use these questions as the focus for a group discussion. Summarise your group's conclusions and share them with the rest of the class. Is there a particular approach to fairness which is favoured by most people?
4. One of the arguments put forward in favour of a more 'equal' society is that equality promotes social cohesion — that is, that people generally get on better together. How does the author respond to this idea?
5. What audience do you think this article was written for? (Consider not only the content and the language of the article but also where it was published.)

Below is a speech made by Paul Keating when he was Prime Minister of Australia.

Paul Keating's Redfern Speech

10 December 1992

The speech below, on indigenous issues, was given by the then Prime Minister of Australia, Paul Keating, at Redfern Park in Sydney. Redfern is an inner city suburb of Sydney with an historically large Aboriginal population.

Ladies and gentlemen,

I am very pleased to be here today at the launch of Australia's celebration of the 1993 International Year of the World's Indigenous People. It will be a year of great significance for Australia. It comes at a time when we have committed ourselves to succeeding in the test which so far we have always failed. Because, in truth, we cannot confidently say that we have succeeded as we would like to have succeeded if we have not managed to extend opportunity and care, dignity and hope to the indigenous people of Australia — the Aboriginal and Torres Strait Island people.

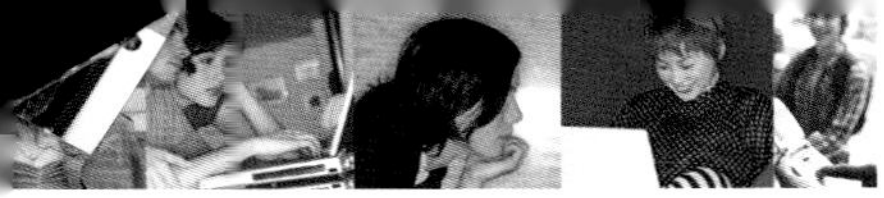

This is a *fundamental* test of our social goals and our national will: our ability to say to ourselves and the rest of the world that Australia is a first rate social democracy, that we are what we should be — *truly* the land of the fair go and the better chance.

There is no more basic test of how seriously we mean these things. It is a test of our self-knowledge. Of how well we know the land we live in. How well we know our history. How well we recognise the fact that, complex as our contemporary identity is, it cannot be separated from Aboriginal Australia. How well we know what Aboriginal Australians know about Australia.

Redfern is a good place to contemplate these things. Just a mile or two from the place where the first European settlers landed, in too many ways it tells us that their failure to bring much more than devastation and demoralisation to Aboriginal Australia continues to be our failure. More I think than most Australians recognise, the plight of Aboriginal Australians affects us all. In Redfern it might be tempting to think that the reality Aboriginal Australians face is somehow contained here, and that the rest of us are insulated from it. But of course, while all the dilemmas may exist here, they are far from contained. We know the same dilemmas and more are faced all over Australia.

That is perhaps the point of this Year of the World's Indigenous People: to bring the dispossessed out of the shadows, to recognise that they are part of us, and that we cannot give indigenous Australians up without giving up many of our own most deeply held values, much of our own identity — and our own humanity. Nowhere in the world, I would venture, is the message more stark than it is in Australia…

We simply cannot sweep injustice aside. Even if our own conscience allowed us to, I am sure, that in due course, the world and the people of our region would not. There should be no mistake about this — our success in resolving these issues will have a significant bearing on our standing in the world. However intractable the problems seem, we cannot resign ourselves to failure — any more than we can hide behind the contemporary version of Social Darwinism which says that to reach back for the poor and dispossessed is to risk being dragged down. That seems to me not only morally indefensible, but bad history.

We non-Aboriginal Australians should perhaps remind ourselves that Australia once reached out for us. Didn't Australia provide opportunity and care for the dispossessed Irish? The poor of Britain? The refugees from war and famine and persecution in the countries of Europe and Asia? Isn't it reasonable to say that if we can build a prosperous and remarkably harmonious multicultural society in Australia, surely we can find just solutions to the problems which beset the first Australians — the people to whom the most injustice has been done.

And, as I say, the starting point might be to recognise that the problem starts with us non-Aboriginal Australians.

It *begins*, I think, with the act of recognition. Recognition that it was we who did the dispossessing.

We took the traditional lands and smashed the traditional way of life.

We brought the diseases. The alcohol.

We committed the murders.

We took the children from their mothers.

We practised discrimination and exclusion.

It was *our* ignorance and *our* prejudice.

And *our* failure to imagine these things being done to us.

With some noble exceptions, *we* failed to make the most basic human response and enter into their hearts and minds.

We failed to ask — how would I feel if this were done to me?

As a consequence, we failed to see that what we were doing degraded all of us…

The message should be that there is nothing to fear or to lose in the recognition of historical truth, or the extension of social justice, or the deepening of Australian social democracy to include indigenous Australians. There is everything to gain. Even the unhappy past speaks for this.

Where Aboriginal Australians have been included in the life of Australia they have made remarkable contributions. Economic contributions, particularly in the pastoral and agricultural industry. They are there in the frontier and exploration history of Australia. They are there in the wars. In sport to an extraordinary degree. In literature and art and music.

In all these things they have shaped our knowledge of this continent and of ourselves. They have shaped our identity. They are there in the Australian legend. We should never forget — they helped build this nation. And if we have a sense of justice, as well as common sense, we will forge a new partnership.

As I said, it might help us if we non-Aboriginal Australians imagined *ourselves* dispossessed of land we have lived on for fifty thousand years and then imagined ourselves told that it had never been ours.

Imagine if *ours* was the oldest culture in the world and we were told that it was worthless.

Imagine if *we* had resisted this settlement, suffered and died in the defence of our land, and then were told in history books that we had given up without a fight.

Imagine if non-Aboriginal Australians had served their country in peace and war and were then ignored in history books.

Imagine if *our* feats on sporting fields had inspired admiration and patriotism and yet did nothing to diminish prejudice.

Imagine if *our* spiritual life was denied and ridiculed.

Imagine if we had suffered the injustice and then were blamed for it.

It seems to me that if we can imagine the injustice then we can imagine its opposite. And we can *have* justice.

I say that for two reasons: I say it because I believe that the great things about Australian social democracy reflect a fundamental belief in justice. And I say it because in so many other areas we have proved our capacity over the years to go on extending the realism of participation, opportunity and care…

…I think we are beginning to see how much we owe the indigenous Australians and how much we have lost by living so apart.

I said we non-indigenous Australians should try to imagine the Aboriginal view. It can't be too hard. Someone imagined this event today, and it is now a marvellous reality and a great reason for hope.

There is one thing today we cannot imagine.

We cannot imagine that the descendants of people whose genius and resilience maintained a culture here through fifty thousand years or more, through cataclysmic changes to the climate and environment, and who then survived two centuries of dispossession and abuse, will be denied their place in the modern Australian nation.

We cannot imagine that.

We cannot imagine that we will fail.

And with the spirit that is here today I am confident that we won't.

I am confident that we *will* succeed in this decade.

Thank you.

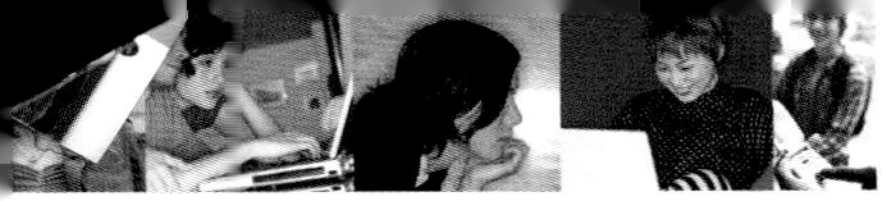

Refer to the section on Speeches in Chapter One if you need assistance with this learning activity.

Learning activity **3.19**

1. Annotate the speech with examples of the following oratorical (speechmaking) techniques:
   - repetition
   - emphasis
   - references to history
   - rhetorical questions
   - inclusive statements (use of 'we' and 'us')
   - appeals of various kinds (to patriotism, to a sense of justice)
   - examples of words and phrases used to position the listeners to agree with his point of view.
2. Why do you think that the speaker uses the word 'imagine' so often?
3. Summarise the reasons the speaker puts forward to argue for a change in the attitudes towards indigenous people and the ways in which they are treated.

OPINION

There's cash to splash, but not for disadvantaged

RICHARD MCENCROE

Thousands of Australians have little and need much at a time when governments are holding billions of dollars in surplus.

Budget surpluses — politicians love them, and voters and international ratings agencies are comforted by reports of spare bickies in the tin. The word evokes a sense of plenty. Reports of mega-surpluses from Canberra and the state capitals reassure heavily mortgaged suburbanites that real austerity or struggle will remain the lot of our forefathers, at least for now. The response is an almost universal call for tax cuts. But is the problem that governments tax us too much, or spend too little?

People in the 'burbs have had it drummed into them by Peter Costello that surpluses, coupled with some modest tax cuts and a little rainy day savings, add up to low interest rates. So for them it's all good. The usual suspects from the big end of town and those championing small and medium enterprises leap on the surplus figure like seagulls onto a chip, then squawk for tax cuts. Newly elected president of the Victorian ALP, Bill Shorten, has also joined the chorus.

Their logic, it seems, is that a big surplus is evidence that tax rates are too high. Calls for reductions are often accompanied by calls for more efficient collection methods, which is a little curious, given we are collecting more than we can spend.

But for many Australians, those same surplus reports simply deflate spirits and add insult to injury. They are the Australians, many of whom are indigenous, who live with the futility and despair that arise from woefully inadequate basic levels of government spending.

An impeccably preened Treasurer boasting of a budget in surplus when such need exists is a cruel, if subtle, reinforcement of the status quo. It signals to the community that the Government is satisfied it is doing enough and any more money collected will be considered surplus.

Surpluses are easily achieved when governments neglect their responsibilities to deliver services and infrastructure the market cannot. If the expenditure bar is set too low, or what is initially allocated to a particular sector or initiative is well below what would redress the market's failure, then budget surpluses are an unsurprising outcome. Rather than political musts, as they have been fashionably regarded for a decade, budget surpluses, especially tens of billions of dollars worth, should be viewed more cynically than they are.

With tens of billions in the kitty, one could be forgiven for thinking every Australian now has equality of opportunity and access, and we have billions in change. Should a society that allows, for example, its elders to be mistreated and underfed, and indigenous babies to die in infancy at three times the rate of non-indigenous children have a surplus?

A stark — and to my mind the most shameful — example of the often tragic flaws of fiscal arrangements in this country is the appalling disadvantage and lack of opportunity that exists in many remote indigenous communities in the Northern Territory. I have spent some time this year working with representatives of government and community groups in the NT. I have been troubled by the idea that Australian society can be both the custodian of whopping federal, and in some cases state, budget surpluses and allow such entrenched disadvantage to fester.

Thousands of Australians are born lucky every year. Thousands are born unlucky. I recently became a father for the third time. We live in Melbourne so we are lucky. We have access to roads, health care, education, transport, telecommunications and shops that stock what we need.

Other Australians, like many I met this year, will be born into chronic disadvantage in terms of education, health care and transport. Can you imagine the outrage if our children turned up to school and did not have desks, or enough teachers or books? It happened to hundreds of children this year in Wadeye, a NT community.

Those children don't have a made road to their community, and nothing like the health, higher education, employment and counselling services available to other Australian children. Talk about a forgotten people. More children were born in the Wadeye community than anywhere else in the NT last year, but have access to none of the services we southern state dwellers take as given. The substance abuse epidemic and other social problems in many NT communities are on a scale that requires a huge shift in resourcing if they are to be remedied.

The Victorian budget surplus is tracking about $7 billion, about half the size of the anticipated Commonwealth surplus. If we were living in a state where the Government kept up its end of the bargain with the taxpayer and where, for example, if you were mentally or physically unwell and in need of care, that care was available, and where the public transport system was efficient and reliable, and our educational standards and facilities world class and accessible to all, then a surplus would be good news. But we don't, and that's the problem. What the Victorian Government is in effect saying is that keeping that money for a rainy day is more important than health, education, infrastructure and a range of other things that are needed now. If you are waiting for a mental health bed, or a special needs teacher, or a hospital bed, bad luck. Your governments, federal and state, have billions available but not for you.

So, what to do? Rather than starting the annual budget process by looking at what was spent last year and tweaking it according to promises and deals made, how about governments begin from the point of view of allocating funds according to need? The annual budget cycle is tight. Even if governments were inclined to look comprehensively and critically at a sector and allocate funds according to need, the annual processes don't allow the time.

The Government has billions, but thousands of Australians have little and need much. Surely it's time for the 'I'm all right, Jack' attitude to taxation and spending to end. I'm all for careful budgeting, but let's be honest about what our real needs are, so we can work out if there really is a 'surplus'.

Richard McEncroe, a former senior economist in the state Department of Treasury and Finance, is a consultant to the Federal Government.

Learning activity **3.20**

1. What point of view is the author arguing in this opinion column?
2. According to the article, which groups in Australian society believe that the news of a budget surplus is 'all good'?
3. What impression does the author seek to create when he says that those who are happy with the budget surplus '... leap on the surplus figure *like seagulls onto a chip*, then *squawk* for tax cuts'?
4. The 'status quo' is the situation as it exists at the present. A 'reinforcement of the status quo' therefore refers to something that serves to make sure that things stay the way they are. What is meant by this expression as used in the article: 'a cruel, if subtle, reinforcement of the status quo'?
5. Comment on the effect of the use of words such as 'futility', 'despair' and 'woefully inadequate'.
6. What impression does the author seek to create of the Treasurer when he describes him as 'impeccably preened'?
7. How does the author use his personal experience and situation to emphasise his point of view?
8. Examine the elements of the cartoon:
   (a) Why do you think the cartoonist depicted the Treasurer as Santa Claus?
   (b) What does the sack represent?
   (c) Who are the various disadvantaged groups represented here?
   (d) How are the words 'Ho! Ho! Ho!' used here?

Fairness in a global context

In this section we will look at the beginning of a photo essay (a story told in photos), a poem and a website — each of which has something to say about the issue of justice from a global, rather than Australian, point of view.

Learning activity 3.21

1. Look at the title of the photo essay. How does it extend the impact of the photo of the Turkish women?
2. The text chosen to accompany the photograph contains many words with positive connotations. What are some examples and why do you think the author chose to use these words?
3. Examine the framing of the photograph. What is the central image? Why do you think the photographer chose to frame the photograph in this way?
4. Examine the angle from which the women have been photographed. What effect do you think the photographer hoped to achieve by using this particular angle?

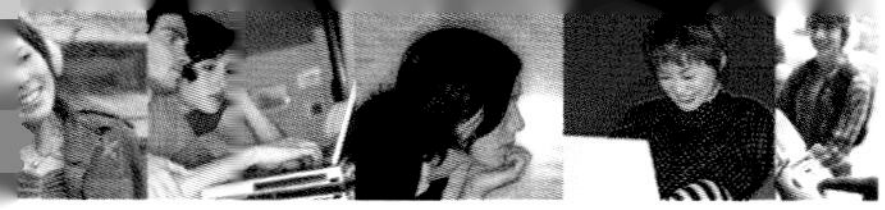

Aboriginal Charter of Rights

We want hope, not racialism,
Brotherhood, not ostracism,
Black advance, not white ascendance:
Make us equals, not dependants.
We need help, not exploitation,
We want freedom, not frustration;
Not control, but self-reliance,
Independence, not compliance,
Not rebuff, but education,
Self-respect, not resignation.
Free us from a mean subjection,
From a bureaucrat Protection.
Let's forget the old-time slavers:
Give us fellowship, not favours;
Encouragement, not prohibitions,
Homes, not settlements and missions.
We need love, not overlordship,
Grip of hand, not whip-hand wardship;
Opportunity that places
White and black on equal basis.
You dishearten, not defend us,
Circumscribe, who should befriend us.
Give us welcome, not aversion,
Give us choice, not cold coercion,
Status, not discrimination,
Human rights, not segregation.
You the law, like Roman Pontius,
Make us proud, not colour-conscious;
Give the deal you still deny us,
Give goodwill, not bigot bias;
Give ambition, not prevention,
Confidence, not condescension;
Give incentive, not restriction,
Give us Christ, not crucifixion.
Though baptized and blessed and Bibled
We are still tabooed and libelled.
You devout Salvation-sellers,
Make us neighbours, not fringe-dwellers;
Make us mates, not poor relations,
Citizens, not serfs on stations.
Must we native Old Australians
In our land rank as aliens?
Banish bans and conquer caste,
Then we'll win our own at last.

Kath Walker

This poem was prepared and presented to the 5th Annual General Meeting of the Federal Council Aboriginal Advancement, held at Adelaide, Easter 1962.

Learning activity 3.22

1. Who is speaking in the poem on the previous page?
2. Who is being addressed?
3. The poem makes use of the following techniques:
   - a series of contrasts
   - repetition
   - use of imperatives.

   Annotate the poem to identify examples of each of these techniques.
4. What do you notice about the placement of 'positive' words in each of the lines? What effect does this have? (Read the lines aloud to note where the emphasis occurs.)
5. In your opinion, is this an effective poem? Why or why not?

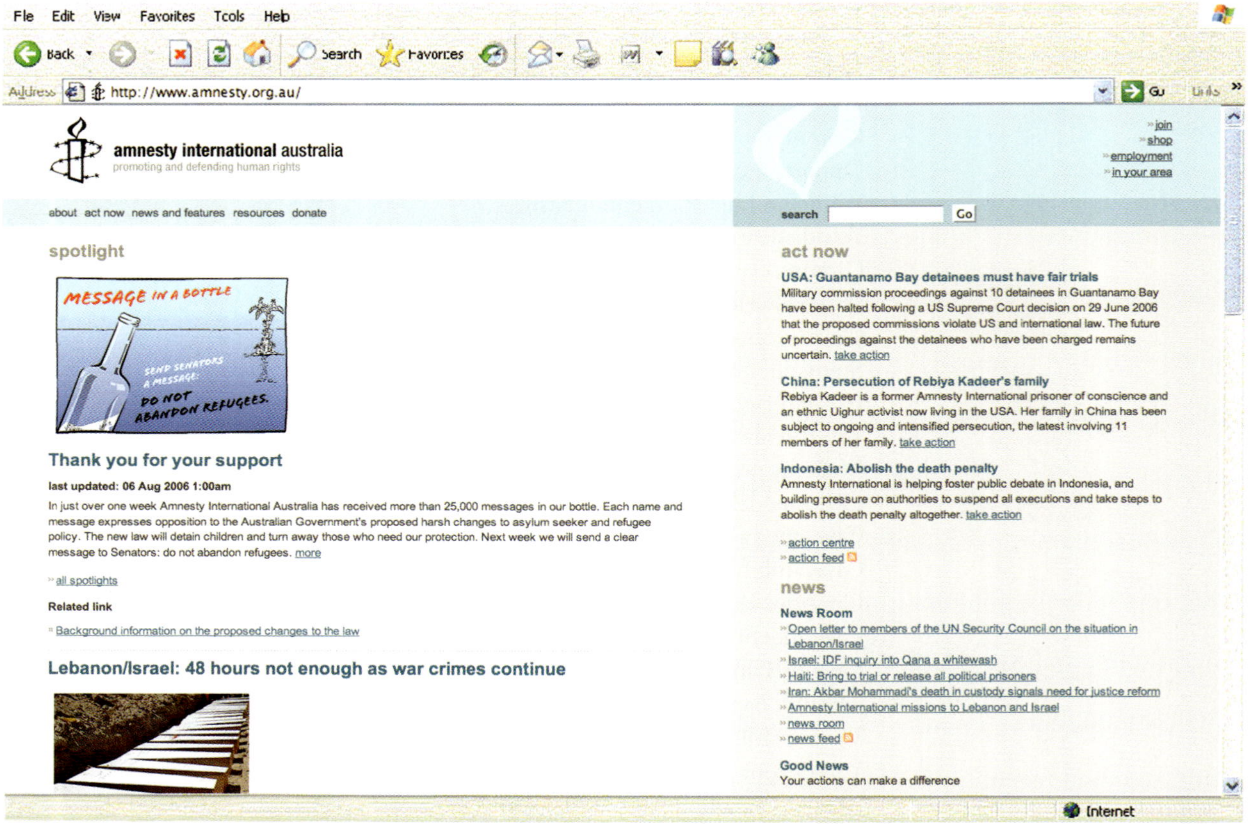
File Edit View Favorites Tools Help

Address http://www.amnesty.org.au/

amnesty international australia
promoting and defending human rights

» join
» shop
» employment
» in your area

about act now news and features resources donate

search Go

spotlight

MESSAGE IN A BOTTLE
SEND SENATORS A MESSAGE:
DO NOT ABANDON REFUGEES.

Thank you for your support

last updated: 06 Aug 2006 1:00am

In just over one week Amnesty International Australia has received more than 25,000 messages in our bottle. Each name and message expresses opposition to the Australian Government's proposed harsh changes to asylum seeker and refugee policy. The new law will detain children and turn away those who need our protection. Next week we will send a clear message to Senators: do not abandon refugees. more

» all spotlights

Related link

» Background information on the proposed changes to the law

Lebanon/Israel: 48 hours not enough as war crimes continue

act now

USA: Guantanamo Bay detainees must have fair trials

Military commission proceedings against 10 detainees in Guantanamo Bay have been halted following a US Supreme Court decision on 29 June 2006 that the proposed commissions violate US and international law. The future of proceedings against the detainees who have been charged remains uncertain. take action

China: Persecution of Rebiya Kadeer's family

Rebiya Kadeer is a former Amnesty International prisoner of conscience and an ethnic Uighur activist now living in the USA. Her family in China has been subject to ongoing and intensified persecution, the latest involving 11 members of her family. take action

Indonesia: Abolish the death penalty

Amnesty International is helping foster public debate in Indonesia, and building pressure on authorities to suspend all executions and take steps to abolish the death penalty altogether. take action

» action centre
» action feed

news

News Room

» Open letter to members of the UN Security Council on the situation in Lebanon/Israel
» Israel: IDF inquiry into Qana a whitewash
» Haiti: Bring to trial or release all political prisoners
» Iran: Akbar Mohammadi's death in custody signals need for justice reform
» Amnesty International missions to Lebanon and Israel
» news room
» news feed

Good News

Your actions can make a difference

Internet

Learning activity 3.23

1. What is the purpose of this website? Which features led you to this conclusion?
2. Who is the likely audience for this website? What kind of relationship is established between the site and its audience? Which features help to do this?
3. Identify the main campaigns in which Amnesty International is currently focusing its activities and say which ones, if any, you find significant and why.
4. What do you think is the purpose of the 'Good News' section?

See pages 13–14 for assistance in writing an analytical response.

Don't forget to edit and proofread. See pages 97–8 for some guidelines.

Assessment tasks | Exploring and presenting themes or ideas

Choose one or more of the following assessment tasks. Be prepared to explain, either orally or in writing, why you chose to use specific language structures and features.

1. Select an aspect of the *It's not fair!* theme and develop *a piece of writing* in which you explore your own ideas on the topic. For example:
   - Write an analytical essay on one of the following topics:
     - 'At the root of all injustice is poverty and inequality.' Do you agree?
     - 'Justice for one group of people might mean that sacrifices need to be made by others. That's why justice is sometimes hard to achieve.' Discuss.
     - Are you hopeful that justice for all can be achieved in Australian society? Explain.
   - Write a poem that describes a particular example of injustice.
   - Write a monologue in which someone who has been unfairly treated tells his or her story.
   - Write a short story that describes an example of a personal injustice and how it was dealt with.
   - Write an analytical essay in which you explore the Australian value of a 'fair go'.
   - Write a feature article on the work of Amnesty International.
2. Select an aspect of the *It's not fair!* theme and develop a multimodal text in which you explore your own ideas on the topic. For example:
   - Create a website that focuses on arousing awareness about injustices done to a particular group of people.
   - Create a photographic essay that contrasts the lives of the 'haves' and the 'have nots'.
   - Create an audiovisual presentation on the work of someone who has devoted their life to working for social justice.
   - Create an anthology of collected poems or short stories on the theme of justice. Design a suitable way of presenting these, with accompanying visuals, and write an introduction in which you explain your choices in terms of their relevance to the theme.

See below for the criteria for assessment.

Criteria for assessment

Your assessment task will be assessed according to the following criteria. Read them carefully before you begin your task; while working on your task, check your progress against the criteria and then review your completed task against the criteria before submitting it to your teacher.

Knowledge and understanding of the content of set text/s. This includes, where relevant:

- use of direct quotes from the set text/s
- use of direct reference to ideas suggested in the set text/s
- use of indirect reference to ideas suggested in set text/s
- discussion of some of the complexities of the theme or issues arising from the context.

Understanding of the relationships between audience, purpose, context and form. This includes:

- identification and discussion of audience and purpose of own and others' texts
- selection of a form appropriate for a specified audience, purpose and context
- identifying, discussing and using language (visual and/or **verbal**) appropriate to the specified audience, purpose, context and form
- planning and revising to achieve coherence of audience, purpose, context and form.

Ability to construct a written or multimodal text using the features and structures of the chosen form. This includes, where relevant:

- relevance of response to the set topic
- clear and coherent point of view supported by evidence from the set text/s
- control of spelling, punctuation and syntax
- use of **non-verbal** and visual language as appropriate to the chosen form, for example, colour, font, camera angles and shots.
- coherent organisation.

CHAPTER 4

Exploring technology and communication

The focus in this chapter is on how different **information and communication technologies,** such as digital and online technology, influence the ways in which authors create text. In addition to examining the features of a number of different texts, this chapter will also look at some of the issues surrounding these technologies and ask you to respond to these. You will also have the opportunity to experiment with the creation of texts that use the technologies.

The digital divide

Before we start this chapter it might be useful to examine one of the significant issues in relation to the use of technologies — what is referred to as the *digital divide*. This term is used to describe the fact that not all people — even within Australia, and certainly in developing countries — have the same access to computers and the internet. Apart from economic reasons (some people simply cannot afford to use these technologies), there are other reasons such as inadequate literacy and technical skills and the quality of the connection services and internet speed.

This digital divide, it is argued, has significant consequences. For example, those without access to efficient technological services are deprived of access to some kinds of entertainment and, more importantly, to information. Government departments are increasingly making important information available via government websites and those without access to the internet are deprived of the opportunity to access information that could be vital to their everyday lives.

Learning activity **4.1**

1. In groups, discuss the following questions about your own experience of the digital divide and present a summary of your findings to the class.
   - Who are the technology users among your family and friends?
   - Why are some people not technology users? What factors prevent them from being technology users?

- Are there certain technologies that some people use that others don't? (Consider the computer, the internet, email, chat, discussion groups, mobile phones, texting, iPods etc.)
- Can you see any pattern in who uses which technologies? Is the pattern linked to the purpose of the technology?
- Where do the technology users make use of these technologies — at home, at work, at school or at university?
- What advantages do you think technology users have over non-technology users?
- In your opinion, should governments play a role in seeking to lessen the impact of the digital divide?
- In your opinion, can schools play a role in seeking to lessen the impact of the digital divide?

2. Examining advertisements for technology can tell you a great deal about who the advertisers think is likely to use their product. Examine the following three print advertisements and answer these questions.

(a) Which groups in society are targeted by these advertisements?

(b) Is there a difference in the kinds of technology that are shown for each group?

(c) Which groups in society are not targeted by these advertisements as technology users?

(d) How does each of the advertisements seek to appeal to its target market?

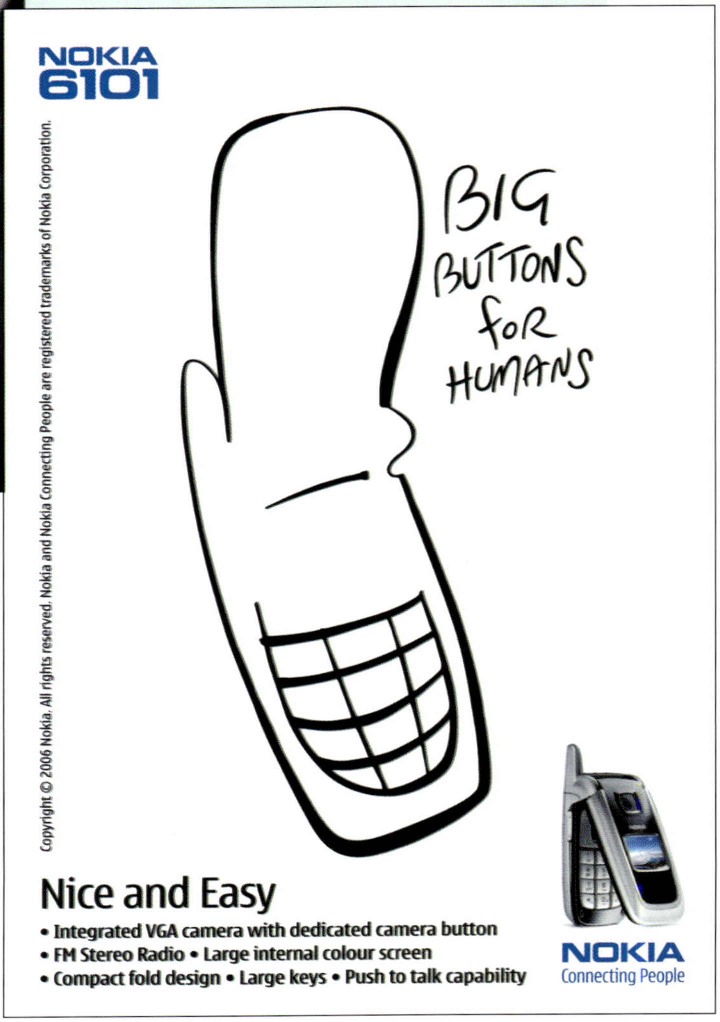

SMS

SMS (Short Messaging Service), along with email, has seen a dramatic increase in the degree to which individuals communicate with each other. Millions of text messages are sent each day. People make arrangements, keep in touch, make enquiries, pass on information, share experiences — all by SMS. And it is not only individuals who make use of this technology. Businesses use text messages as a way of communicating with customers and their employees; politicians promote themselves and their polices via text messages; 'reality' TV shows use the technology to facilitate interactive text voting; charities and nonprofit organisations use text messages to raise funds; and international relief efforts and emergency operations have been made somewhat easier as a result of the convenience of text messages.

MMS (Multimedia Messaging Services) is an enhancement of SMS and allows users to add sounds and video to their electronic print texts to create **multimodal** texts.

An acronym is an abbreviation which uses only the first letter in a number of words. For example, FYI — for your information.

SMS has seen the evolution of a texting language which typically abbreviates words, omits vowels, and uses acronyms, numbers and symbols to communicate. The limits of the technology — a small screen or display area and a limit of 160 letters or symbols — and the comparatively more expensive cost of voice calls on mobile phones have encouraged these changes to language. This is a perfect example of how the form (SMS) and the **context** (technology) influence the use of language.

@ = "at"	msg = "message"	w = "with"
atb = "all the best"	w/o = "without"	wknd = "weekend"
bcnu = "I'll be seeing you"	xlnt = "excellent"	no1 = "no-one"
xoxox = "Hugs and Kisses"	b4 = "before"	oic = "oh, i see"
pcm = "please call me"	cu = "see you"	1 = "one, won"
2 = "too, to, two"	2day = "today"	f2t = "free to talk"
ruok = "are you ok/okay"	2moro = "tomorrow"	2nite = "tonight"
gonna = "going to"	sum1 = "someone"	4 = "four, for"
u = "you"	gr8 = "great"	h8 = "hate"
luv = "love"	ur = "you are"	thnq = "thank you"

Examples of shorthand versions of words and phrases

Symbols ('smilies') used to convey emotions

: -)	(a smile)	I'm happy.
; -)	(a wink)	I'm joking.
: -D	(mouth open)	I'm surprised.
: -O	(mouth wide open)	I'm screaming.

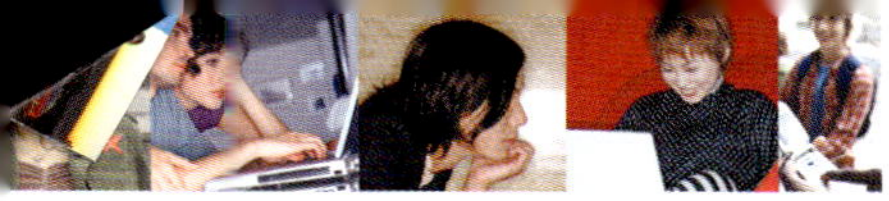

Learning activity 4.2

1. Write a text message that incorporates each of the following features of texting language:
   - abbreviated words
   - words without the vowels
   - an acronym
   - numbers to represent syllables
   - symbols to convey emotion or **tone**.
2. The language used in a text message is appropriate for the form, the audience and the purpose. What might happen to the clarity and accuracy of communication if the following were written in the language used for text messages? Explain your answer.
   - a railway timetable
   - a legal document
   - a poem

Some teachers have argued that the increasing use of SMS by students will have an adverse impact on their ability to write in more conventional ways. Read the following articles about the effect of texting on literacy and answer the questions.

Texting 'is no bar to literacy'

LUCY WARD, SOCIAL AFFAIRS CORRESPONDENT
THURSDAY DECEMBER 23, 2004
THE GUARDIAN

It's gr8 news 4 skools. Claims that the explosion in text messaging among children is eroding youngsters' literacy skills appear to be unfounded, according to research.

A study comparing the punctuation and spelling of 11- and 12-year-olds who use mobile phone text messaging with another group of non-texters conducting the same written tests found no significant differences between the two.

Both groups made some grammatical and spelling errors, and 'text-speak' abbreviations and symbols did not find their way into the written English of youngsters used to texting.

According to the author of the research, the speech and language therapist Veenal Raval, the findings reflect children's ability to 'code switch', or move between modes of communication — a trend familiar to parents whose offspring slip effortlessly between playground slang and visit-the-grandparents politeness.

But the study did find that the pupils familiar with text messaging wrote significantly less when asked to describe a picture or an event than those who did not use mobiles, potentially fuelling concerns that the quality and expressiveness of children's writing could be at risk even if their spelling is not.

The study, conducted at the department of communication and science at City University in London, comes amid growing concern in some quarters over the potentially damaging effects of new technologies on children's ability to communicate effectively using conventional means.

According to the mobile telecoms consultancy Mobile Youth, 700,000 (20%) of primary school children own mobile phones and the under-10s are the fastest-growing section of Britain's mobile phone market.

The leap in the popularity of mobiles and text messaging among children and teenagers over the past five years has prompted concern that pupils' literacy skills could suffer.

Texting puts a premium on speed and concision, leading to the creation of a host of abbreviations and acronyms incomprehensible to the untrained reader, together with symbols or 'emoticons', such as smiley faces, to express emotions.

Chief examiners' reports on trends in public examinations have begun to note instances of texting language in exam scripts. Some cases — including a 13-year-old Scottish pupil who wrote an entire description of her summer holidays in text-speak — have provoked concern among some teachers.

But despite widespread speculation there is little research into the potential influence of texting on children's writing.

According to Mr Raval's small-scale study, which focused on 20 youngsters, children have developed an ability to switch between two forms of language when texting or writing standard English.

Pupils were given a spelling test and conducted two writing exercises designed to replicate situations where they might normally text, such as describing something they had done the previous day, held in formal classroom conditions.

Mr Raval said: 'The fear that has been put across in the media is that children don't understand the need to code switch – that is, switch between standard English grammar for an exam or essay and what is acceptable when you are communicating on a social level. In fact, they are capable of that switch, just as bi- or tri-lingual children might speak English at school and a mother or father tongue at home.'

While the text-experienced children wrote much less than those without mobiles, concision was not necessarily a bad thing, he argued. 'Whether that is a positive or negative effect is up for debate. It depends on the situation or the subject studied. A science exam might require brief answers which might not be appropriate in a literature exam.'

A spokesman for the Qualifications and Curriculum Authority, which oversees public examinations, said the authority was interested in the research, and believed more investigation was necessary into the effect of texting on written communication.

It was important that children could communicate in a range of ways 'depending on the communication channel they were using', he said.

A National Union of Teachers spokeswoman welcomed the research, saying abbreviation used in texting could even boost literacy skills by helping children to learn about how words divide into syllables.

Learning activity **4.3**

1. What was the **source** of the research on which this article is based? Do you think it was comprehensive research? Explain your answer.
2. What were the findings of the research? Do you think that the headline given to this article reflects those findings? Explain your answer.
3. What was the opinion expressed by the spokeswoman from the National Union of Teachers?
4. This article refers to the practice of code switching. How many times each day do you code switch? Why do you need to do this?

Online communication

Emails

Emails are electronic mail messages composed and transmitted on a computer system or network. This technology has revolutionised the world of business and personal communication, with billions of emails being sent every day.

Like text messages, some emails make use of abbreviations such as acronyms. FYI, for example, and LOL, TTYL. They also make use of symbols such as 'smilies', intended to compensate for the fact that we can neither hear nor see the person with whom we are communicating via the email and therefore need extra clues to help us understand the intended tone of a particular comment. See some examples on page 122.

Learning activity **4.4**

1. Here are two emails. One is a personal email sent by someone to a friend, while the other is an email that has a more formal purpose.

From: princess254@hotmail.com
Sent: Tuesday, 17 January 2006 10:35:54 AM
To: jobaby@hotmail.com
Subject: everything

Hi there
just wondering how it's all going.... holidays OK? parents? (no dramas here anyway so I'm happy :-)

My cousin came down from Sydney for a few days. spent a lot of time in the city. took her around Melbourne central, out to chaddie, chapel st, brunnie st, up to the dandenongs. spent heaps of course. Mum wasn't pleased, but whoa! it's family what can u do? Wish you could come and stay. We'd *really* have a goooooooood time. ;-)

Starting to get ready for school (aaagh!) again. got my books yesterday. being a good student and starting to read the English books. feel up for it at the moment so might as well. you?
tell me what u're up to. (how's J – dare i ask?)
bfn
XX

From: leejones@yahoo.com
Sent: Monday, 17 July 2006 11:24:45 AM
To: JMaloney@business.com.au
Subject: missing cheque

Dear Mr Maloney
I received your cheque on June 24 and posted it to my credit union for banking on June 26. Unfortunately it seems to have gone astray in the mail.

Would it be possible for you to arrange for the cheque to be cancelled and a new one reissued?

Thank you for your assistance.

Regards
Lee Jones

Examine the use of language in each email. Annotate features to draw attention to the way in which the language use varies according to the purpose and audience of the email.

2. How might the language used in a letter be different from that used in an email? Rewrite the personal email above in the form of a letter and comment on the changes that you made to the language and structure.

In the business world billions of emails zip around the world every day. This means, of course, that individuals receive many emails each day in their inbox. Some they are interested in, some they are not. The following article explains that the way in which email newsletters are written has become very important because this will determine whether or not they are read by the recipients.

The key to email: a two-second grab

BY DAVID WALKER
JUNE 15, 2004

To communicate online, and particularly in email, you have to overcome the greatest dilemma of online communication: the online world has infinite space and infinitely small attention spans.

Content creators feel they can write at inordinate length, putting into the message not only their key idea but all the fine detail they think is important. After all, they think to themselves, it's not as if all this stuff has to be crammed onto a poster or even into a brochure.

Yet content recipients sit at the other end, making brutal, two-second decisions about what to look at and what to ignore, based on viewing no more than 20 words of that content. Even if they read, they skim. Or they save the email for another day, making it even less likely they will ever see its full content.

The result: the sender's writing a booklet, but the recipient's treating it like a roadside billboard. You're writing 1000 words. They're reading 10 — on a good day.

Why is this particularly true of email? Because the stakes for the user are so high here. Many email users are now trying to deal with much higher spam volumes than ever before. For these people, email has lost its innocence. They don't have time to linger over email; they want to empty their inbox and get on with it. So they sit, dropping most of their incoming messages down the pit with their delete key. You probably already operate in this brutal fashion. So does everyone else.

All this stands out in the email studies from the Nielsen Norman group, whose most famous principal, Jakob Nielsen, has just been in Australia holding seminars about — among other things — the challenges of email communication. Over the past decade no one else has been so accurate in predicting trends in the evolution of internet media. And Nielsen Norman's published studies are models of clarity.

Nielsen Norman first published a major study of email newsletter usability in 2002. Reading it, you saw anew how users of the time treated email newsletters like old-fashioned postal letters.

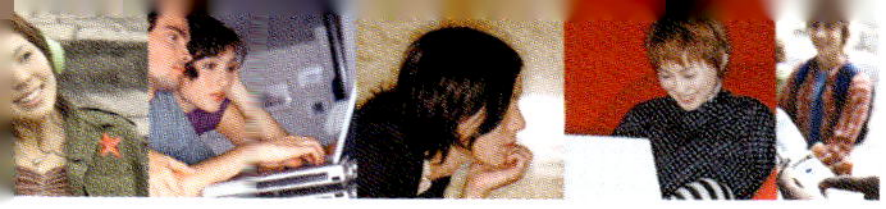

'Newsletters feel personal because they arrive in your inbox,' said the study. 'You have an ongoing relationship with them. In contrast, websites are things you glance at when you need to get something done or find the answer to a specific question.'

Nielsen Norman discovered users who didn't want to unsubscribe from newsletters because 'it doesn't feel good to sever the relationship'.

Nielsen Norman has updated its study and concluded that the email audience is getting still tougher and smarter. More people can tell the difference between email and spam; more people use spam filters to get rid of unwanted emails (with anti-spam technology, that means users are often reporting innocent newsletters as spam); they are concentrating more on email that helps them get something done.

'There is pretty much a "what have you done for me lately?" phenomenon at play, where newsletters have to justify their space in the inbox on a daily basis,' the researchers conclude.

Most importantly, users are weighing up email messages in even less time, scanning rather than reading. 'In our first study, 23 per cent of the newsletters were read thoroughly. In our second study, two years later, only 11 per cent of the newsletters were read thoroughly,' Nielsen Norman reports.

Email newsletter authors, and anyone else writing messages from organisations to individuals, must take a clear lesson from this: people are throwing away most of your information, and you can't fight the trend. Craft your email newsletters to sum up your message in subject lines, FROM addresses, opening lines and headings — the stuff Jakob Nielsen calls microcontent.

Yet the company remains confident of the future of the best newsletters, although that is a future of two-second decisions by users.

Learning activity **4.5**

1. What was the source of the information used by David Walker to write this article?
2. Complete this sentence: A 'two-second grab' is ....
3. Explain what the author means by 'the greatest dilemma of online communication'.
4. According to the article, there are three ways in which email recipients respond to email received:
   -
   -
   -
5. In what ways, according to the article, is the 'email audience getting still tougher and smarter'?
6. What was the purpose of this article? Quote evidence from the article to support your answer.

Email etiquette

See pages 164–5 for information about how to structure a business letter.

Just as there is a certain etiquette or protocol attached to the writing of a business letter, there is also a set of rules about writing emails. These rules are designed to make the communication clear and accurate and to create a good impression of the sender (and their organisation, if the sender is writing a business email).

Many businesses have an email policy which they distribute to their staff. These policies often include advice as follows:

- do not include graphics in the body of the email
- do not use ALL CAPITALS
- check your message and the name and address of the person to whom you are sending the email before sending
- begin your message with an appropriate greeting
- keep paragraphs short
- finish your message with an appropriate sign-off
- do not forward someone else's email without permission
- complete the subject line and keep it short
- if you are forwarding an email, delete any email addresses
- don't use emoticons ('smilies') in a formal email.

Of course, much of this advice is also relevant for personal users of email. Another piece of advice, relevant to personal users, is the need to have a formal email address for formal emails. Why might this be a good idea?

Examples of informal email addresses:
jacquibaby@yahoo.com
speedster@hotmail.com
pinkslippers@hotmail.com
broadshoulders@bigpond.com

Learning activity **4.6**

For each of the above dot points, explain why you think this advice would be included in an email policy.

Emails and privacy

While email technology has resulted in an enormous increase in the number of personal and business communications which occur every day, it has also created new concerns for those using that technology. The number of spam emails generated not only causes annoyance, but also raises concerns about the ability of systems to cope. An overload of spam mail can cause networks to crash while 'phishing' is a fraudulent practice which raises security issues. The following article provides advice about how to respond to 'phishing'.

'Phishing' emails reeling email users in

July 2006

Email users, already facing an avalanche of spam email (unsolicited, bulk email), are now also the targets of 'phishing' emails. Phishing emails contain hoax messages that instruct consumers to supply personal information in their reply email or after clicking on the supplied weblink. Essentially, phishing emails form part of an identity theft scam.

Consumers are often sceptical about the chance of email users falling for such a scam as, on the surface, it appears as if it is simply a blatant request for sensitive personal information. Such a request would normally be rejected out-of-hand and, perhaps, reported to the appropriate authorities. However, the 'catch' with phishing emails is in the detail. The messages often purport to be from respected institutions (often financial institutions) or businesses such as the Commonwealth Bank, ANZ bank, Citibank or eBay. They appear to have legitimate 'From:' addresses that infer that they have come directly from the institution or business. The messages also often contain official sounding

language, and the exact signature, confidentiality and copyright line that is used by the purported sender.

Email users are often alarmed into responding to the messages due to the nature of the instructions. The email messages may claim that the institution or business is conducting an audit of its accounts and requires the consumer to click through to a fake website at which account details and passwords can be entered to 'confirm' that they are indeed the owner of that account. The threat of account closure may be used to motivate the consumer to follow the instructions. Another example of a phishing email may have a supposed business that uses an internet shopping function on their website, apparently emailing their customers to alert them about internet shopping fraud. They will request that the customer click through to a (mock) website where they can re-enter credit card and address details to confirm that they are the holders of the internet shopping account. Even if no personal details have been requested, opening an attachment in the email or clicking on a weblink may allow keylogger spyware to be installed on your computer to steal details directly. There are many versions of phishing email scams; however, all will ultimately request personal details such as credit card numbers, passwords, address, name, phone number, date of birth and bank account numbers.

This modern-day scam requires consumers to be extra vigilant about unsolicited emails and about clicking through to websites contained within 'official' sounding emails. Use the following hints to protect yourself:

- Don't go into 'instant reply mode' after receiving an email. Take the time to read through the email carefully and judge its authenticity. Don't automatically follow the instructions.
- Never click on a weblink in an email unless you are confident beyond doubt that it is legitimate.
- If you do click on a weblink and find that the site looks quite authentic, be careful. The websites will often looking amazingly like the actual institution or business's websites, as website forgers are quite skilful.
- Note that financial institutions will never contact its customers by email to request account details or passwords.
- Move quickly if you believe you've been scammed or if you're wondering if it is a scam. Contact your financial institution or legitimate business and ask them to confirm that the email is authentic. They will advise on your next step.

Instant messaging

Instant messaging is a private text conversation between two people conducted in real time over the internet. Instant messaging makes use of a language similar to that used in texting, and users can send graphics, files, photos and sounds to each other as part of the conversation.

Chat rooms

A chat room is part of a website where users with common interests can communicate with each other in real time. Users have a user name, or virtual identity, and type their messages into a text box. Once again, the language of texting is commonly used in chat rooms.

Transcript from a chat room

You are in Movies:1

Indicates which chat room you are currently in

Carlo_9813: yr fav movie?
Soccerstar_93 left the room.
Tiffanygal: joined the room.
Sandralol: loved saw 1 but I just went to see Saw 2 I was really disappointed
Carlo_9813: yeah. not as good. what about king kong?
Yossimospats: 3 hours - ur joking. 2 long 4 me!
Sandralol: no it was great - definitely worth a look
Tiffanygal: boooring! they could have told that story in half the time... But Naomi watts was good.
Sandralol: yeah. I really like her, what about her in 24 grams. See that?
Carlo_9813: brilliant. And how about Sean Penn. Man, is he something!
Jojobelle left the room.
Pollyanna_312 left the room.
Loudman55 joined the room.
Tiffanygal: so carlo yr fav movie?
Carlo_9813: animation's my thing
Cudaniel: me too let's talk about that.
Sandralol: I'm outta here. cu
Carlo_9813: bye
Loudman55: sup?
Sandralol left the room.
Cudaniel: cel or computer?
Carlo_9813: computer
Tiffanygal: hi loudman remember me?
Cudaniel: which movies?

Bold type indicates visitors who are engaged in chat

Names of visitors

Use of texting language

Inconsistent use of capitals, more likely to be lower case

Visitors are made aware of who enters and leaves the room.

More than one conversation going on at the same time

Derives from What's up? Wassup? Sup?

Elsewhere on the screen there may be a list of who is currently signed in to the chat room. Not everyone who signs in will be engaged in the chat. Visitors who watch but don't participate are called 'lurkers'.

Chat room security

Many people have security concerns associated with chat rooms. These concerns centre on the fact that people can hide behind virtual identities and may not be as trustworthy as they seem, and there has been a lot of advice directed at chat room users to ensure their protection. In particular, there is concern about the way in which children use chat rooms. Read the following article and answer the questions.

How to Keep Safe in Chat

- **Be careful who you trust online** and remember that online friends are really strangers. People online, no matter how long you have been talking to them or how friendly they are, may not be who they say they are.

- **Meeting someone you have only been in touch with online can be dangerous.** If you feel that you 'have to' meet, then for your own safety you must tell your parent or carer and take them with you — at least on the first visit — and meet in a public place in daytime.
- **Stay in charge in chat.** Keep your personal information secret when chatting online (name, address, telephone number, mobile number, private email address, picture), even if people ask for this. Although it can be tempting to reveal more than you normally would in online friendships, giving out personal information can make you vulnerable.
- **Check your profile and make sure it doesn't include any personal information** (name, address, telephone number, mobile number, private email address, picture).
- **Get away from an unpleasant situation in a chatroom by logging out** (this just takes one click) or by changing your screen name.
- **Think before you answer private messages.** It can be harder to end a conversation in a private chat than in a public chat. A private chat may end up being more personal than you like.
- **Use a nickname**, not your real name, and a nickname that is not going to attract the wrong type of attention.
- **Look out for your friends** and do something if you think that they are at risk.
- **Tell your parent or carer** if someone or something makes you feel uncomfortable or worried.
- **Learn how to keep/save a copy of the conversation in chat** — this may be useful if you want to report something.
- **Learn how to block/ignore people.**
- **Check you know how to report something** you feel uncomfortable about to the chatroom provider.

Learning activity **4.7**

Answer the following questions by annotating the above article.

1. Who is the audience for this article?
2. What is its purpose?
3. How does the use of language reflect the purpose and audience of the article?

Discussion groups and message boards

Discussion groups are part of a website where users with common interests can communicate with each other by 'posting' comments, but this does not happen in real time. That is, users cannot get an instant reply to their comment or question but must return to the site on another occasion to see if someone has posted a response.

Discussion groups are often moderated; that is, someone is in charge of reading comments and keeping the discussion 'on track' by posing a question or comment for the participants to respond to. Many university lecturers make use of discussion groups for the students doing their subjects.

Message boards or forums are similar in purpose and form. Users ask queries or post comments and then wait for another user or users to reply. The Lonely Planet Thorn Tree is an example of a message board on which users post queries about travel destinations.

Example of a forum

New York

travel forum

Today Search Who's on Log in Help

Reply to this topic

New York

Lazydaisy Posted: 15 March 2006 7:43am	what would be a good itinerary for someone who has three days to spend in new york? what are the must–sees?
Campman Posted: 15 March 2006 9:10am	Central Park could occupy an entire day. So much to see there – people-watching is the best thing!
Lazydaisy Posted: 16 March 2006 8:12am	thanks. how easy is it to get around? are the subways safe? Is it easy to buy tickets for buses? Some places want you to have exact money which can be a pain.
Erica Posted: 17 March 2006 9:05am	Ny is the easiest city in the world to get around. Just buy a daily or weekly Met ticket at any subway and you can use it on buses and trains. If you travel around by bus you see everything but it's sloooow. The subway is fast but you don't see anything along the way. My best Ny place is the Met. You can spend a whole day there too.
Jackie4561 Posted: 19 March 2006 10:56pm	Some ny areas worth wandering around: Madison Ave between about 72th and 86th – rich, rich, rich! Lower East Side – more genuine, lots of students, a bit gritty. Greenwich – ok – pretty enough but a bit artificial. Upper west side around Columbus university, Chelsea ... ah well, just about anywhere really ...
Mai–ling Posted: 19 March 2006 11:15pm	To make the most of your time you really should plan it quite carefully. You don't want to be wasting time on public transport so plot out your route so that you're not crossing and recrossing Manhattan. I suggest starting right down the 'bottom' at Battery Park with a visit to the museum of the American Indian. From there you could make your way up Fifth Avenue to F.A.O. Schwarz – an amazing toy shop that even adults would find fascinating – and then, almost across the road, rent a rowboat at the boathouse in central park. Build in some time to sit on a seat somewhere in the Park and watch the passing parade. It's a wonderful insight into a great city. You might finish off the day with a baseball game at Yankee Stadium or a Broadway Show. (Visit the Half-Tix booth at Times Square for cheap tickets.)

Name of person posting the query or reply

Date and time of the posting

Original query

Icon which indicates whether the user is on- or offline

Print icon converts text to print-friendly version (without all of the formatting)

Responses

Language use varies: some texting language, some more conventional

Visitors are required to register

Username:

Password:

Login Cancel

Forgot your password?

Visitors are required to register before they can post queries or replies.

Learning activity 4.8

Write a reply to the following message posted on a travellers' forum. Use Mai-ling's posting in the above forum as your model, and write about 100 words.

> I'm hoping someone can help me with this. I'm travelling from London to Perth and have a two-day stopover in Melbourne in May. What should I do? See? I'm an 18 year old guy, vegetarian, like the outdoors, sport, girls (of course) and music (rock, rhythm, blues . . .)

Ezines

An ezine is an electronic magazine. Some ezines are sent by email to people on a distribution list, while others are published on the internet. Ezines — or zines — are often non-commercial, small-circulation magazines produced and distributed by their editors. Many of them survive for only a few issues.

In Australia there are, however, a couple of ezines that have been very successful in providing an outlet for views alternative to those that are published in the mainstream media. To read them, visit the website for this book and click on the first two Ezine weblinks for this chapter (see 'Weblinks', page 252).

Learning activity 4.9

You will need to go online in order to answer the following questions.

1. Who is responsible for the publication of each of the ezines you visited online?
2. What information can you find on the ezine about these people or organisations?
3. How does the ezine appear to be financed? (Take note of the kinds of advertising that occur on the site. Might any of these advertisers possibly influence the material that is posted on the site? Explain your answer.) Does the ezine have links with other publications or organisations?
4. How has the technology of the internet allowed for an interaction between the creators of the ezine and their users?
5. Do you think that the ezine has a particular target audience? If so, what is the nature of that audience and which aspects of the ezine helped you to draw that conclusion?

Websites

Reading a website requires the reader, who is usually referred to as the 'user', to:

- read and understand print
- recognise the significance of the elements of the design of the web page (font size, colour and style, placement of text and images, and the meaning of icons)
- identify links and make decisions about whether or not to access them according to the purpose in reading the website
- understand how to navigate around a website, scrolling down, using back and forward buttons and side and top menu bars and reading breadcrumbs
- have a visual memory for what they have seen on the screen.

'Breadcrumbs'
Breadcrumb navigation locates the current webpage in the context of a navigation path so that the user knows how s/he has reached a particular page.

A web page is not read in a linear way. Firstly, users scan the accessed web page to see what is there. Their eyes focus on images or print that demand their attention and then they make a series of choices about how to access the information provided by the website. The design of a website therefore needs to reflect the ways in which the users will actually use the technology available to them. A website which provides large chunks of information in a single column occupying the entire screen and unaccompanied by any graphics is not one which is making full use of the technology available. Nor is it one which is likely to appeal to a user who is familiar with the range of technological possibilities offered by the online environment.

Here is the home page of the website for Tourism Australia. Aimed particularly at potential visitors to Australia, this website makes comprehensive use of online technology and offers readers the opportunity to select from many different features. Websites are constantly changing — either updating information, changing their 'look' or ceasing to exist — visit the website for this book and click on the Tourism Australia weblink (see 'Weblinks', page 252).

The top menu provides a series of **hyperlinks** to extra information.

A search facility is provided.

Invitation to users to interact with the site by subscribing to the newsletter

The website uses visuals as a way of engaging user interest.

Links to information in the form of videos and articles

Side menu provides extra information.

There is a video which explains aspects of the site.

Readers are encouraged to use the site in an interactive way.

Learning activity **4.10**

Print the home page of your favourite website. Using the annotated web page above as a model, write annotations for your web page to highlight its structure and features, and the way in which it makes use of the technology.

Design features to avoid:

- too much white space on the page
- too much text on the page
- a single column of text which spreads across the page
- headlines whose font is too light or too small
- lack of contrast between the text and the background
- underlining — use bold and italics instead
- uneven spacing between paragraphs
- too much hyphenation
- too many different fonts

The design of a website

Any review of a website will pay attention to the 'look' of the website. It will analyse the creator's choice of font size, colour and style, the placement of text and images, the ease with which users can navigate around the website and the use of features such as **animation**. It will answer questions such as:

- Is the font of a readable size?
- Does the colour selected for the font and the background make it easy or difficult to read?
- Is the font style easy to read?
- Does the font style reflect the content and purpose of the website?
- Are headings sufficiently differentiated?
- Are there large chunks of text on the screen that require the user to scroll in order to read?
- Does the site make use of frames?
- Are these easy to use?
- If the site is a large one, does it make use of breadcrumbs to help the users know where they are?
- Are the images selected appropriate for the content of the page or site? (Do they relate to the content or are they just there for design purposes?)
- Is there a side or bar menu?
- Do the back and forward buttons help to navigate the site?
- What role does advertising play on the site? Does it make use of banner advertisements? Pop-ups? Are the text and images in the advertisements static or moving? How much does the advertising element interfere with reading the site?

Learning activity **4.11**

In groups, select a website and apply the above questions. Present your findings to another group or to the class.

The reliability of a website

Most importantly, the users' response to a website depends on their purpose in accessing it and the degree to which the website meets that purpose. One of the primary purposes for which the internet is used is to seek information, and of course the user needs to know that the information is reliable.

Learning activity **4.12**

In pairs, use the following table to help you explore the reliability of a selected website. Share your findings with another pair.

How accurate and comprehensive is the information on this website?	(a) Very accurate (b) There are mistakes either in the information or the spelling and grammar. (c) There is a great deal of information on the subject. (d) There is very little information on the subject and it tends to be general in nature.

Who is responsible for this website? (Is this author qualified to present this information?)	(a) The author is a reputable organisation or an individual who is an authority on the subject. (b) There is no evidence that the author is an authority or expert on the subject.
Is the website biased in the way it presents information?	(a) The website is designed to change the viewer's point of view and information is 'slanted' in order to achieve this. (b) The information is presented in a manner that is generally free from bias.
Is the information on the website current and up to date?	(a) The information has been recently updated. (b) It is difficult to tell how recently the site was updated. (c) The website contains information that is out of date.

Blogs

See pages 91 and 99 for examples of blogs.

A 'blog' is a particular kind of website which is created by an individual as an online journal. Some blogs are famous, such as the Baghdad Blog which was written by an Iraqi to record what was happening in Iraq around the time of Saddam Hussein's overthrow and the US invasion. Some blogs are more personal and almost have the status of a diary, while others are used by their creators as a means of showcasing their artistic design or musical talents. Journalists working in a freelance capacity are using their blogs to publish articles that would perhaps not otherwise appear in the mainstream media.

Learning activity **4.13**

In pairs, discuss the following questions:

1. Have you any experience of blogs? Explain.
2. What, in your opinion, makes a good blog?
3. What do you see as the privacy issues associated with blogs?
4. Are there precautions that you think teenagers should take if they wish to create a blog? Explain your answer.

Datashow presentations

A datashow presentation allows a presenter to enhance his or her presentation with extra material such as a print summary, graphics, photographs and video. The size of the screen determines the amount of material which can appear on any one slide and the size of any of the individual components must take into account their ability to be clearly seen and read by the audience.

Here are the first few slides from a datashow presentation.

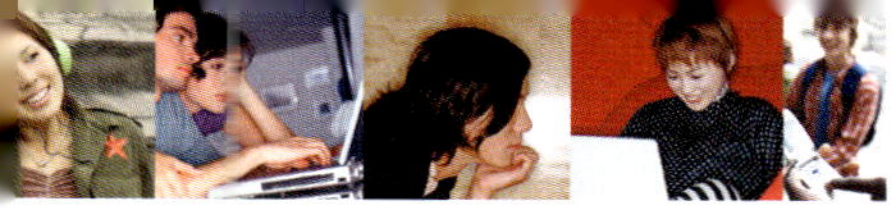

Title screen is clear and uncluttered. A large font is used.

Consistent background is used for all slides.

Each slide has a heading.

The colour of the background makes the font easy to read.

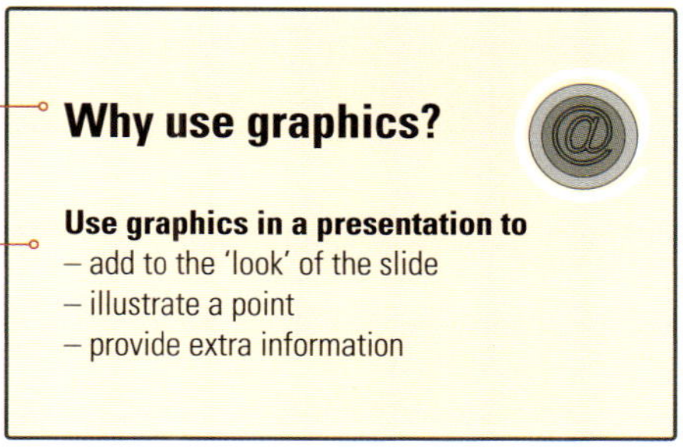

Headings are all in the same font style and size.

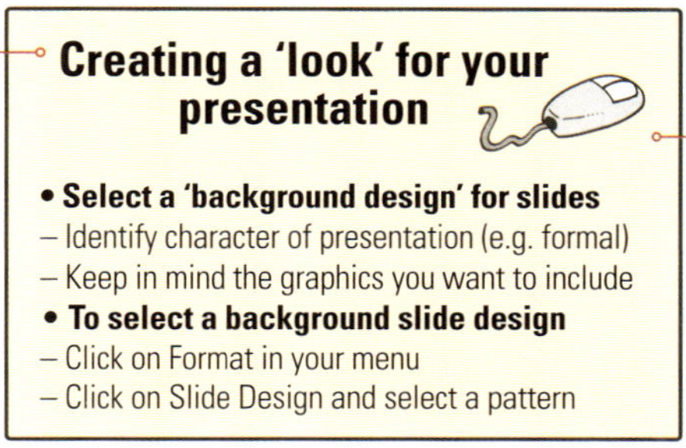

Graphics are used to enhance the 'look' of the slide.

Information on each slide is limited to a few, easy-to-read, points.

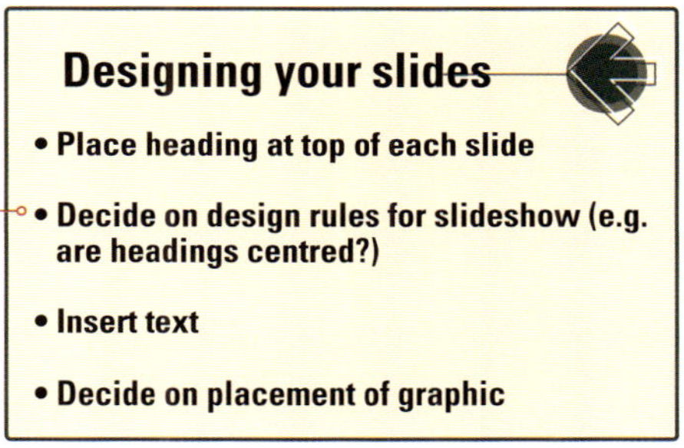

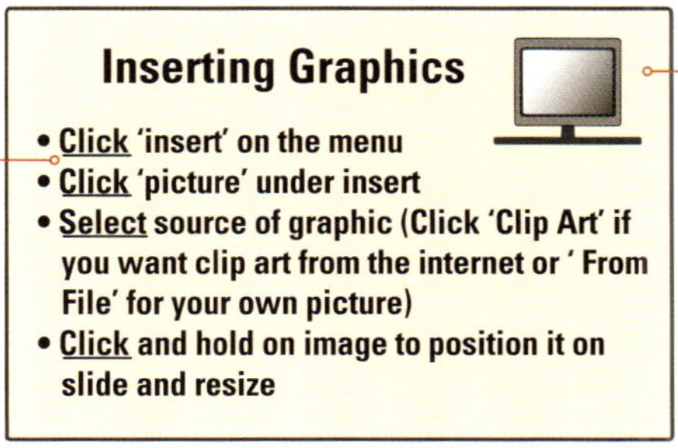

The positioning of graphics is consistent on each slide.

Language is the language of instruction. Imperative **verbs** are used throughout.

Learning activity **4.14**

When making a presentation supported by a datashow one of the worst things a presenter can do is simply to read from the slides. The speaker's notes that accompany each slide should therefore expand on the information depicted on the slide and should try to avoid simply repeating what is already on the slide.

Write the speaker's notes that you think should accompany one of the above slides.

Learning activity 4.15

Complete the following table by drawing on the information in this chapter. This will provide you with a summary of the relationships between the text forms created by information and communication technologies and their audiences, purposes, structure and language features. At the end of the table there is space to add other forms not discussed in this chapter.

Texts created by information and communication technologies				
Form	Structure	Language features	Possible audience/s	Possible purpose/s
SMS message	Unstructured/ Informal	Word/symbol limit; unconventional sentences; abbreviations; use of acronyms	Usually friends but also potential customers (advertising by SMS)	Variety — information, transaction, queries etc.
MMS message				
Email				
Instant messaging (online)				
Chat room conversations				
Postings on a discussion group, message board or online forum				
Ezine				
Web page				
Blog				
Datashow presentations				
Other				

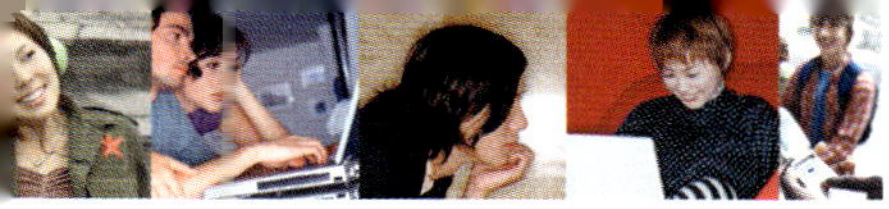

Verbal language in online texts:

- Keep language appropriate to the audience.
- Keep language consistent from one page to another.
- Keep sentences short.
- Use 'point form' (bulleted lists, like this one) whenever possible.
- Use the active, rather than the passive voice.

Assessment tasks | Creating and presenting with communication technology

Choose one or more of the following assessment tasks. Be prepared to explain, either orally or in writing, why you chose to use specific language structures and features.

1. Be creative. Tell a short story through a series of text messages and emails. (For example, imagine a conflict created by an email/SMS message that has been read by the wrong person.) Your short story must have at least two characters and a plot. (How might you present this short story using technology?)
2. Write a series of emails for different audiences:
   (a) to a friend overseas, drawing attention to a number of your favourite websites. Include:
   - descriptions of the purpose and audience for each of the sites
   - URLs as hyperlinks to particular pages in the site, with descriptions of what can be found on those pages

   (b) to a member of Parliament to petition for change to an aspect of our society that is of concern to you (for example, treatment of refugees, an environmental issue, train fares)
   (c) to your grandmother or older relative, describing a recent family holiday or event and including photographs as attachments.

   Submit these emails to your teacher electronically.

Strategies | Before you start

Consider the kind of language that is appropriate
(a) to the form in which you are writing (i.e. the email)
(b) to the audience for which you are writing.

3. Use the information in the article on phishing (pages 128–9) to design a community awareness brochure on that topic. This brochure would be of the kind that is made available free to those who visit the local library. You might use a software program such as Publisher to help you do this.
4. Teach someone how to send a text message. Prepare a multimodal presentation (sound, visuals and text). Your instructions should not only include information about how to do this, but should also provide information about SMS language. You could deliver your presentation to a group who is unfamiliar with texting.
5. The ezine crikey.com claims to 'go where the other media won't go'. Examine this claim. Choose an issue currently being discussed in the media. Read newspaper reports and letters to the editor on the issue. Watch the television news. Then read what crikey.com has to say on the same issue. Is the coverage any different? How? To find this site, visit the website for this book and click on the last Ezine weblink for this chapter (see 'Weblinks', page 252).
6. Create your own website on a topic of your choice. Your website should have between 5 and 10 screens and include text, hyperlinks and images. It could also include sound and animation if you wish. Explain the choices that you made in creating your website either orally or in writing.
7. Design and create your own blog. Who is your audience? What is the purpose of your site? As well as journal entries and visuals such as photographs, include links to other sites that you find particularly interesting. Remember the advice about protecting your identity and make sure you don't include anything that could reveal who you are, where you live, the school you attend and so on.

Be clear about the audience and purpose of your written or multimodal text.

Consider the influence of audience and purpose on the verbal and or **visual language** of your text.

8. Design a datashow with accompanying speaker's notes on a topic of your choice. In the datashow include graphics and, if you wish, video.
9. Create a digital cookbook on a CD-Rom which includes text, sound and video.
10. Create a digital children's book on a CD-Rom which includes, text, sound and video.
11. Create a multimodal text which focuses on the year in which you were born (or, if you prefer, the year in which someone close to you was born). Research key national and international events that occurred in that year, find photographs (and video, if you like), include interviews (for example, with your parents). Add any other features that you find interesting. Present the text on a CD-Rom.
12. Write an essay on one of the issues surrounding the use of information and communication technologies in society. Include a list of the resources you consulted and don't forget to acknowledge any ideas or direct quotations.

See below for the criteria for assessment.

Criteria for assessment

Your assessment task will be assessed according to the following criteria. Read them carefully before you begin your task; while working on your task, check your progress against the criteria and then review your completed task against the criteria before submitting it to your teacher.

Knowledge and understanding of the content of set text/s. This includes, where relevant:

- use of direct quotes from the set text/s
- use of direct reference to ideas suggested in the set text/s
- use of indirect reference to ideas suggested in set text/s
- discussion of some of the complexities of the theme or issues arising from the context.

Understanding of the relationships between audience, purpose, context and form. This includes:

- identification and discussion of audience and purpose of own and other's texts
- selection of a form appropriate for a specified audience, purpose and context
- identification, discussion and use of language (visual and/or verbal) appropriate to the specified audience, purpose, context and form
- planning and revising to achieve coherence of audience, purpose, context and form.

Ability to construct a written or multimodal text using the features and structures of the chosen form. This includes, where relevant:

- relevance of response to the set topic
- clear and coherent point of view supported by evidence from the set text/s
- control of spelling, punctuation and syntax
- use of **non-verbal** and visual language as appropriate to the chosen form (for example, colour, font, camera angles and shots)
- coherent organisation.

CHAPTER 5

Exploring the workplace

Work is a very large part of people's lives and for this reason job satisfaction and working conditions are extremely important. In this chapter you will read a number of texts which explore some of the issues associated with the workplace and have an opportunity to discuss and respond to the content.

Throughout this textbook the emphasis has been on the interconnection of audience, purpose, form, **context** and language. In the context of the workplace that interconnection is particularly important. We will therefore examine the language, structures and features of some common forms of workplace communication before you write or create your own workplace texts or texts that explore workplace issues.

What is a workplace?

A workplace is anywhere that work takes place. It might be a home office where only one person works; it might be a small shop where two or three people work; it might be the factory of a small business where 30 people work; or it might be an office environment in a large enterprise which employs hundreds of people.

Learning activity 5.1

What kinds of workplaces are you familiar with, either through personal experience or through friends or family?

Make a class list for later reference. You might consider using this list as a resource to identify guest speakers or people who can be asked for information to assist you in exploring workplace issues.

What are some of the issues surrounding the workplace?

By workplace 'issues' we mean difficulties, concerns or topics that have particular relevance to the workplace. There are some issues that apply generally across workplaces (health and safety issues, for example) but which have particular application in different workplaces. The safest way of operating a specific piece of machinery would be relevant to a particular factory, perhaps, while health issues arising from working in air-conditioning would be more relevant to an office environment.

Learning activity 5.2

Do a class brainstorm to identify a list of the general issues related to the workplace context. (This activity will be useful not only in preparation for the exploration, but also to identify issues that perhaps will not be covered in this chapter but which you might like to pursue individually at a later time.)

Strategies | Before reading

Scan the article, paying particular attention to the headings and to what appears in bold print in order to gain a sense of what the article will be about.

Work–life balance

Achieving a work–life balance has two aspects. There are many unemployed people and part-time or casual workers who would like to work more hours, and many full-time workers, particularly working mothers or white-collar workers, who seem to feel that their work is taking over their lives. The old five-days-a-week model, 9 to 5, is rapidly becoming something of the past, and many workers complain that they would like more time to spend with their families and on their own leisure activities. The frustration that they feel about this situation can be stressful both on themselves and their families, and as a result can impact on the efficiency and commitment that they bring to their working lives.

The following article addresses this issue. It is annotated to draw attention to the way in which it has been constructed by the author. Read it and answer the questions that follow.

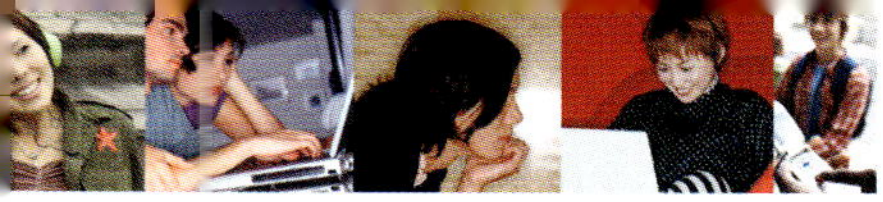

Work and life: strike a balance

Instructional mode: the purpose of the article is to provide advice. The author addresses himself directly to the reader and constantly refers to 'you' and 'your'. This has the effect of making the advice seem quite personal.

The use of imperative **verbs** is a characteristic of a piece of instructional writing.

This section provides a brief summary of the focus of the article and is designed to encourage the reader to read the entire article.

Do you find it hard to balance your work and your personal life? If you do, you're not alone. Whether you're a full-time, outside-the-home worker with a family at home; a VCE student with a part-time job and extra-curricular activities; a full-time at-home worker (looking after children); or a carer, you undoubtedly battle to find time for everything. Most of us tend to skew our lives, so that we devote more time to work than we do to our personal lives.

It is important that you look after your own mental, physical and emotional self. If you don't, your effectiveness and quality of input at work and the quality of time spent with others is greatly reduced because you may be stressed and exhausted.

To do this, you need to set boundaries to ensure that your life is well-rounded. Workers need to look realistically at the proportion of hours spent at work compared to hours spent with family, at play or looking after themselves, and then act to restore balance. In a similar way, VCE students should be encouraged to mix in extra-curricular activities (such as sport, involvement in community groups, music, social get-togethers and part-time work) with their school and study timetables.

Why the long hours at work?

This section is only relevant for those workers who can choose whether or not they work overtime.

Although workers spending long hours at work is not a new occurrence, there are now more modern reasons for the long hours.

Explanation of the reasons behind a work–life imbalance. Presented in dot points for easy and clear reference

- **Information and communication technology.** Computers, email, blackberries, mobile phones and scanners are examples of ICT tools that have allowed us to blur the boundaries between work, home, cars, planes and overseas locations (to name a few). With the use of ICT tools, many workers can now work from a number of locations, and are not office bound. While this can work to both the employee's and employer's advantage, it also means that work can cross over to such an extent that it is part of work, home, travel and holidays.
- **World-wide businesses.** Businesses with offices all over the world, or with clients in other countries, work with multiple time zones. Employees often need to be available outside normal business hours to deal with urgent queries from people working in a different time zone.

- **Less support for carers.** Our society is no longer as family centred as it was. Where, once, family and extended family would help share carer roles, it is now often left to one person. Government resources for carers are limited and are sometimes not accessible for those living in remote communities.
- **Fairer family roles.** Although the primary carer of children is usually still a woman, the roles within a family have shifted a little, so that the primary carer will often work outside the home, as well. This means that there are more people who are juggling the responsibilities of both outside- and inside-the-home work.

Techniques to re-set the balance

Examines the reasons for working overtime

Before looking at ways to help provide more balance in your life, it is important to note that, for some people, working some paid overtime hours (or working more hours to further a career) is a financial necessity. To these people, creating a balance is not as easy. However, if you are one of these people, make sure that you have taken time out to critically assess whether it is a necessity, or whether you are financing *wants*, rather than *needs*. Working long weeks can lead to exhaustion, missing family life, leaving the brunt of care work to others and neglecting your friends, so it is important to periodically reassess your life. If you decide that you need more balance, you could try these tips:

The use of imperative verbs is a characteristic of a piece of instructional writing.

- **turn off work-related communication tools.** That is, if it's not part of your role to be available outside business hours, switch off the work mobile, log out of work email and turn off the fax once you've finished your allocated hours.
- **make plans for the weekend that involve your family, friends, or yourself only.** Don't be tempted to cancel these plans to work instead.
- **don't work into the night.** Ensure that you get the sleep that you need, so that you are not overly tired the next day. If you aren't productive due to lack of sleep, then the cycle is simply repeated once you work into the night to make up for lack of efficiency during the day.
- **incorporate some exercise into your week.** Exercise leads to a physically healthier body that can withstand the demands of life more easily, and encourages a good night's sleep.

- **talk to a professional.** Find a counsellor, psychologist or doctor with whom you can talk through your problems. That's what they're there for. Sharing problems with a professional can help reduce your stress levels and mental fatigue.
- **don't take your work on holiday.** Holidays are very important for protecting your mental and physical health, and for spending quality time with friends and family. Leave your work at work.
- **keep the communication lines open.** If problems or tension crop up at home or in your personal life, calmly talk them through with the people involved. Similarly, away from the heat of the moment, talk to work colleagues if there is an issue at work. Don't bottle up negative feelings about problems or work ridiculous hours to solve a work problem, as they might be resolved by talking them through.

Creating a balance in your life is never easy: there is a good chance that you will always feel that you should spend more time on an aspect of your life. However, this is not an excuse for not taking action when your life has a definite, unjustifiable skew towards work. Take a moment now to ask yourself, 'Am I happy with the way I have balanced all aspects of my life?'

Concludes with a direct question to the reader, designed to engage him/her in the next step

Learning activity **5.3**

1. Scan the article to identify any unfamiliar words. Highlight them and, in pairs, discuss possible meanings. Check with someone else or a dictionary if you are still uncertain what some words mean.
2. Who do you think is the intended audience for this article? Quote evidence from the article to support your point of view.
3. What factors does the author believe should be taken into account by a worker when s/he is deciding whether or not to work overtime? Use your own words to list the factors.
4. In the section headed 'Techniques to reset the balance' the author suggests several strategies that might be adopted in order to 'juggle the demands of career and personal life'. Read these suggestions and identify the kinds of behaviour that the author believes make it more difficult for workers to achieve a work–life balance.

The following is an extract showing postings from an online forum of an Australian newspaper. The issue being discussed is a report that drew attention to the excessive working hours of young Australians.

YOUR SAY FORUM

The long, long working week

Is this true? The latest research out of Europe says that it's actually young Australians who are working some of the longest hours in the western world. Are you one of those young Australians? Tell us about your experience.

Re: The long, long working week

Sure it's true. I regularly work 70 hours a week, but it really doesn't bother me. I'm single, have no relationship commitments and I want to put myself in a solid position before I venture into such territory. Working long and hard will let me do this. The rewards are definitely there, so it's crazy to bellyache about it.

Posted by: Jack on December 14, 2006 at 7.20 am

Re: The long, long working week

There are very few jobs where you actually *have* to work long, long hours. If you insist on the ground rules from the start — 'Yes, I am going home at 6 pm.' — *and* you do your job effectively and well, you'll earn respect rather than negative attention. I started a new job six months ago and established exactly that kind of expectation about my working hours, and have had no negative feedback at all. I wonder, however, whether that's because I'm a woman, and a mother. If I were a male, I'm not sure whether the situation would be the same. It's almost as if I have an 'excuse', but what excuse can a man offer?

Posted by: Kathy on December 14, 2006 at 9.30 am

Re: The long, long working week

The rewards probably aren't really there at all. Have you ever calculated your hourly rate based on the number of hours you've worked that week?

Posted by: Stu on December 14, 2006 at 9.31 am

Re: The long, long working week

Many of us do in fact have family and relationship commitments. I work long hours too, but I can't say I enjoy it and I know it's definitely having an impact on my domestic situation. The money is fine, but, as the cliché says, it can't buy happiness. And I think that the job satisfaction issue is relevant here, too. Not only do I work long hours but I work them for a corporation whose ethics are definitely on the nose. I wonder how much longer I'll continue to take the money and run.

Posted by: Zhang on December 14, 2006 at 9.32 am

The long, long working week

Anyone who is working 70 hours plus has other options. If you're working these kinds of hours, you're obviously in a professional position and you've got a bit more bargaining power than someone who is working 35 hours a week in a non-professional capacity. Negotiate your situation. I did, and now I work four days a week, twelve hours a day, and that gives me three free days each week. It can be done, if you're prepared to relinquish some of your status. (Part-timers definitely don't have the same status as those who work full-time, whatever anyone says.)

Posted by: Ann on December 14, 2006 at 9.35 am

The long, long working week

Well, my guess is that you'll continue to take the money for a fair while yet. How can you afford to do otherwise? I know a few people who have opted out, gone for the sea change or whatever it is they call it, and the romance soon fades. Unless you're 50+ there's no way you can be satisfied with a dull, pedestrian lifestyle once you've tasted the cut and thrust of life in the CBD.

Posted by: John on December 14, 2006 at 11.14 am

The long, long working week

Oh, really? The 'dull, pedestrian lifestyle' is only for those over 50? If young people weren't so shallow and superficial, so fixed on immediate gratification, perhaps they, too, would be able to slow down and find pleasure in things other than those associated with money and prestige.

Posted by: Elaine on December 14, 2006 at 12.05 pm

The long, long working week

Do long working hours equal greater efficiency? I doubt it. I see my staff here in the office at 7.30 am, but I also see them making endless cups of coffee, going downstairs for a quick smoke, chatting with each other about the football and checking their private emails. It's usually at least 9 before they really start work. The rest of the day is much the same — lots of small time-wasting breaks. It's no wonder they have to stay on past 5 pm to catch up with their work. If they worked more efficiently during a shorter time at work, everyone, including me, would be much happier.

Posted by: Lou on December 14, 2006 at 2.16 pm

The long, long working week

Ann, I think you're completely wrong when you say that all people working 70+ hours per week have other options. I personally know several people who are working these kinds of hours in very lowly paid jobs. If they didn't work those hours they'd never survive. (We're rapidly going the way of the US where some people are in such poorly paid full employment that they have to go to charitable institutions for handouts to keep them going.)

Posted by: Li on December 14, 2006 at 3.19 pm

Learning activity **5.4**

1. Work in pairs to analyse the postings made on this topic. Use this table to record your findings.

Who is the author of this posting?	Which aspect/s of the topic is s/he commenting on?	Is this a direct reply to another posting? If so, whose posting?	What is the main point s/he wishes to make?	Does the posting contribute positively to the topic of the discussion? Explain your response.
Jack				
Kathy				
Stu				
Zhang				
Ann				

John				
Elaine				
Lou				
Li				

2. Write a short summary (about 100 words) of the main aspects of the discussion.
3. What do you think are the advantages and disadvantages of the online forum as a way of expressing and exchanging opinions? Provide at least two advantages and two disadvantages.

Bullying at work

Bullying in a school context is an issue with which many students are familiar. But bullying is not confined to the interactions of students. Unfortunately, it is also a feature of many workplaces, and from time to time we hear of court cases in which a victim sues those who have bullied him or her, or sues the employer who allowed the bullying to occur. Often these are cases of physical intimidation, but there are other actions, such as verbal abuse or psychological harassment, that are also regarded as bullying.

Following is an extract from the *Guidance Note on the Prevention of Bullying and Violence at Work*, a Victorian Government publication. It appears on the Victorian WorkCover website which provides advice to employers and employees about work-related issues. Read the annotations and then answer the questions.

Preventing workplace bullying

Informational purpose

1 WHAT IS BULLYING?

Different font size for different classes of headings

Bullying can occur wherever people work together. Under certain conditions, most people are capable of bullying. Bullying is not always intentional. Sometimes people do not realise that their behaviour can be harmful to others.

1.1 Defining workplace bullying

Signifies a sub-section

Workplace bullying is repeated, unreasonable behaviour directed toward an employee, or group of employees, that creates a risk to health and safety.

Within this definition:

*‘**unreasonable behaviour**’ means behaviour that a reasonable person, having regard to all the circumstances, would expect to victimise, humiliate, undermine or threaten*

*‘**behaviour**’ includes actions of individuals or a group, and may involve using a system of work as a means of victimising, humiliating, undermining or threatening*

*‘**risk to health and safety**’ includes risk to the mental or physical health of the employee*

Shading draws attention to the definition and an explanation of it.

Bold type highlights important points.

The following types of behaviour, **where repeated or occurring as part of a pattern of behaviour,** could be considered bullying:

Lists are presented in dot points for ease of understanding.

- verbal abuse
- excluding or isolating employees
- psychological harassment
- intimidation
- assigning meaningless tasks unrelated to the job
- giving employees impossible assignments
- deliberately changing work rosters to inconvenience particular employees
- deliberately withholding information that is vital for effective work performance

This list is not exhaustive. Other types of behaviour may also constitute bullying.

Note: An employee may be a manager or supervisor.

Different font size for different classes of headings

What is 'unreasonable' behaviour?

'Unreasonable' refers to behaviour that a reasonable person, having regard to all the circumstances, would expect to humiliate, intimidate, undermine or threaten.

In this context, a '*reasonable person, having regard to all the circumstances*' means a hypothetical reasonable person who has observed the situation. '*...having regard to all the circumstances*' does not mean that this hypothetical person has total knowledge of every aspect of the situation. Rather, this person knows as much as the alleged bully could reasonably be expected to know.

What is 'repeated' behaviour?

'Repeated' refers to the persistent nature of the behaviour, not the specific form the behaviour takes. Behaviour is considered 'repeated' if an established pattern can be identified.

It may involve a series of diverse incidents—for example, verbal abuse, deliberate damage to personal property and unreasonable threats of dismissal.

The author has anticipated questions likely to be asked about the definition or points that s/he wishes to clarify further.

What about a single incident?

According to the definition, a single incident of bullying-style behaviour does not constitute workplace bullying. However, since an employer has a general duty to provide his or her employees with a safe workplace and safe system of work, single incidents of bullying-style behaviour should not be ignored or condoned.

If the behaviour displayed during a single incident of bullying-style behaviour involves a physical attack or threat of physical attack, it may be dealt with under the guidance note as on instance of occupational violence [see Part Two].

The case study is annotated to show how it demonstrates the elements of bullying.

Repeated unreasonable behaviour

Shading draws attention to the definition and an explanation of it

The behaviour created a risk to health and safety.

This case study demonstrates all of the elements of the definition of workplace bullying used in this document.

Case Study: Bullying

A project officer was subjected to bullying by a colleague over a number of months. The behaviour directed at the project officer was hostile and harassing and included:

- **often finding fault with his work when it was inappropriate to do so**
- **regularly subjecting him to offensive verbal abuse**
- **threatening to get him sacked and telling him that he and his family would end up in the gutter, and**
- **publicly making disparaging comments about his relationship with his wife.**

A number of incidents were witnessed by other employees. The colleague's bullying tactics had an adverse psychological effect on the project officer. Normally positive and outgoing, he became severely stressed and anxious. Eventually, he was unable to continue working for the organisation due to stress injury.

1.2 Sources of bullying

Bullying usually comes from a source inside the workplace.

- An employee may bully another employee.
- An employer may bully an employee or group of employees.
- A group of employees may bully an individual or another group of employees.

Lists are presented in dot points for ease of understanding.

Clients and customers may also bully employees. The guidance on managing the risk of occupational violence can be used to address the problem of bullying perpetrated by clients and customers [see Part Two].

1.3 Managerial actions

This guidance note is not intended to diminish an employer's managerial prerogative to direct and control how work is done in their organisation other than in terms of ensuring, so far as is practicable, the health and safety of employees.

The guidance note is not intended to cover poor or bad management practices on their own, because they are not considered bullying.

The guidance note does not cover situations where an employee has a grievance about legitimate and reasonable:

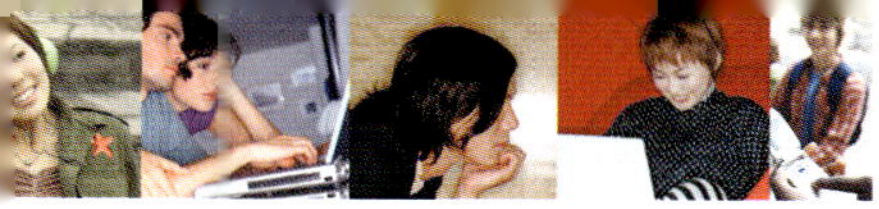

- performance management processes
- disciplinary action
- allocation of work in compliance with systems.

The guidance note does not treat business processes, such as the implementation of organisational change or downsizing, as incidents of bullying. However, they may contribute to producing an environment where bullying is more likely to occur [see Section 7.2].

2 PREVENTING WORKPLACE BULLYING

The prevention approach used in this guidance note is based on the premise that bullying can occur in any workplace, given certain circumstances. While an organisation might appear to be free from bullying, it still may be happening.

Suggests reasons why bullying might not be reported

Bullying can be difficult to detect. Incidents of bullying may not always be reported because employees might:

- fear retribution or 'payback' from the bully
- believe that no-one will act on the problem
- fear being labelled 'weak' or 'whinging'
- think that reporting will affect their career prospects
- accept bullying as a normal part of work culture.

As bullying can occur wherever people work together, this guidance note recommends that employers implement a range of complementary prevention measures.

The recommended prevention measures in Figure 1 (below) are designed to reduce the likelihood of bullying occurring.

The use of a diagram supports the text and illustrates the process of implementing prevention measures.

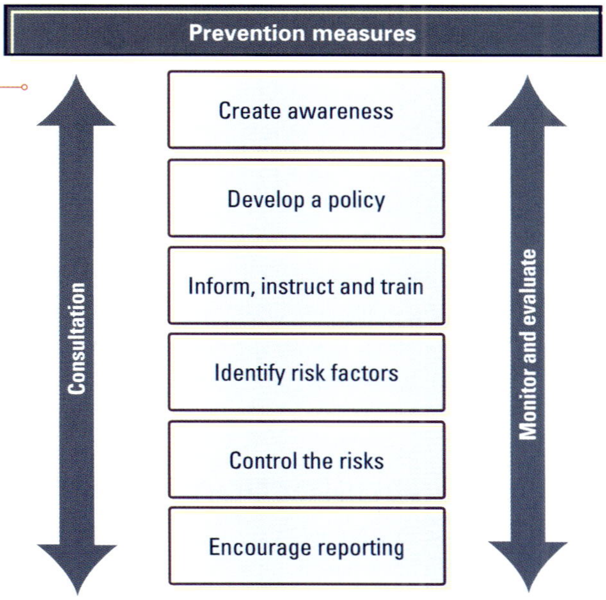

Figure 1

Because any one measure by itself will not adequately reduce the risk of bullying, it is important that these measures are used in conjunction with each other.

An employer may, in consultation with health and safety representatives, decide the order in which to implement these measures in their workplace. Sections 4 to 9 of this guidance note describe each of these prevention measures and how to implement them.

Once the measures have been put in place, an employer should check that they have been implemented correctly and monitor their effectiveness.

Learning activity **5.5**

1. Scan the article to identify any unfamiliar words. Highlight them and, in pairs, discuss possible meanings. Check with someone else or a dictionary if you are still uncertain what some words mean.
2. Who is the intended audience for this guidance note? Quote two pieces of evidence from the guidance note to support your answer.
3. Who else, other than the intended audience, might be interested in the information contained in this guidance note? Name one other group.
4. If this information were written for a different audience, the language in which it is written would need to be changed. Choose a paragraph and rewrite it for a different audience, changing the language where necessary.
5. How does the way in which the guidance note is structured or set out help the reader to access the information?
6. What, according to the guidance note, is the difference between workplace bullying and 'an instance of occupational violence'? Give an example of occupational violence.
7. What are some of the reasons why workers might be unprepared to report workplace bullying?
8. What are the 'complementary prevention measures' that are recommended?
9. Look at the diagram. Explain what is meant by the two-headed arrows.
10. If you were to rewrite this information for a web page, where would you use **hyperlinks**? Highlight the words or **phrases**. Are there particular graphics or photos that you think would increase understanding of the content?
11. If possible, view an episode of *The Office*, Series One. In your opinion, is there evidence of bullying in this workplace? Use the definition of workplace bullying provided in this guidance note to help you make and explain your decision.

Job satisfaction

In the extract on pages 160–2 from the science fiction novel, *The Space Merchants*, George could hardly be said to have experienced much job satisfaction. But what is job satisfaction and what makes a job satisfying? Various surveys seek to measure

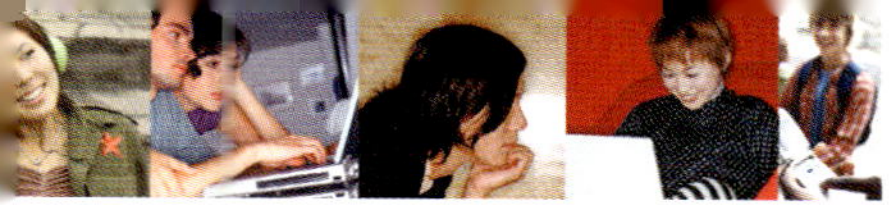

this and the results of some surveys have been published. One such Australian survey, conducted nationally and presenting the opinions and attitudes of over 1000 workers aged 15 years or over found that:

- 77% of workers were positive about the treatment they received from their immediate manager
- 76% were satisfied or very satisfied with the way in which people at work got on together
- 74% were positive about their level of job security
- 20% indicated that their pay was not fair and reasonable
- 22% were dissatisfied with their career prospects over the next 2 years
- 23% distrusted senior management
- 24% expressed dissatisfaction with the balance between the time they spent working and the time they spent with family and friends
- 29% were dissatisfied with the level of stress experienced at work.

Moreover, research from the Australian Institute tells us that one in five Australians are turning away from long hours and high income to 'down-shift'. In other words they are leaving jobs that are too demanding, and giving up their high incomes to take up other work which is often part-time. Often they move house and go to live in the country, where the pace of life in general is regarded as slower and, perhaps, healthier.

Below is an example of a job satisfaction survey. It is not the same survey that was undertaken in the Australian survey referred to above.

Read the survey and answer the questions that follow.

Job satisfaction survey

Please tick the boxes which show how much you agree with the following:

	Strongly agree	Partly agree	Neutral	Partly disagree	Strongly disagree
Role					
My job is secure	☐	☐	☐	☐	☐
I am happy with my workload	☐	☐	☐	☐	☐
My working hours are flexible	☐	☐	☐	☐	☐
I have an impact on my company's success	☐	☐	☐	☐	☐
I can influence the decisions made by the company that affect me	☐	☐	☐	☐	☐
Self-development					
I am kept up-to-date with new technologies	☐	☐	☐	☐	☐
I participate in staff-development courses	☐	☐	☐	☐	☐
My work includes a variety of interesting tasks	☐	☐	☐	☐	☐
I can advance in my position	☐	☐	☐	☐	☐

Interpersonal relationships					
I get along well with my colleagues	☐	☐	☐	☐	☐
My customers/clients are happy with what I do for them	☐	☐	☐	☐	☐
I get along well with my manager/ supervisor	☐	☐	☐	☐	☐
I am given appropriate feedback by my manager/supervisor	☐	☐	☐	☐	☐
My supervisor/manager is a good leader	☐	☐	☐	☐	☐
My supervisor/manager has good communication skills	☐	☐	☐	☐	☐
Remuneration					
I am satisfied with my salary	☐	☐	☐	☐	☐
My salary is acceptable for my position	☐	☐	☐	☐	☐
My salary is linked to a fair appraisal system	☐	☐	☐	☐	☐
I am rewarded well for my work through a bonus/reward scheme	☐	☐	☐	☐	☐
Overall job satisfaction					
I am satisfied with my job	☐	☐	☐	☐	☐
I understand the company's objectives	☐	☐	☐	☐	☐
I am satisfied with my company	☐	☐	☐	☐	☐

Learning activity **5.6**

Write the statements from the survey that seek to find out the respondents' opinions about each of the following:

- whether they think there are opportunities to be promoted
- whether they like the people they work with
- whether they believe the company makes certain that they get training to improve their performance
- whether they believe that their opinion is valued
- whether they believe they are able to work shorter hours on some days and longer hours on others
- whether they believe that their supervisor/manager is clear when giving instructions or providing information and feedback
- whether they believe that they are being paid appropriately
- whether they believe that their performance in the job is taken into account when their salary is decided.

Read the following interview with male nurse, Kenley Arndt, to identify the aspects of his work that give him job satisfaction.

Rural nursing

Why/how did you become interested in nursing?

People often ask, why did you choose nursing? Indeed, my mother often asks why I didn't become a doctor instead! My first experience with nurses came at a very young age. I used to suffer with croup a lot when I was younger, and because we lived only one street behind our local hospital, I would often end up there being treated for croup. During these times, I developed a fascination with how and what nurses did. The nurses that looked after me were caring, kind and filled with humour. When I left hospital, they would let me take oxygen masks and tubing home. I used to play 'pretend hospital' at home with my teddy bears, pretending I was the nurse!

Where and what did you study?

I studied a Bachelor of Nursing (pre-registration) at the University of Southern Queensland in Toowoomba. It was there that I first discovered my interest in rural and remote nursing, as placements were often at smaller country hospitals, rather than in the big city hospitals. I have also studied a Master of Nursing (Perioperative) by part-time distance education through the University of Western Sydney. However, I have found that I am compelled to work in rural healthcare settings, rather than in the operating theatre. I am hoping to convert my postgraduate degree to a rural and remote specialty, with further study via distance education.

What is the most rewarding aspect of your job?

People often say that the patients are the most rewarding aspect of being a nurse. While this is true, I have to say that the people I have worked with over the years make the job memorable. Nurses are caring people, filled with compassion and a sense of duty. They are great people to work with every day, it is often these people you spend time with dealing with some of life's most depressing issues, such as pain or death. I don't think the ordinary person would be able to cope with some of the things my colleagues and I have to face each day at work. It is for this reason I think that the nursing time is the most rewarding aspect of my job.

What's the most challenging thing about your job?

Nursing is constantly changing. In fact, in the short time I have been in the profession, things have changed even since I did my training. The population is ageing and technology is increasing at an alarming rate. Consumers are becoming more health care conscious, and most chronic diseases are on the increase. Keeping up with these changes can be challenging. It involves the need to immerse yourself in new and exciting information, and being able to comment or trial new ways of being. I don't think I could survive in nursing without the ability to embrace change.

What are the most memorable moments?

The most memorable moments I would say I have encountered in nursing are the beginning and end of life. Seeing the smile on a new mother's face as a baby is lifted to her chest for the first time, or seeing the relaxed and peaceful facial expressions of a dying patient are ingrained in your mind forever as a nurse. Nurses are people who get to enjoy these important life occasions every day. How many people can say they see a baby being born every week, or that they were there in the last dignified hours of a patient's life. In nursing, we are rewarded

with these milestones, and sometimes we get so wrapped up in what we're doing, we forget how lucky we are.

What would you advise for nurses interested in your area?
Rural nursing is very different to working in a metropolitan hospital. Nursing in rural locations can expose you to so many different experiences. One day you could be caring for a dying patient in their own community, the next day you could be assisting in the retrieval of a multi-trauma patient. There is flexibility and the chance to learn new things. Many 'city' nurses find it hard to make the transition to nursing in rural locations. But given time, they become as good if not better than the country nurses. Rural nurses make a real connection with the people in their community. We remember patients' first names, their families and everything about them. To us, our patients are real people, not a number or a surgical procedure.

Why would you encourage someone to become a nurse?
Nursing is definitely a career that is progressing in leaps and bounds. While Australia may be behind in some aspects, we are gradually introducing changes that will see us as one of the best health care providers into the next century. There is a huge amount of autonomy in nursing. You don't have to become a doctor to change people's lives, nurses do it every day, on every shift, with every interaction or intervention. Nursing is a career that you will find challenging, interesting and inspiring. We need nurses who are not afraid to take the challenge of changing someone's life. If this sounds like you, check out nursing. You'll be surprised!

Learning activity **5.7**

1. Scan the article to identify any unfamiliar words. Highlight them and, in pairs, discuss possible meanings. Check with someone else, or a dictionary, if you are still uncertain about what some words mean.
2. In what kind of publication do you think this interview might have appeared? Explain your answer.
3. What do you think is the purpose of this interview? Which aspects of the interview lead you to this conclusion?
4. According to Kenley Arndt, which aspects of his job give him job satisfaction? Identify two aspects.
5. Examine Arndt's response to the question 'What are the most memorable moments?' How does his use of language work to persuade the reader that nursing is a 'special' kind of job?
6. Are there any extra questions that you would like to ask Kenley Arndt? Explain.

Learning activity **5.8**

Interview two people you know about their jobs and write up the interviews, using the rural nursing interview as a model.

Health issues in the workplace

Occupational health and safety is a significant aspect of the workplace. Legislation seeks to ensure that employers provide safe working environments for their workers, and each industry has a significant number of specific safety regulations to ensure that this is the case. Most workplaces have a Health and Safety Representative who works with the employer on behalf of the employees to ensure that the working environment is safe and to respond to workers' concerns.

The WorkSafe Victoria website provides information about a number of safety issues, including those which arise from working with asbestos, chemicals, explosives, forklifts, hazardous substances, waste and machines, and in situations such as those that are particularly noisy or outdoors in the sun.

It's probably fairly easy to imagine the health and safety issues that arise from the situations listed above. But what about working in an office? Do a quick class brainstorm to identify the health and safety issues associated with working in an office environment.

Perhaps you mentioned issues such as the quality of the air-conditioning and lighting; and you probably mentioned something to do with RSI or repetitive strain injury, which is associated with repeating the same movement over and over again, as in using a keyboard, for example; or even back and neck injuries associated with sitting at a computer all day. You might also have mentioned the word *ergonomics*.

What is ergonomics? According to the website created by Ergonomics in Australia, ergonomics is essentially about 'fitting work to people'. It's the process of designing or arranging workplaces, products and systems so that they fit the people who use them.

Workers who spend much of the day at their computers are often provided with ergonomic information about their workstation.

Here are two examples of that kind of information.

Ergonomics in the Seated

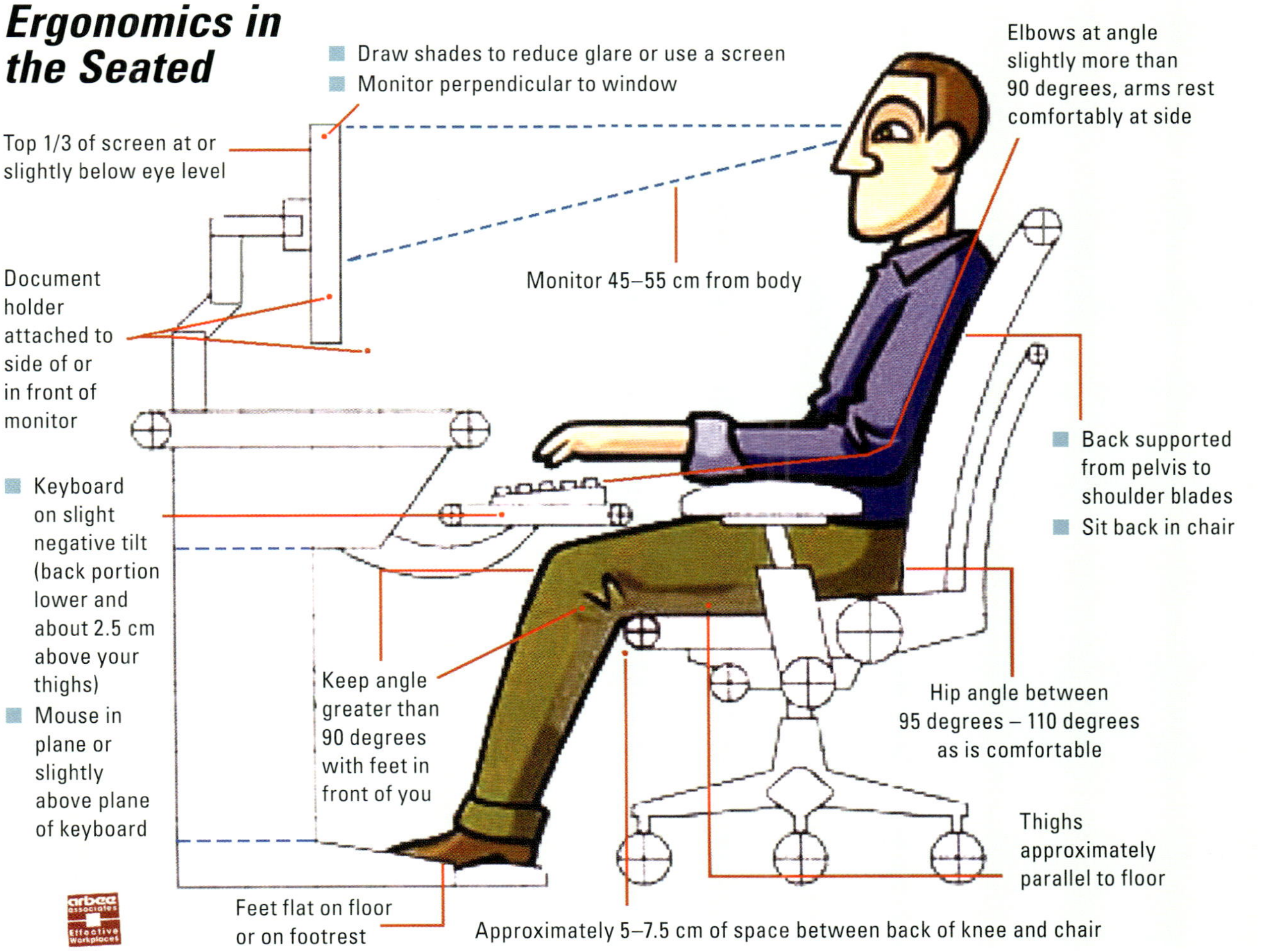

5 Tips for using a laptop computer

1. **Un-ergonomic laptops** — the design of laptops violates a basic ergonomic requirement for a computer, namely that the keyboard and screen are separated. In the early days of personal computing, desktop devices integrated the screen and keyboard into a single unit, and this resulted in widespread complaints of musculoskeletal discomfort. By the late 1970s, a number of ergonomic design guidelines were written and all called for the separation of screen and keyboard. The reason is simple — with a fixed design, if the keyboard is in an optimal position for the user, the screen isn't and if the screen is optimal the keyboard isn't. Consequently, laptops are excluded from current ergonomic design requirements because none of the designs satisfy this basic need. This means that you need to pay special attention to how you use your laptop because it can cause you problems.
2. **Laptop user type** — how do you use your laptop? Are you an occasional user who works on your laptop for short periods of time or are you a full-time user with the laptop as your main computer? Occasional users will have less risk of problems than full-time users. All users should pay some attention to how they use their laptop, but full-time users may have more problems.
3. **Laptop posture** — as indicated above, laptops violate basic ergonomic design requirements, so using a laptop is a tradeoff between poor neck/head posture and poor hand/wrist posture.
   - **Occasional users** — because the neck/head position is determined by the actions of large muscles, you are better off sacrificing neck posture rather than wrist posture. For occasional use:
     - find a chair that is comfortable and that you can sit back in
     - position your laptop in your lap for the most neutral wrist posture that you can achieve
     - angle the laptop screen so that you can see this with the least amount of neck deviation.
   - **Full-time users** — if you use your laptop at work as your main computer you should:
     - position this on your desk/work surface in front of you so that you can see the screen without bending your neck. This may require that you elevate the laptop off the desk surface using a stable support surface, such as a computer monitor pedestal.
     - use a separate keyboard and mouse. You should be able to connect a keyboard and mouse directly to the back of the laptop or to a docking station.
     - use the keyboard on a negative-tilt keyboard tray to ensure a wrist neutral posture
     - use the mouse on an adjustable position mouse platform
     - follow the postural guidelines for working at a computer workstation.
4. **Laptop dimensions** — many laptops offer large screens (15" plus) and can work as desktop replacements (giving the viewing area of a 17" monitor). However, think about where you will most use your laptop to help you choose the best size. The larger the screen the more difficult it will be to use this in mobile locations (e.g. airplane, car, train). There are a number of smaller notebook and ultraportable laptops on the market. Consider issues of screen size and screen resolution. A small screen (e.g. 12.1") will be useful in mobile settings, but if the resolution is high (e.g. XGA – 1024 × 768) make sure that you can read the screen characters and can easily

use the input device to point to areas on the screen. The smaller the laptop, the smaller the keyboard, so make sure that you can comfortably type on a keyboard that may be only 75% the size of a regular keyboard.

5. **Laptop weight** — if you are a mobile professional who will be frequently transporting your laptop, think about the weight of the system. By the word 'system' I mean the weight of the laptop plus the required accessories (e.g. power supply, spare battery, external disk drive, zip drive, CD-RW). Many lightweight portables can become as heavy as regular laptops when you add the weight of all of the components together. If your laptop plus components weighs 10lbs or more, then you should certainly consider using a carry-on bag that you can pull along. If you want a smaller bag and can comfortably carry your laptop, consider a good shoulder bag design.

Article by Professor Alan Hedge, Cornell University, 16 October 2004

Learning activity **5.9**

1. Each of these texts is aimed at a different audience. (The diagram is for those who work at a computer station, the online article is written for those who use laptops.) Do you think that the text form chosen by the author/s in each case is an appropriate one? Explain your answer.
2. According to the information in the diagram, what parts of the body require particular protection when working at a computer workstation? How would you go about finding out whether or not the information in this diagram is correct?
3. Look at the online article. Why is it necessary, in ergonomic terms, for the computer screen to be separate from the keyboard?
4. According to the online article, what particular problems are faced by the users of laptops?
5. What was the **source** of the online article? Do you feel comfortable about the reliability of the information it supplies? Explain your response.
6. Analyse the posture you adopt when using a computer or laptop. Take a photograph or draw a diagram. What conclusions can you draw? How can you improve the situation?

'No wonder your arm aches. Shackles should be placed at eye level. Man, it's an ergonomic nightmare down here.'

Explain how this cartoon uses ergonomics as the basis for its humour.

What is the future of work?

What will work be like in the future? Will we work from home, using computers and the internet? Will we be working fewer or longer hours? In the 1980s, predictions focused on a likely decrease in working hours and a corresponding increase in leisure time. But that scenario hasn't come to pass.

Will you be working well past your sixtieth birthday? Present predictions say there will be fewer people in the workforce in the future and, because people will be living longer, they will need to work longer in order to finance their retirements. Government policy at the moment seeks to encourage workers to remain employed after retirement age in order to relieve the government of the financial burden of providing pensions for those who are no longer working. Perhaps in future the official retirement age will be extended.

But maybe there will be fewer jobs to go around anyway. What kinds of threats are posed by off-shoring (for example, off-shoring of the technology industry to countries like India) or by globalisation, which sees lower-paid workers in other countries competing with higher-paid workers in this country for the same job?

Will work for the vast majority of people simply become increasingly mundane and less creative?

In *The Space Merchants*, a science fiction novel by Frederick Pohl and CM Kornbluth, the authors imagine a world which is run by advertising agencies. The main character, who works for the ad agency, Fowler Schocken, has been kidnapped by a rival agency and put to work as a consumer. In these extracts he describes his daily life, which is dominated by particularly boring and routine work.

The Space Merchants

Scum-skimming wasn't hard to learn. You got up at dawn. You gulped a breakfast sliced not long ago from Chicken Little and washed it down with Coffiest. You put on your coveralls and took the cargo net up to your tier. In blazing noon from sunrise to sunset you walked your acres of shallow tanks crusted with algae. If you walked slowly, every thirty seconds or so you spotted a patch at maturity bursting with yummy carbohydrates. You skimmed the patch with your skimmer and slung it down the well, where it would be baled, or processed into glucose to feed Chicken Little, who would be sliced and packed to feed people from Baffinland to Little America. Every hour you could drink from your canteen and take a salt tablet. Every two hours you could take five minutes. At sunset you turned in your coveralls and went to dinner — more slices from Chicken Little — and then you were on your own. You could talk, you could read, you could go into trance before the day-room hypnoteleset, you could shop, you could pick fights, you could drive yourself crazy thinking of what might have been, you could go to sleep.

Mostly you went to sleep.

I wrote a lot of letters and tried to sleep a lot. Pay-day came as a surprise. I didn't know two weeks had slipped by. It left me owing Chlorella proteins only eighty-odd dollars and a few cents. Besides the various assignments I had made, there were the Employee Welfare Fund (as closely as I could figure that one out, it meant that I was paying Chlorella's taxes); union dues and instalment on the initiation fee; withholding tax (this time my own taxes); hospitalization (but try and get it, the older men said) and old age insurance.

One of the things I faint-heartedly consoled myself with was the thought that when — *when*, I always said firmly — I got out I'd be closer to the consumers

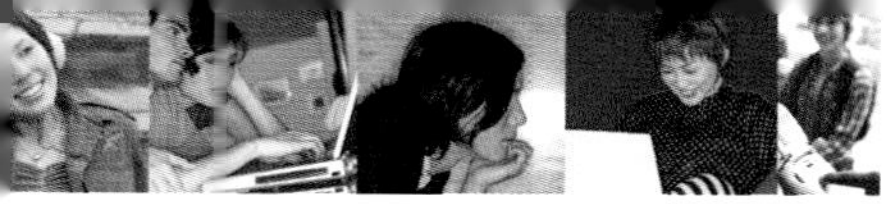

than any ad man in the profession. Of course at Fowler Schocken we'd had our boys up from the ranks, mostly scholarship kids. I knew now that they had been too snobbish to give me the straight facts on consumers' lives and thoughts. Or they hadn't cared to admit even to themselves what they had been like.

I think I learned that ads work more strongly on the unconscious than even we in the profession had thought. I was shocked repeatedly to hear advertising referred to as 'that crap'. I was at first puzzled and then gratified to see it sink in and take effect anyway…

And so I went through another day, up at dawn, breakfast, coveralls and goggles, cargo net, skimming and slinging for blazing hour after hour, dinner and the day-room and, if I could manage it, a chat with Herrera.

'Fine edge on that slicer, Gus. There's only two kinds of people in the world: the ones who don't take care of their tools and the smart ones.'

Suspicious look from under his Aztec brows. 'Pays to do things right. You're the crumb, ain't you?'

'Yeah, First time here. Think I ought to stay?'

He didn't get it. 'You *gotta* stay. Contract.' And he went to the magazine rack.

Tomorrow's another day.

'Hello, Gus. Tired?'

'Hi, George. Yeah, a little. Ten hours swinging the slicer. It gets you in the arms.'

'I can imagine. Skimming's easy, but you don't need brains for it.'

'Well, maybe some day you get up-graded. I think I'll trance.'

And another:

'Hi, George. How's it going?'

'Can't complain, Gus. At least I'm getting a sun-tan.'

'You sure are. Soon you be dark like me. Haw-haw! How'd you like that?'

'*Porque no, amigo?*'

'Hey, *tu hablas, español! Cuando aprendiste la lengua*?'…

And another day — an astonishing day.

I'd been paid again, and my debt had increased by eight dollars. I'd tormented myself by wondering where the money went, but I knew. I came off shift dehydrated, as they wanted me to be. I got a squirt of Popsie from the fountain by punching my combination — twenty-five cents checked off my pay-roll. The squirt wasn't quite enough so I had another fifty cents. Dinner was drab as usual; I couldn't face more than a bite or two of Chicken Little. Later I was hungry and there was the canteen where I got Crunchies on easy credit. The Crunchies kicked off withdrawal symptoms that could be quelled only by another two squirts of Popsie from the fountain. And Popsie kicked off withdrawal symptoms that could only be quelled by smoking Starr cigarettes, which made you hungry for Crunchies… Had Fowler Schocken thought of it in these terms when he organized Starrzelius Verily, the first spherical trust? Popsie to Crunchies, to Starrs, to Popsie?

And you paid six per cent interest on the money advanced you.

It had to be soon. If I didn't get out soon I never would. I could feel my initiative, the thing that made me *me* dying, cell by cell, within me. The minute dosages of alkaloid were sapping my will, but most of all it was a hopeless, trapped feeling that things were this way, that they always would be this way, that it wasn't too bad, that you could always go into trance or get really lit on Popsie or maybe try one of the green capsules that floated around from hand to hand at varying quotations; the boy would be glad to wait for the money.

It had to be soon.

'Como 'sta, Gustavo?'

He sat down and gave me his Aztec grin. *'Como 'sta, amigo Jorge? Se fuma?'* He extended a packet of cigarettes.

They were Greentips. I said automatically 'No, thanks. I smoke Starrs; they're tastier.' And automatically I lit one, of course. I was becoming the kind of consumer we used to love. Think about smoking, think about Starrs, light a Starr. Light a Starr, think about Popsie, get a squirt. Get a squirt, think about Crunchies, buy a box. Buy a box, think about smoking, light a Starr. And at every step roll out the words of praise that had been dinned into you, through your eyes and ears and pores.

'I smoke Starrs; they're tastier. I drink Popsie; it's zippy. I eat Crunchies; they tang your tongue. I smoke—'

Gus said to me: 'You don't look so happy, Jorge.'

'I don't feel so happy amigo.' This was it. 'I'm in a very strange situation.' Wait for him, now.

'I figured there was something wrong. An intelligent fellow like you, a fellow who's been around. Maybe you can use some help?'

Extracts from *The Space Merchants*, by Frederick Pohl and CM Kornbluth

Texts on the theme of work:
Death of a Salesman — Miller (play)
The Apprentice — TV series
Spotswood — film
Metropolis — film
Scales of Justice — TV series
The Grapes of Wrath — Steinbeck (novel)
Selected episodes of *Australian Story* — TV program produced by the ABC.

Learning activity **5.10**

1. Identify at least six words and phrases which indicate that these extracts come from a science fiction novel and explain your selection.
2. What is the setting of this extract? How do you know?
3. What aspects of the narrator's job make it particularly boring?
4. What do you think George, the narrator, means when he says '… I'd be closer to the consumers than any ad man in the profession'?
5. What is the pattern of the B labour contract?
6. Why do you think the authors included several examples of **dialogue** between Gus and George?
7. How did the consumers in this society try to ease the difficulties of their lives?
8. Certain words and phrases in the extract echo advertisements for various products. What are some examples? Why do you think the authors chose to include them in the extract?
9. A feature of one kind of science fiction is the way it draws on elements of the present to depict a less-than-ideal future. What elements of the present have the authors of this novel used in order to construct their view of the future?

Form, context, audience and purpose

The authors of each of the texts discussed so far made choices about the form, context, audience and purpose of their writing, which in turn shaped the language they used to create their texts. These same choices will need to be made by you as the author of a text that discusses an issue relevant to a workplace context. Look at the table on purpose, audience, form and context on pages 91–2 before you complete the next learning activity.

Words and phrases which can be used to describe language:
formal
informal
colloquial
conversational, friendly
simple, clear
complex or sophisticated word choice
elegant
poetic, lyrical, full of **imagery**
short, **simple sentences**
long, **complex sentences**
technical terms, **jargon**

Learning activity 5.11

For each of the texts you have read so far in this chapter, identify the form, the context, the audience and the purpose. In the last column describe the kind of language in which the text is written.

Text	Form	Context	Audience	Purpose	Language
Work and life: strike a balance					
Your say forum					
Preventing workplace bullying					
Job satisfaction survey					
Rural nursing					
Ergonomic diagram					
5 Tips for using a laptop computer					
The Space Merchants					

Workplace texts

The workplace texts that we will discuss in this section include the different kinds of written and **multimodal** presentations that occur in the world of work: letters, faxes, emails, reports, discussion papers and datashow presentations. Business relies on effective communication and accurate information, so it is important to be aware not only of the specific conventions of each of the above forms, but also to recognise the impact of careful presentation. This means having a knowledge of layout and being prepared to edit and proofread drafts carefully.

Language

The language of workplace documents needs to be clear and precise. Using a greater number of words is not necessarily the way to achieve this. If there is a simple way to say something, using a few words, this is more effective than opting for a longer and often unwieldy expression. For example, why say 'due to the fact that' when you can simply say 'because'? Similarly, 'during the month of February' can be simply expressed as 'in February'.

Clichés also detract from the clarity of a communication. Avoid phrases such as 'the bottom line' or 'in the final analysis'. What expression or word might you use instead of these?

Because sexist language can cause offence, it is usually avoided in workplace documents.

Business letters

In our personal lives, letters seem to be becoming less and less relevant, replaced in many cases by email communication or the telephone.

In businesses, however, letters are still a common form of communication, although faxes and emails are increasingly used to send messages that are either urgent or less formal. It is also important to note that letters, faxes and emails are a record of communication. You can refer to what has been said in them in a way that you cannot easily do with a telephone call.

Letters have many purposes: they can be written to inform, complain, persuade, request and instruct, and the audience can be members of the public, other businesses or organisations.

Parts of a letter

Letters contain the following parts:

- the address of the sender of the letter (usually contained in an organisation's printed letterhead)
- the name and address of the person to whom the letter is being sent; if the person is part of an organisation, his or her title will also be included — for example, 'General Manager'
- the date
- a greeting ('Dear Mr Roberts', 'Dear Sir', 'Dear Madam', etc.)
- the body of the letter — this is a paragraph or series of paragraphs containing the message
- the ending, or close — the formal ending to a letter is traditionally 'Yours faithfully' if you do not know the person to whom you are writing, or 'Yours sincerely' if you do know the person; other endings can be chosen according to how well you know the recipient of the letter, but it is safest to end a letter with one of the two shown here
- the name and title of the writer
- a signature.

There might also be a 'footer' at the bottom of the page that indicates where the letter is electronically filed. It could look like this:

j:management/correspondence/jones.doc

This tells you the drive and the names of the folders and the document, for easy reference.

Layout conventions

Layout conventions are rules for how to set out letters. It is important to observe these conventions because the person reading the letter will make judgements about the writer based on how well the conventions have been observed. Someone who does not obey the conventions of letter writing might be judged to be lazy, ignorant or rude, and this judgement would reflect on the business he or she represents.

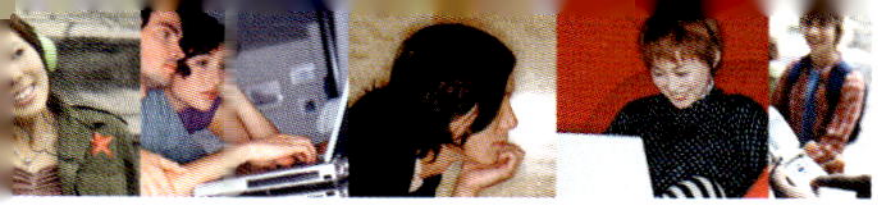

Usually a business has its own 'house style', a preferred way of setting out all documents, including letters.

Although there are a few basic layouts for letters, by far the most commonly used is the full-block style, in which every line commences on the left-hand margin.

Full-block layout

CUMBERLAND DRAPES
431 Ashworth Street
Fitzroy 3065

(The letterhead contains the name and address of the firm that is sending the letter.)

19 February 2006 *(Date)*

Ms A. Mayfield
93 Lanty Road
BAYSWATER. 3153

(Name and address of the person to whom the letter is being sent)

Dear Ms Mayfield, *(Greeting)*

Thank you for the opportunity to quote for the supply of drapes for your home.

We are pleased to advise you that we have now prepared a quote which we submit for your approval.

To supply and fit drapes in Fleur No. 314, Grange Hermitage, for four rooms: $3395.

The order will be placed when we receive your instructions to proceed, and we guarantee delivery within three weeks. We will require a deposit of $1000, with the remainder payable upon delivery.

This quote is current for three months.

We look forward to hearing from you and assure you of our prompt and efficient service.

(Message)

Yours faithfully *(Closing)*

[ ] *(Signature)*

Leanne Bracco *(Name of person who is sending the letter)*
Manager *(Title or position)*

The language of letters

What is regarded as appropriate language in a business letter is more formal than the language that you would use in a personal letter, unless you know the reader quite well. 'Thanks for writing', for example, would rarely be appropriate in a business letter. Instead, you would say 'Thank you for your correspondence' or 'Thank you for your letter'. Similarly, 'Thanks for your help' would be phrased as 'Thank you for your assistance', and 'I look forward to your reply' would be more formal than 'Hoping to hear from you soon'.

Learning activity **5.12**

Make any amendments or additions that you think are necessary in order to make the following an acceptable business letter. Consider not only the elements of the layout but also the content of the letter. Does the sender provide enough information, for instance?

Tuesday April 3
99 Hodson St., Ballarat, 3350

To
JF Records
Lonsdale Street
Melbourne.

Dear Sir
I bought this DVD two weeks ago but it will not play properly. The picture breaks up and the sound is wrong. I am mailing it to you because I cannot get there in person.
Can you please arrange for a replacement?

Thanks
Kerry

Faxes

Faxes are a quick and relatively cheap way of sending messages, including graphics, illustrations and photographs. The cover sheet includes the firm's logo, address, fax and telephone numbers, space to indicate the name and position of the person sending the fax, the date, the subject and the number of accompanying pages. The actual message on the cover sheet is often quite brief.

Fax

To: Calvin Cole
Morris and Associates
TELEPHONE/FAX: 5952 2201
FROM: Susie Ng
Email: susieng@netspace.net.au
TELEPHONE/FAX: 03 9419 4049
DATE: October 10
SUBJECT: Request
No. of pages: 1

Dear Calvin
Thank you very much for sending me the cheque for reimbursement of the faulty goods.

I am, however, embarrassed to tell you that I have misplaced it. Would it be possible for you to arrange for the cheque to be cancelled and reissued?

The details are as follows:

Susie Ng Cheque no. 19288 Issued September 2.

Amount $310.00.

Thank you for your assistance.

Yours sincerely

Suzie

Details which define the fax

Provides another way of contacting

Important — in case not all pages are successfully faxed

Polite greeting

Content or message

Polite sign-off

Signature

Learning activity 5.13

Use a fax template (Microsoft Word has a number from which you can choose) to write one of the following faxes. In each case you will need to make up the name of the firm or person to whom you are writing, and their fax number, as well as your own contact details.

1. You have created a number of graphs and now want to seek expert advice as to whether you have interpreted the data correctly. You decide to send three pages of graphs to someone who might be able to help you. Write the fax you will send.
2. You have been asked to fax a copy of a conference schedule to an overseas visitor who will be attending. Write the fax that will accompany the schedule.
3. Your boss urgently wants a quote for some new equipment (you decide what it is). Write the fax.

Emails

Refer to pages 125–9 for a discussion of emails, including the use of appropriate language in a business email, compared with a personal email.

The email can include a message and an attachment, which might be a print document or a graphic. The recipient is able to work directly on the material that has been sent, reformatting it as required, and saving it to disk or hard drive.

If you have access to internal email at your school, complete the following activities.

Learning activity 5.14

Work in pairs. You need to have a letter checked before you send it. Send an email message to a colleague (your partner), attach the letter and ask him or her to check it. When the other student has received the email, he or she should open the attachment and check it as requested before sending it back. Use the Track Changes and Insert Comment functions in Word on a computer to review the letter.

(Any other piece of writing will be suitable for this activity since the emphasis is on using the technology and editing a document.)

Discussion papers

A discussion paper is used as a way to investigate the popularity and feasibility of an idea. That is, an idea is proposed, the arguments for and against its implementation are discussed and certain people are invited to respond. For example, a manager might decide that there is a need for in-house training in a certain field. The idea might be described in a discussion paper, and the reasons, advantages and possible difficulties are explained.

A discussion paper could take the following format:

- Introduction
- Elaboration (the idea described in detail)
- Rationale (the reasons behind the idea)
- Advantages
- Disadvantages

Reports

Reports are written, and sometimes oral, communications that are used for a variety of purposes:

- to record recurring events such as monthly sales or the proceedings of a particular committee
- to report progress, for example, of a particular project
- to describe or inform about unusual events such as an accident
- to give information that could be used as the basis for a decision
- to analyse a situation and persuade the audience to adopt a particular course of action.

Reports can be short or long, depending on their purpose, and often include graphic presentations or spreadsheets. Reports that are informative in nature are likely to be shorter than those which seek to analyse and persuade their audience.

The audience for a report might simply be your employer — as in the case of a project report — or it might be an entire sales team, the board of directors or franchisees.

Learning activity 5.15

Write one of the following short reports.

1. Your supervisor requires an incident report that describes an accident in which a workmate was slightly injured. Include details such as date, time, place, witnesses, how the accident occurred, what injuries were sustained by the victim and what assistance was given (and by whom) to the injured person.
2. Your boss needs an inspection report that describes vandalism to the firm's property — two car windscreens were smashed, tyres slashed on three trucks, bolt-cutters used to open main gate, paint splashed over showroom window. Include the date that the damage occurred, the time it was discovered and by whom, and what action has been taken.

Datashow presentations

Datashow presentations are a very common form of workplace communication. Workers make presentations to fellow workers, senior management and clients in order to persuade, instruct and inform. Their presentations need to look not only professional but must also be clear and concise in terms of content.

Refer to page 137 for an annotated example of a datashow.

Learning activity 5.16

Use the following table to make a summary of the features of the various workplace texts we have discussed above.

Type of workplace text	Purpose/s	Language	Features
Business letter			
Fax			
Email			
Discussion paper			
Report			
Datashow presentation			

Assessment tasks |

Creating and presenting workplace texts

Choose one or more of the following assessment tasks. Be prepared to explain, either orally or in writing, why you chose to use specific language structures and features.

1. Create and present a picture of a particular workplace in a video or PowerPoint presentation with voice-over. Specify your audience and purpose.
2. Australia is said to be facing a skills shortage, but young people don't seem to want to take on apprenticeships. Use this situation as the basis for one of the following tasks:
   (a) Write an article for a specific audience explaining why young people aren't interested in apprenticeships.
   (b) Design a campaign to persuade young people to enter into apprenticeships. Your campaign should include the script of a radio or television advertisement and a print advertisement. (See chapters 6 and 7 for more information about the features of advertisements.)
   (c) Design and conduct a survey to find out why apprenticeships don't seem to be attractive to young people. Write up the survey results in the form of a **feature article** for a specific audience.

3. Do you have a casual job? Keep a print or digital journal in which you record your experiences 'on the job'. Focus, for example, on the people you meet, your exchanges with them, incidents that you find challenging or rewarding, the skills you acquire.
4. Choose a workplace issue to research and prepare an oral, written or multimodal report for a specific audience and purpose. For example, you could interview a number of people about the issue of job satisfaction, explore the health and safety issues related to specific kinds of employment, or find out more about suggested ways of handling conflict situations.
5. How is work depicted in popular culture? What values are associated with work? What are the respective roles of men and women in relation to work? Analyse, for example, a selection of films, television shows and song lyrics in order to answer these questions. How accurate is the depiction, in your opinion? Present your findings in an oral, written or multimodal form.
6. What do you think work will be like in the future? Create an imaginative oral, written or multimodal text that depicts your vision for the future. For example, write a science fiction story, or create an oral presentation that instructs workers of the future on some aspect of their work, or create a multimodal text that warns workers of the future about a safety aspect of their work.

See page 248 for information about making an oral presentation.

Don't forget to edit and proofread.

7. Here are some descriptions of situations in which a business communication needs to be written. Read the descriptions to decide which form of communication — an email or a business letter — would best suit this situation. Explain the reasons for your choice and then write one of the communications in the form you have selected.
   (a) Your business wants to order catering for a special lunch to be held in a fortnight's time. You have been asked to get some quotes from catering firms. There will be eighty people at the lunch, ten of whom are known to be vegetarians, so their needs will have to be taken into account. This should be a light lunch that includes both sweet and savoury dishes. It will be buffet style. The quotes need to include beverages — orange juice, tea and coffee. Your firm has a kitchen that can be used by the caterers, but all preparation will need to take place off-site and they will need to provide all crockery and cutlery.
   (b) Your business is unhappy with the degree of technical assistance it is currently receiving and wants you to get quotes from some other computer firms. You will need to provide a list of the equipment that you are currently using — computers, printers and scanners — and an estimate of their respective ages. You need to know the procedures followed by the business you are writing to, the estimated maximum waiting period for service and the nature of their charges.
   (c) An employee who has worked with your business for thirty years is retiring. Your boss wants to thank him for his commitment to the business over such a long period and to wish him well for his retirement. (During the time he has been at the firm he has worked in a number of different positions, working himself up to the level of Senior Manager. He has been noted for his excellent relationships with both staff and customers and his ideas have led to several profitable innovations for the business.)
8. You wish to establish a social club for the employees of your firm. Write a discussion paper putting forward the proposal.

9. You are aware of an unsafe work practice. Write a discussion paper, to be sent to section managers, suggesting a way or ways in which safety on the job could be improved.

10. As Equal Opportunity Officer for your business, you have had several complaints from female staff about the way they are treated by some of the men. Write a discussion paper suggesting rules that could be implemented by the business to make certain that it is complying with the *Equal Opportunity Act 1995*.
11. Prepare and present one of the following as a datashow presentation, with accompanying speaker's notes:
    (a) provide instructions for using a particular piece of equipment or performing a particular process
    (b) provide information about an issue of relevance to the workplace
    (c) provide information about a product or service offered by a business, prepared for a prospective client and designed to persuade the client to purchase.

See below for the criteria for assessment.

Criteria for assessment

Your assessment task will be assessed according to the following criteria. Read them carefully before you begin your task; while working on your task, check your progress against the criteria and then review your completed task against the criteria before submitting it to your teacher.

Knowledge and understanding of the content of text/s read for this area of study. This includes, where relevant:

- use of direct quotes from the text/s
- use of direct reference to ideas suggested in the text/s
- use of indirect reference to ideas suggested in the text/s
- discussion of some of the complexities of the theme or issues arising from the context.

Understanding of the relationships between audience, purpose, context, form and language choices. This includes:

- identification and discussion of audience and purpose of own and other's texts
- selection of a form appropriate for a specified audience, purpose and context
- identification, discussion and use of language (visual and/or **verbal**) appropriate to the specified audience, purpose, context and form
- planning and revising to achieve coherence of audience, purpose, context and form.

Ability to construct a written or multimodal text using the features and structures of the chosen form. This includes, where relevant:

- relevance of response to the set topic
- clear and coherent point of view supported by evidence from the set text/s
- control of spelling, punctuation and syntax
- use of **non-verbal** and **visual language** as appropriate to the chosen form — for example, colour, font, camera angles and shots
- coherent organisation.

using language to persuade

VCE UNITS 1 & 2

CHAPTER 6

Using language to persuade in print and non-print texts

In the next three chapters the focus is on examining how language is used to persuade readers and viewers to a particular point of view. We're talking here about language in its widest sense: **verbal language** (language that makes use of words), **visual language** (colour, symbols, design), and **non-verbal language** (facial expressions and gestures, as well as sounds and music).

Chapter Eight will also examine the ways in which an argumentative text can be structured and the role of arguments and evidence in supporting a thesis. The kinds of texts that we will examine will be those that seek to persuade us to do something or believe something and they will include print, non-print and **multimodal** texts.

After we have examined how language works in this **context**, you will have the opportunity to create your own persuasive texts.

Verbal language

Verbal language, the language that makes use of words, either in writing or in speech, is evident in persuasive texts such as **editorials**, letters to the editor, opinion columns, essays and reviews. It is also evident in speeches where it is accompanied by non-verbal language (such as gestures and facial expressions) and in multimodal texts such as print and television advertisements, where visual language enhances the verbal message. To identify and analyse how language is being used in a persuasive text it is necessary to consider all of the forms of language that the author has employed.

Let's start by looking at some of the common verbal techniques used by the authors of persuasive texts.

Verbal persuasive techniques

The connotations of words

The dictionary meaning of a word is its denotation. The **connotation** is the emotional meaning associated with the word. For example, both 'kill' and 'slaughter' essentially mean the same thing, but the word 'slaughter' has a different connotation to that associated with 'kill'. If a man is said to have been killed, we understand that he has lost his life. If, on the other hand, he is described as having been *slaughtered*, we imagine that his death was particularly horrific and that excessive violence was used to end his life.

Therefore, if a writer wishes to emphasise the horror of duck-hunting, for example, he or she would be more likely to say that the ducks were slaughtered, rather than killed.

Authors of texts that seek to persuade consider very carefully the connotations of the words that they use. They use specific words to elicit from their readers the kind of response that they want.

Learning activity **6.1**

1. In the following sentences the words printed in italics all have negative connotations. Rewrite the sentences and change the words to ones that have a positive or favourable connotation. The first one is done for you.
   (a) The family lived in a *shack*. (The family lived in a *mansion*.)
   (b) His approach to life is very *reckless*.
   (c) That model is so *skinny*!
   (d) The after-shave had a strong *stench*.
   (e) With great *cunning*, the President achieved exactly what he wanted.
   (f) The lawyer's *accomplice* was not available for comment.
2. Read the following. Identify the words and **phrases** that have a favourable connotation and explain how they work. The first word with a favourable connotation is 'mansion', which conveys the idea of a large and attractive home — one which is much better than the average house.

   The mansion is situated in a quiet, leafy street in the fashionable suburb of Kent. Built of sturdy brick, it is an imposing structure that nestles in a beautifully landscaped garden of exotic trees and shrubs. The architect-designed residence comprises four spacious bedrooms, a dramatically high-ceilinged living area and a state-of-the-art kitchen. The floor-to-ceiling window in the period bathroom looks out over a private and peaceful fernery.

Anzac Day march

Appeals

Those wishing to persuade us to adopt their point of view often seek to tap into values and views that we hold dear. They seek to position the reader or listener to agree with them by appealing to a view or value that is important to the reader.

Appeals to tradition

If a writer or speaker wants to argue against a proposed change, he or she will often use an appeal to tradition. For example:

- 'We've always done it like this…'
- 'This practice has a long and noble history.'
- 'Our forefathers fought for this.'

The readers or listeners are meant to feel that if they do not support the writer's point of view, then they are undervaluing the importance of tradition.

The **documentary** *Bowling for Columbine* explores the idea that the media deliberately create a climate of fear. See pages 218–19 for activities associated with this documentary.

Appeals to fear

There are many kinds of fear to which a writer or speaker can appeal. There is the fear of change, the fear of loss and the fear of violence. For example:

- 'If this happens, then we will see a vast increase in crime.'
- 'If we allow the government to do this, individual rights will be severely eroded.'
- 'This could lead to social unrest.'
- 'People will lose their jobs if this goes ahead.'

Because of the possibility of these fears being realised, the readers or listeners are more likely to be persuaded to agree with the point of view being put forward.

Appeals to 'family values'

'Family values' are based on the importance of the family as a 'unit'. Families are thought to value such things as security, belonging, caring and nurturing.

For example, the following claims might appeal to or be of interest to people who value the family.

- 'Working mothers are unable to give sufficient attention to their children.'
- 'Corporate businessmen working long hours are alienated from their families.'
- 'Insecurity in employment is preventing couples from starting families.'
- 'Unemployed parents cannot afford to buy Christmas presents for their children.'
- 'The breakdown of the family in our society is leading to an increase in drug-taking among adolescents.'

Special concern for the vulnerable (the children and the aged) are central to these family values. If it can be demonstrated that a proposal benefits or threatens families, readers and listeners may be persuaded accordingly.

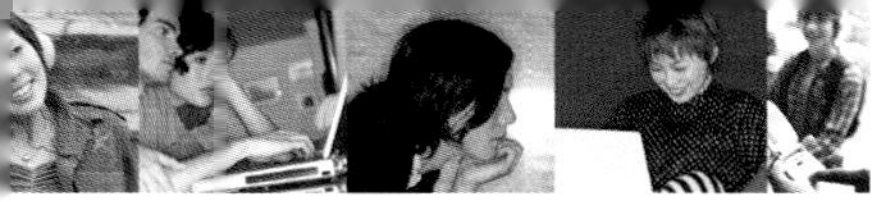

However, as the following article demonstrates, perhaps appeals to the notion of 'family' might mean different things to different readers.

Just what is this thing called family?

BY HUGH MACKAY

Politicians espouse family values, but they're looking backwards.

Let's hear it for The Family! All together now, 'Ahh.' The family is back in vogue. For a while, we were so caught up in gender issues we forgot to acknowledge that the family is where a nation's character, values and outlook are formed.

For better or worse, we are the products of our familial origins — genetic, social, economic and cultural. In spite of life's refining influences, we remain remarkably, defiantly true to label. (As the English poet Philip Larkin so eloquently put it: 'They f– – – you up, your mum and dad.')

In a reasonably robust family, children learn about loyalty and mutual obligation. That's where they make the painful discovery that they are not at the centre of the universe after all, and that being a member of a community — even one as small as a nuclear family — entails some responsibility for other people's wellbeing.

If we're lucky, families are also where we learn, by example, the most important lesson of all: the need to take other people seriously, to listen to them, and to accept them as they are. If we don't experience unconditional acceptance in the family, it's unlikely we'll find it easy to accept, let alone embrace, 'otherness' later on.

So three cheers for families and, yes, let's do all we can to support and encourage them.

But a new, darker note has recently entered the rhetoric about families. When politicians advocate 'family values' and want to preserve the integrity of the family, are they simply stating the obvious, or is there another agenda?

We can only guess what that agenda might be, but it's hard to avoid the suspicion that 'family' is becoming a code word for 'conservative' and that we are being urged to extol the virtues of a *particular kind of family*. This is the family that existed before the gender revolution, before the birthrate plummeted to an all-time low and before the 'average' Australian household shrank to the point where the fastest-growing type is the single-person household.

Of course, household statistics are different from population statistics. Most *people* still live in larger households, but more than 50 per cent of *households* now contain only one or two people. Talk of 'family' seems remote from the growing number of Australians who are not living in conventional family groups — especially those who, left over from a divorce, are living alone involuntarily. And with the marriage rate at a 100-year low and more than 40 per cent of contemporary marriages predicted to end in divorce, it looks as if married-with-children is only one of several 'normal' expectations among young Australians.

While it's true that about 80 per cent of dependent children live with both their natural parents, that figure can blind us to the changing nature of family life. In most families, for instance, both parents work, and that has had a dramatic effect on family dynamics.

And what about the one million children who live with only one of their natural parents? They will inevitably have different, and perhaps even more pressing, emotional needs than children living with both their parents, especially if an unwelcome step-parent has entered the scene.

Consider the implications of the mass migration of 500 000 kids who regularly move between the homes of their custodial and non-custodial parents. That's tough for kids who were never consulted about custody and access arrangements that might seem to them to have been hewn out of the rock of their parents' bitterness.

The repeated agony of child-swapping is tough for the parents, too. 'We meet at a park to hand the kids over, and my ex can scarcely look me in the eye,' says one anxious mother who has recently been inducted into the ranks of parents of migratory children. 'He never sticks to our arrangements, which hurts and disappoints the kids,' says another.

It can also be tough for the neighbourhood — that micro-community of friends who might otherwise provide a stable gang, especially on weekends, for children who are bruised or confused by their parents' shenanigans — and for the grandparents and the rest of the extended family who must come to terms with fractured families and the shifting kaleidoscope of in-laws and 'outlaws'.

When politicians praise the joys of family life, are they remembering that almost 25 per cent of families with dependent children are single-parent families, and that those parents are often suffering from a shortage of time and money? They typically operate on a shorter fuse than parents with partners; their patience and sense of humour can be sorely tested by the demands of single-parenthood.

If we're interested in putting families first, those in most urgent need of support and protection are the single-parent families. They, along with blended families, step-families, transient and dysfunctional families, are the ones for whom 'family impact statements' are overdue. They will also be the families most grateful for this week's decision by the Industrial Relations Commission to grant parents the right to request part-time work while they are responsible for the care of young children.

Yes, the family is still the place where, as children, we learn about 'family values': loyalty, acceptance and mutual obligation. But it's not the place it once was and fewer of us live there, as adults, than ever before. If we're interested in nurturing the rich diversity of family life, 2005-style, we should not be looking in the rear-view mirror; we should be seeking ways to help those struggling to deal with the revolutionary changes engulfing them.

Perhaps the nuclear family is in decline; perhaps we're about to rediscover the strength of the extended family, or even the surrogate extended family. Perhaps parent co-operatives and community-based family services are about to come into their own. In the meantime, if I were a politician I'd be using the word 'family' very, very carefully.

The Age, 12 August 2005

Learning activity 6.2

Each of the following statements is based on information in the article. For each statement, decide whether it is true or false and then support your answer with evidence from the article.

1. Families have a strong influence on an individual's views and values.
2. Politicians have an out-of-date view of what is meant by a 'family'.
3. The author believes that families are an important part of the structure of society.
4. The concept of family is a changing one.
5. The author is sympathetic to the needs of single-parent families.

Appeals to compassion

A description of the plight of the underprivileged is an appeal to the readers' or listeners' sense of compassion. Sometimes this might also be designed to elicit outrage and a desire to take some action to rectify the situation. For example, a description of the condition of those living in a war-afflicted zone or in the aftermath of a disaster can be used to encourage donations to a special fund.

Appeal to readers who want to do something that will have long-term consequences

The majority of the images in links are of children — to appeal to the reader's desire to protect and care for the young

The reader's compassion is appealed to in order to help change this situation.

'Stop children dying' — a very strong appeal to responsibility and compassion

Warm fuzzy name for the gift catalogue — allows readers to imagine the impact their gift might have

The name of the appeal taps into the reader's desire to help and protect the young and defenceless.

An appeal to the reader's desire to do something positive

Words such as 'crisis' and 'disaster' are designed to elicit a compassionate response from readers.

Appeals to self-interest

Appeals to self-interest can take many forms. For example, if a writer or speaker shows readers or listeners that they will be better off in some way as a result of a particular proposal, they may be more likely to agree with the proposal. Statements such as those below are appealing to self-interest.

- 'Residents of the City of Kingsville should realise that if the government's proposal goes ahead, there will be an increase in tourism to the area.'
- 'If you vote for my party, interest rates will not go up.'

Appeals to group loyalty

With this sort of appeal, the readers or listeners are positioned so that they feel they should support the point of view out of loyalty to a particular group. For example:

- 'If this proposal goes ahead, then many of your fellow workmates will lose their jobs.'
- 'Students should stand together on this issue.'

Appeals to patriotism

The term 'un-Australian' is an example of an appeal to patriotism. When a politician or commentator uses this term, the reader or listener is made to feel that supporting a particular point of view or action is not a patriotic thing to do. References to national interest, Australia's position in the world and its economic well-being are other examples of this sort of appeal. For example:

- 'We must take this action if Australia is to be a credible force in our region.'
- 'We must not change the flag because Australian soldiers fought under it in past wars.'
- 'Australian performers are capable of great things!'

Although 'un-Australian' can be seen as an appeal to patriotism — we 'true' Australians wouldn't want to identify with behaviour or ideas that are regarded as 'un-Australian' — it can also be seen as a term of chastisement, a way of reprimanding particular ideas or behaviour. The following Opinion column by Hugh Mackay explores the meaning of this term.

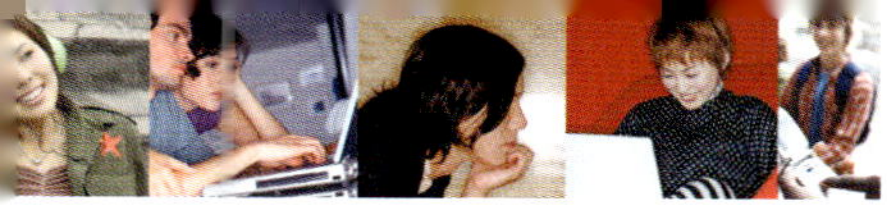

Just who is un-Australian?

It's the new term of chastisement, but what exactly does it mean, asks Hugh Mackay.

'It's un-Australian,' Dick Smith asserted last week, as he railed against the seven-year detention of Peter Qasim, the Kashmiri asylum seeker recently transferred from the Baxter detention centre to an Adelaide psychiatric ward. 'We drove him mad,' Smith said on ABC radio, and then repeated his charge: 'It's un-Australian'...

Surely it's 'Australian' to do whatever Australians do. It's Australian to smuggle drugs in and out of the country. It's Australian to minimise your income tax payments to the point where you're not actually pulling your weight as a taxpayer. It's Australian to cheat if you can get away with it — at work (PriceWaterhouseCoopers reports 47 per cent of companies have suffered some form of corporate crime, mostly committed by employees), on the sporting field (the 'professional foul', for instance), or in personal relationships (where, these days, cheating on your partner scarcely counts as cheating at all).

It's Australian to drink and drive, get hopelessly into debt, lie to secure an advantage — whether political, commercial or personal — and engage in merciless and slanderous gossip. It's Australian to give vent to our xenophobia through outbreaks of racism, to reserve our nastiest prejudices for indigenous people, and to worship celebrity.

Sound a bit negative? Not at all. It's Australian to do such things because, however uncivilised they may seem, it's human to do them. The Dutch do them; so do South Africans, Turks, Indonesians, British, Italians, Brazilians, etc. Like everyone else on the planet, Australians are a mixture of good and bad, noble and shameful, exemplary and slippery.

So, to balance the ledger, I ought to acknowledge that it's entirely 'Australian' (but also entirely French, Korean, etc.) to help neighbours in distress, to bake cakes for fund-raising stalls, to give our children clear moral guidance and to respond to the needs of strangers. It's Australian to befriend the lonely, comfort the sick, pay the taxes we should pay, charge fair prices for our goods and services, make donations to charity without seeking recognition or acknowledgement, cheerfully obey the rule of law, behave with integrity — at work, on the sporting field, in love — and even to celebrate the joys of honest toil.

We're human, OK? So let's not get carried away by hubris: Australians are no better than anyone else when it comes to occupation of the moral high ground. After all, this is the country where many people who opened their hearts and wallets to the tsunami relief appeal then grumbled about the ungrateful Indonesians who dared to convict Schapelle Corby of being a drug courier, as if our charity was part of some implicit trade-off: we'll help your tsunami victims; you let our drug traffickers off lightly.

Let's not assume that if it's praiseworthy or beautiful, it's Australian, and if it's blameworthy or ugly, it's un-Australian. Can you imagine Italians criticising each other for being 'un-Italian'? Have you ever heard of un-Scottish or un-Irish activity? What would un-Swedish behaviour look like?

There was a brief period, it's true, when 'un-American' was in vogue. That was during the hysterical early days of the Cold War when the US anti-communist crusade was in full swing. There was even a congressional committee commissioned to investigate un-American activities. The whole thing fell apart when the neurotic and obsessive ringleader, Joe McCarthy, was both discredited and disgraced, though not before the trashing of countless citizens' reputations.

We should be warned: 'un-Australian' is an ugly word and a signpost to an ugly trend.

The Age, 20 June 2005

Learning activity **6.3**

1. How does Mackay regard the term 'un-Australian'?
2. Mackay first lists a number of different negative forms of behaviour that he calls 'Australian' and then a number of different positive forms of behaviour that he also calls 'Australian'. What point is he making?
3. In the paragraph that begins 'Let's not assume . . . ' Mackay asks a series of rhetorical questions. How does he expect the reader to respond?
4. How does Mackay's use of the 'un-American' example work to persuade readers to his point of view?

Appeals to the desire to be modern

Advertisers make extensive use of this appeal, urging customers to buy the latest in technology, the most up-to-date in fashion or the most recent model car. But there are fashions in ideas, too, and writers and speakers can position readers and listeners to agree with them by indicating that opposing ideas are old-fashioned. For example:

- 'The dinosaurs who resist change must not be allowed to stand in the way of progress.'
- 'We have to change with the times; we cannot become embedded in the past, embracing old-fashioned ideas.'

Appeals to guilt

A feeling of guilt is a powerful emotion, and writers and speakers who make their readers and listeners feel guilty about an issue exercise considerable appeal. For example:

- 'If we sit back and do nothing, this building proposal will go ahead and the surrounding environment will be destroyed.'
- 'If shareholders continue to insist on bigger dividends, companies will improve their efficiency by sacking workers.'

Appeals to a sense of responsibility

An appeal to a sense of responsibility seeks to make the reader feel that there are strong moral reasons for taking action on a particular issue. For example:

- 'We can't just stand by and let this happen.'
- 'For the sake of future generations, we must take action now.'

Refers directly to the reader's responsibility

Use of imperative **verbs** directs the reader to what can be done on a personal level to achieve 'a more sustainable Australia'

Designed to include the reader in accepting responsibility for the environment

HOW WHAT YOU EAT AFFECTS THE EARTH

What we eat in Australia makes up almost half of our impact on the environment. Trying to reduce the damage done by our eating habits is a big step towards achieving a more sustainable Australia and there are many things we can all do in our own lives that will help.

1

WASTE LESS

➜ Australians spend $5.3 billion each year on food we don't eat. This amounts to millions of tonnes of wasted food, plus all the land, water and energy that goes into the cost of producing it. The figure includes leftovers, drinks, frozen or fresh food, and takeaways and restaurant meals. You will make a difference if you buy only what you're likely to eat and cut out the waste.

'You will make a difference' assures the reader of the importance of an individual's actions.

3

BUY ORGANIC

➜ Where possible, buy Australian certified organic produce — remember to check the label. Organic farming doesn't rely on synthetic chemicals, is free of genetically modified organisms and poses a relatively low risk to wildlife, water, land, climate and human health. Organic products are easy to spot on the shelf and buying organic produce sends a signal to other farmers to keep moving towards more sustainable farming methods.

Designed to appeal to the reader's sense of guilt

2

GO LOCAL

➜ Around the world there is a growing movement to 'bring the paddock closer to the plate'. By reducing the distance between the farms that produce food and the dinner tables where it is consumed, it is possible to cut down on the transport pollution that comes from moving food around. You can help by shopping at farmers' markets, or, if shopping at supermarkets, choosing produce from your own state or region, or at least from Australia. You also will be supporting local farmers.

Readers won't want to contribute to pollution.

4

GROW YOUR OWN

➜ Why not try to grow some of your own food at home? That way you'll know that it's organic (if you don't use pesticides or fertilisers). Grow foods that are suitable for the season and climate, and remember to be water wise with your garden.

Appeals to reader's desire to be healthy and fear of illness

5

EAT LESS RED MEAT

➜ Even by developed world standards, the average Australian eats a lot of meat. But times are changing. Nutritionists now caution that eating too much meat can put your health at risk. And according to University of Sydney researchers, meat and other animal products, including dairy, make up the biggest part of our ecological footprint. Just by reducing the amount of meat you eat by one 150 gram serve a week, you can save 10 000 litres of water and 300 kilograms of greenhouse pollution each year.

A direct appeal to be responsible, given the advantages specified

Appeals to a sense of justice

An appeal to a sense of justice or fairness is often used when the rights of two opposing sides come into conflict. The following arguments are examples:

- 'It's all very well to talk about the rights of non-smokers, but what about smokers? Don't they have any rights?'
- 'So single mothers are getting more concessions from the government, are they? Why aren't the disabled being helped too?'

The following editorial appeared in the *Herald Sun* newspaper on 31 December 2005. Read it and then answer the questions that follow.

Fuel for thought

When Victorians are forced to choose between their house and car, it is time to take action on petrol prices.

The *Herald Sun* yesterday revealed that home ownership is being pushed out of the reach of many urban fringe dwellers.

High petrol prices, inadequate public transport and long journeys to work are keeping young Victorians from fulfilling the great Australian dream of home ownership.

The Federal Government takes 34c in excise from every litre of petrol sold. With GST on top of this excise, motorists are taxed almost 40c a litre every time they go to the bowser.

With high petrol prices looking increasingly the rule, it is time the Government cut drivers some slack.

Scrapping the GST on its own excise would be a reasonable step to help John Howard's battlers, many of whom cannot afford to drive their cars out of Struggle St.

If you write your answers to questions in complete sentences, you will be practising the fluency and coherence that will later be an assessment criterion when you complete assessment tasks.

Learning activity **6.4**

1. How does the headline represent a pun or play on words?
2. How do you think the reader is expected to react to the opening statement?
3. '...home ownership is being *pushed out of the reach* of many urban fringe dwellers': If you were to draw this image, what would you see? How does the phrase in italics create a sense of injustice and unfairness?
4. What is the effect of mentioning 'young' Victorians? How is the reader meant to respond?
5. The author evokes the idea of 'the great Australian dream of home ownership'. Why does he mention this and how does he want his readers to respond?
6. Why does the author quote statistics about the Government's share of the price of petrol? How is the reader meant to respond?
7. '...it is time the Government cut drivers some slack' is an example of **colloquial** language. What does it mean?
8. Why do you think the author chose to express this idea in colloquial language rather than in a more formal way?
9. In the last paragraph, the author characterises those who are paying high prices for petrol as 'John Howard's battlers' who live in 'Struggle Street'. Why does he use these terms?

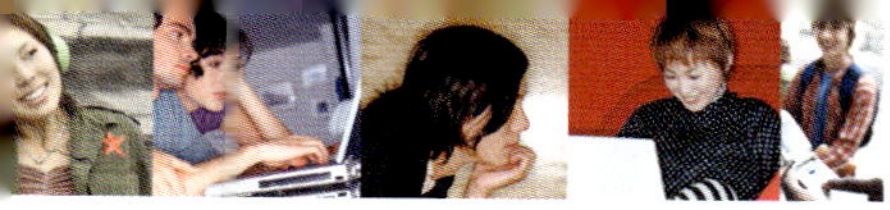

Denigration of opponents

Writers and speakers also position readers and listeners to agree with their point of view by portraying their opponents as foolish, uncaring, dangerous or deceitful. For example:

- 'Town Hall? Clown Hall, more likely, if we consider the Mayor's latest comments.'
- 'When is it going to dawn on the government that their polices are causing untold hardship to country people?'
- 'The short-sightedness of these people is all the more disturbing because they seem to have absolutely no idea what the implementation of this proposal will mean.'
- 'Those behind this latest proposal are shadowy figures who hide from the press and refuse to give any further details.'

Use of inclusive language

When a writer or speaker seeks to identify with the readers or listeners by using **pronouns** such as 'you and me', 'we' and 'our', that writer is identifying as one of us, implying that we are equally affected by the issue and invites readers/listeners to agree with the point of view expressed. The audience is drawn in to the writer's or speaker's concerns. For example:

- 'People like you and me don't want to see this happen. We know how socially destructive it will be, and we don't want our kids growing up in that sort of society.'

Use of jargon

The use of **jargon** can persuade an audience that the writer or speaker is well informed on the topic. If the audience regards the writer as having expertise on an issue, the audience could be persuaded to accept his or her point of view.

The following is an extract from an article by Peter Roebuck which appeared on the sports pages of *The Age* on 3 January 2006. Identify the jargon that demonstrates the author's expertise on the topic. (You might list the words and phrases or underline them in pencil.)

Adversarial captain needs deeds to back his words

'Smith must have been pleased to break his duck as a full-toss was pushed past the bowler. Thereafter his bat was all bristle and bone. Repeatedly the tall left-hander aimed to leg only to send the ball skidding away through the slips. Drives placed towards cover rolled to square leg…

Clearly the South African's technique requires attention. Most particularly he is standing with his feet far apart and crouching low over his bat. At the crease his back is as bent as an arthritic destitute searching for coins in a muddy field. Admittedly batting is an activity best pursued by small left-handers. Nevertheless Smith ought to copy Matthew Hayden by turning his height to advantage. Hayden stands like Alexander before blasting the ball past the bowler. Smith seems to be crawling through trenches.

Standing with pegs a yard apart flattens the toes and limits footwork. Moving into position and transferring weight are important parts of strokeplay. Smith needs to stand upright and dance. He needs to convey intent.'

Use of formal language

Formal language has a distancing effect. It makes the writer/speaker sound well educated and knowledgeable; it removes the heat of emotion from the issue and, for that reason, it can have the effect of making the writer sound reasonable and rational. A reasonable person gives the impression of having considered all aspects of the issue and seems to be presenting a balanced viewpoint. Examples of formal language are likely to be found in the editorials of **broadsheet** newspapers such as *The Age* and *The Australian*.

Honouring our greatest achievers

Word choice indicates an 'educated' vocabulary.

The annual bestowing of honours on our national day has again thrown up some curious choices, as well as conferring deserved recognition on Australians who have worked selflessly for the good of their community. The Companion of the Order of Australia is the highest accolade and this year it was given to just eight citizens. With one notable exception, the recipients are not household names.

Among the academics, health professionals and philanthropists is actress Nicole Kidman, whose award is perhaps compensation for missing out last year when she was the NSW nomination for Australian of the Year. Kidman has achieved notable success — and a sizeable fortune — as an actor. Her citation acknowledges this contribution to the performing arts ['as an acclaimed motion picture performer'] as well as her advocacy for cancer research and other humanitarian causes.

Without wanting to diminish her achievements, this newspaper has reservations about the infiltration of the cult of celebrity into the awards. As we have previously argued, these awards must do much more than merely add to the fame of the already famous.

Designed to appear balanced

Designed to draw attention to a consistent attitude

Prime Minister John Howard may take issue with our assessment. In his address to the nation he complained that, 'too often, history, along with other subjects in the humanities, has succumbed to a postmodern culture of relativism where any objective record of achievement is questioned or repudiated'.

Mr Howard has put on the record his interpretation of the Australian story and how our past has shaped the nation we have become. But this is a continuing narrative and his observations invite further debate. Perhaps one aspect of this could be an exploration of the range of achievements we choose to honour on this day.

Puts the point of view into a broader context, thus perhaps adding weight to the argument

Designed to appear reasonable; 'Perhaps' implies a suggestion rather than a definite call for action

The Age, 26 January 2006

Use of colloquial language

Colloquial language is informal, everyday or conversational language. It is seductive because it is friendly. It invites the audience to share the view being put forward because the writer or speaker seems to be on their wavelength. The audience may in fact be addressed directly, by using the second person pronoun 'you'. There appears to be nothing remote or pretentious about a person who uses such language, so his or her down-to-earth views are probably all right!

We all use this sort of language unconsciously, but a writer may sometimes use it deliberately to achieve a particular effect on the reader.

On the other hand, authors of formal written arguments, such as those which might be written in an academic context, would never use colloquial language. Again, it is the context, audience and purpose of the piece of writing that determines the language that is used.

Tone

When someone speaks to you in a particular **tone** of voice, it is often difficult not to respond accordingly. For example, if you are yelled at, you might find it hard to stay calm and detached. If an instruction is given to you in an authoritative tone, you are more likely to obey than if it were delivered tentatively and uncertainly. If one of your parents speaks to you in a disappointed tone, you will probably feel guilty or ashamed rather than pleased with yourself. Often it is not what is said that is important, but how it is said.

Here are some of the tones that can be adopted, either in speech or writing, to influence the listener or reader.

Reasonable

'It is, after all, only right and fair that all parties should be given time both to prepare and present their cases. Only then will we be in a position to make a decision. To do so before all aspects of the matter have been heard would be foolhardy.'

Outraged

'It is absolutely beyond belief that the Council is yet again changing the parking signs in the main street. Aren't they getting enough revenue out of the motorists already? Aren't they making things difficult enough for business proprietors and their staffs? Apparently not, for here they go again.'

Patronising

'Surely opponents of this change aren't as naive as they seem. I'm certain they must realise what it will mean for all of us if the change fails to be implemented; but perhaps I overestimate them.'

Authoritative

'There is clearly no doubt that we must proceed with the changes as outlined in the report. Research conducted by a reputable agency confirms that this is the most suitable approach.'

Satirical

'Underachieving students would probably perform better if schools changed examinations into a reality show in which students could phone or SMS their answers, or vote for the most popular answer, or even phone a friend.'

Admonishing
'I'm sick and tired of hearing people whinge and moan about the government, the weather, their jobs — the list goes on and on. We should be grateful for what we've got. How would you like to be living in Iraq or Banda Aceh?'

Disgusted
'Why is it that skateboarders have to take over every bit of flat concrete in the city? I'm sick and tired of having to walk around them and watch what they're doing in case they run into me. Can't the Council just provide areas for them and restrict them to these?'

Disappointed
'Recently I visited a park in Greenglade that I hadn't seen in a number of years. It was very dispiriting to see how run-down everything had become. The children's play area badly needed paint, the seats were broken, the grass needed mowing. What a pity that it hasn't been properly maintained so that the public can enjoy it.'

Humorous
'If commuters are avoiding the ticket machines in trams why not install pokies instead? That should raise enough revenue to keep the transport system going!'

Passionate
'More and more these days when I hear our political leaders pontificating, I am deeply ashamed. I am ashamed of the way in which they think they speak for me, the average Australian, when they make statements that lack compassion for our indigenous people, our young, our aged and our unemployed. What can I do to make them see that far from agreeing with them my reaction is one of absolute horror and extreme distress?'

Mocking
'Whacko! Victoria is to have yet another Major Event. Well, that should make all the difference to those who are complaining about lengthy queues and overworked staff in our hospitals. Teachers will be pretty pleased, too, I reckon. It'll make having a prep class of 30 seem so much easier to cope with.'

Learning activity **6.5**

In pairs, read each of the above examples of tone and say how that particular tone is meant to work on the reader. Record your comments in a table like the following:

Example of tone	How this tone is intended to work on the reader
reasonable	Designed to convey the idea that the writer is someone who has carefully considered the issue and is not biased. The reader feels 'safe' with this kind of tone and feels that it is authoritative and able to be believed.

Learning activity **6.6**

Work in pairs to see how many different tones you can use in this exchange:

A: It won't work.
B: Here. Look.
A: Oh.
B: What will we do now?

Learning activity 6.7

Read the following extracts from letters and articles and try to describe the tone in each case.

Pack mentality

BY MAGGIE ALDERSON

...As you know, I'm the kind of twit who packs five cardigans and six pairs of shoes for a weekend in the country, but there have been occasions when I have travelled light, honestly there have. On more than one trip I have heard the blissful words. 'Is that all you've got?' in relation to my luggage, as opposed to the more usual, 'What have you got in here? Dead bodies?'

The Age, 9 May 1998

New push for men to seek help

BY STEVE DOW

Hey, guy, you got a problem? Well, you could try talking it through with the doctor.

Nah, you're right. What would you say?

Maybe, then, you could go to one of those community health centres for a bit of advice and support.

Nah, too girly...

The Age, 7 May 1998

Other persuasive techniques

Repetition

Repeating a statement does not necessarily make it true, but it can certainly make sure that the statement becomes embedded in the minds of the listeners. Advertisers are aware of this fact, which is why television viewers are bombarded with an advertisement several times within the hour over successive nights. Whether you want it to happen or not, the slogan or words of the jingle remain with you.

Politicians use the same tactic, particularly prior to an election, when they decide on a few key phrases to represent their party to the electorate ('Jobs for the young!', 'A better deal for mainstream Australia!'). They then repeat those phrases over and over at every opportunity, so that they become identified in the voters' minds with the party.

In written arguments, repetition can be very effective as a way of driving home a point, as in the following example:

'Capital punishment is wrong because it is a barbaric practice that appeals to a primitive desire for revenge. It is wrong because it requires one human being to take the life of another human being. And it is wrong because, despite all the rhetoric to the contrary, it achieves no useful purpose. That is, it does not act as a deterrent to crime.'

In the previous paragraph, the constant repetition of the words 'is wrong' is intended to reinforce the argument in the minds of the readers.

Repetition is also a very effective feature of a speech. See pages 108–10 for Paul Keating's 'Redfern speech'. You will notice that repetition is a very prominent feature of this speech.

Hyperbole, or exaggeration

Hyperbole (pronounced hy-per-bol-ee) is often associated with mockery or denigration of opposing points of view or their proponents (the people who support those points of view). An idea might be deliberately exaggerated in order to make it appear ridiculous, for example:

'Those who support this ridiculous idea would have us believe that it will dramatically improve the quality of modern living. Of course it will! And it will probably cure cancer, eradicate pollution, improve traffic flow and make the kids go to bed when we tell them!'

Ridicule

Making fun of one's opponents, or mocking the ideas or behaviour of others, is a technique used by some authors to encourage readers to agree with them. At the same time that the viewers or readers laugh, they dissociate themselves from those who are being laughed at.

Read this article by Kerry Cue and either answer the questions or annotate the article in pencil.

This activity and others like it could be done as a class if the article is copied onto an overhead transparency (OHT). Annotations suggested by students can then be made directly onto the OHT.

Mags for the mundane

BY KERRY CUE

Something interesting's happening at the up-market end of the glossy magazine business.

Several new glam titles have been launched in Australia this year, including *Madison* for stylish single women.

US Vogue is releasing a *Men's Vogue* this week, aimed not at the man in the street but, according to the blurb, at 'the man who has already arrived'.

So if you are pre-Ferrari, forget it.

What's really happening in the glossy magazine market is a scramble for that 35-plus reader who's smart enough to earn heaps, but dumb enough to buy anything from the latest fashion atrocity to the coolest and craziest gizmo.

Manolo Blahnik shoes fall into the first category. At up to $1100 a pair, the absurd height of these stilettos is not the issue — although a Paris Hilton clone could commit suicide by simply throwing herself off her strappy heels on a bad hair day.

The problem is girls are allowed to board planes wearing stiletto heels that could slash throats. They're lethal weapons.

As for pointless gizmos, there are many contenders.

My current favourite is the underwater iPod. It exists. So a loaded 35-plus gizmo addict can now surf to a hip-hop beat.

Apart from the 40 pages of ads you must wade through before arriving at an article, the most noticeable change to up-market glossy magazines is that they are now moving more and more up-market.

In a typical hi-gloss mag the handbags are so couture they can only be worn with body paint and your head in a bird cage; the perfume is so expensive it can only be dabbed behind ears designed by Armani.

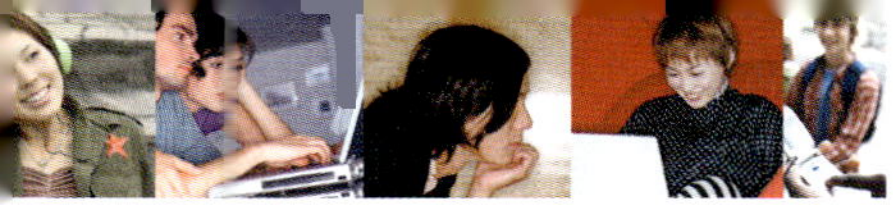

The watches are so up-market they do not tell the time, they flaunt it.

The usual female model is so thin she looks like a pretzel with a pout.

The preferred male model is so young he looks as if he's been sent to sulk outside the headmaster's office in a $3000 linen suit.

And the food is so gourmet each main course has a name that reads like a French novel and a steak the size of a postage stamp.

Meanwhile the people interviewed in these hi-gloss mags all seem to belong to the Rich and Famous A-list.

Our Princess Mary doesn't rate. Well, she's from Tasmania, darling.

The preferred interviewee is so successful he's thinking of taking on Donald Trump as an apprentice and so famous he gives the Pope an audience.

His house is so fabulous his poodle has its own condo with spa, mirrored bedroom and theatrette.

In other words, the reader of the ultra hi-gloss magazine is expected to be so up themselves they could put their hand out their own mouth and wave.

Isn't it time there was a glossy magazine that celebrates ordinariness?

I'd call this publication *Vague Living*, the first hi-gloss magazine to take you inside the lifestyles of the mortgaged and unknown.

Gardens will be based on the survive-or-die school of landscaping.

Meals will be filling and from the *Don't Fuss, They'll Whinge Anyway Family Cookbook*.

Selected female models will boast Venus Williams comfort-padding.

Male models will boast FPHG — Feral Pattern Hair Growth — where hair abandons the head to colonise the rest of the body.

Handbags, perfumes, watches and other products will all be brand name items, but from the iffy Chinese brand lines like Goochee and Am R Nee as well as Victory Toilet Paper and Blast Off Shampoo.

Star Signs will be blunt. Gemini. This Friday to Sunday you're knackered. Stay home and watch the footy.

And interviewees would work hard, renovate their homes using the Sydney Harbour Bridge Method (by the time they've finished at one end, they have to start again at the other), love a back-to-basics barbie and think our Princess Mary is lovely.

But would anyone buy this magazine? I doubt it.

Once Australians wanted to be seen as average Aussies with an average house, average car and average bathroom.

Now most Australians want to be seen as above average. The problem is standards keep rising.

And staying above average has become a helluva lot of hard work.

Herald Sun, 6 September 2005

Learning activity **6.8**

1. Who does Kerry Cue identify as the target audience for the new glossy magazines?
2. What aspect of the new magazines leads her to this conclusion?
3. Give two examples of how she uses ridicule to mock each of the following:
   (a) the products advertised in the magazines
   (b) the models portrayed in the magazines
   (c) the people who are interviewed for the magazines.
4. What point of view is Kerry Cue arguing in this article?

Rhetorical questions

A rhetorical question is one to which no answer is really expected; it is asked for effect only. Someone who poses a rhetorical question knows there is only one answer, and that answer confirms the point of view of the writer (or speaker).

For example, someone arguing against the screening of violent programs on television, because of their alleged tendency to increase violence in the community, might ask the following rhetorical question:

'Do we want our children growing up in a world where they are threatened with violence on every street corner?'

Clearly, the reader can only answer 'no' to such a question, even if the reader disagrees with the general argument.

Use of statistics

Authors often quote statistics in support of a point of view. Readers can be persuaded by statistics because they give the appearance of being objective and 'true'.

- Ninety-seven per cent of people agreed with the proposition.
- The survey found that three-quarters of those interviewed said they supported the idea.
- It is estimated that several thousands of people have contracted some kind of cancer as a result of the use of mobile phones.

Persuasive? Maybe.

Before you decide whether or not you want to be persuaded by the above use of statistics, you might want to ask:

- 'Ninety-seven percent of what?' (How many people are we talking about here? Ten? A hundred? A thousand?)
- How many people were actually interviewed? Where was the survey conducted?
- How many is several thousands? And what is the **source** of this vague statistic?

See page 230 for a further discussion on the use of statistics and the questions readers need to ask before they agree to be persuaded by them.

Learning activity **6.9**

Here are several texts about the same topic. Read the texts and complete the questions that follow.

Schoolies lessons

The annual phenomenon known as Schoolies Week is a headache for parents, police and some participants.

The partying is a well-earned chance to unwind after a year of hard work.

But there is an unfortunate aspect — excess drinking, drug use and the presence of older outsiders bent on mayhem.

Some adults want the schoolies celebrations ended. They brand them as nothing more than tourist promotions that exploit the young.

Certainly police must show no mercy to those who lead astray young people through alcohol, drugs or incitement to violence.

But it would be a great pity if the actions of a few denied schoolies the chance to let their hair down.

Herald Sun Online, 24 November 2005

A week to be wary of

BY ROBYN RILEY

Boys smashed in the face with broken bottles, girls bingeing on vodka, designated buses ferrying children fresh out of school on trips to buy drugs…

These are our children we are talking about and this is the culture we have all helped to create.

It's no wonder I am not a big fan of Schoolies Week.

For starters, it no longer is a week, more like a month, which, in a sense, is symptomatic of the problem: give 'em a bit of leeway and they'll want more.

That's what has happened isn't it? When my parents left school, they finished on the Friday and started work on the Monday. When I left school, we let our hair down with a couple of parties and then it was upwards and onwards to the real world.

But then some children were treated with a trip to Queensland to mark the end of high school — something we adapted of course from our American cousins — and pretty soon it was considered a basic right: 'Mum, you've got to let me go, all the kids are going'.

And now every parent is confronted with this awful dilemma; how to afford your children with the freedom and responsibility that every 18-year-old takes for granted while at the same time providing them with hope and some semblance of security?

I don't profess to know the answer, but we are not doing our children any favours by indulging them during Schoolies time.

And yes, I am aware that an awful lot of children manage to have the time of their lives and return to their parents relatively unscathed. I'm sorry, but when my children are 18, I will be telling them that it is a risk that I am not prepared to take.

What staggers me here is how parents willingly provide the not inconsiderable funds for their children to go to the Gold Coast and elsewhere and then just cross their fingers that nothing will happen.

I understand children have a lot of pressure on them these days, that jobs are harder to get and Schoolies Week represents a letting-off of all those pressure valves that come from years of study.

I also know that children get plenty of time out as it is, that from October to February is one long party for many of them and that there is a growing army of children who take the following year off from either joining the work force or heading to uni, so they can 'chill' and enjoy the last vestiges of their teenhood.

My children are still years away from this, but already I am telling them not to get their expectations up for Schoolies Week. I tell them that I trust them enough to go somewhere nice with their friends, but not to a Schoolies hotspot where predators are known to be hovering and drugs and excessive alcohol and violent acts are just a part of the landscape.

All I know is that we can't keep blaming the bad elements and we can't keep blaming our children. Sooner or later, parents are going to have to start parenting.

Herald Sun Online, 4 December 2005

Schoolies week used to be fun

Robyn Riley in her article 'A week to be wary of' reminds me of my experience of Schoolies Week back in 1996.

I can't tell you how different it was then. Yes, we liked having a few drinks, but I can't remember things really getting out of control. What I do remember is laughing heaps and having lots of fun with my mates.

It's totally different now, and much nastier.

In particular, it seems that it's the girls whose behaviour has really got worse. When I was at Schoolies, the girls weren't into binge drinking and a lot of the guys weren't either. Now it seems that everyone is into it, and that's worrying because they're not only into binge drinking during Schoolies Week — they're doing it every weekend!

Jack Tatler

Learning curve

I take offence at Robyn Riley's Schoolies Week article.

My goal has been to teach strength, independence, love and respect to my children.

My son has reached adulthood, has his driver's licence, works part-time and has finished his VCE.

Saving hard for his first holiday with his mates was exciting and his father and I enjoyed watching him organise it. He had our blessing to enjoy his first real taste of independence.

He knows life is about making choices and that there are consequences for your actions.

We are not bad parents for letting him go to Queensland.

Jill and Gary Craven, Langwarrin

Schoolies week

Fuss over nothing

Robyn Riley is all worked up over Schoolies Week. She says it indicates a much wider problem in the community and that parents are pretty much to blame.

Well, I'd like to know where she got her facts from. Has she been to Schoolies Week or has she just been watching the beat-ups on commercial current affairs programs?

Because I can tell her, I *have* been there. I've just got back from Surfers and my experience was nothing like Robyn's fantasy.

Lloyd Tilojic

Answer the following questions:

1. What is the issue referred to in all of these texts? Explain in full.
2. Complete this sentence. The point of view put forward in the editorial is that...
3. Complete this sentence. Robyn Riley's point of view is that...
4. Which letters agree with Riley's point of view?
5. Which of the following tones is adopted by the editorial?
   - outraged
   - reasonable
   - admonishing

   Explain your answer and support it with direct quotes from the editorial.
6. Read the opening paragraph of Robyn Riley's article. What response was Riley attempting to evoke in her readers? Explain.
7. The three dots at the end of the first paragraph of Riley's article imply that...
8. Complete this sentence. Riley uses 'our' and 'we' because she wants readers to feel...
9. Give and explain examples of how Riley attempts to make parents feel guilty about allowing their children to go to Schoolies Week.
10. What is the effect of Riley's use of the word 'staggers' ('What staggers me here is...')?
11. What kind of reader would be likely to be persuaded by Riley's point of view? Why?
12. What reader values are appealed to in 'Schoolies week used to be fun'? Quote from the letter to illustrate.
13. How does 'Fuss over nothing' use denigration of opponents as a persuasive tactic?
14. What tone is adopted by the author of 'Learning curve'?
    - angry
    - disappointed
    - reasonable

    Explain your answer and support it with direct quotes from the letter.
15. What reader values are appealed to in 'Learning curve'? Quote from the letter to illustrate.
16. Do the other texts reflect the same values as 'Learning curve'? Explain.

The above learning activity guided you through the analysis of a number of different texts on the same issue. The following assessment task requires you to produce your own analysis of the language choices without a set of guiding questions. The following process should help you to do this:

(a) annotate the editorial wherever you can see examples of the verbal persuasive techniques outlined above
(b) group together persuasive techniques of the same kind — for example, appeals to the reader's sense of justice and fair go. Each 'group' could later be discussed in a separate paragraph.
(c) For each group, provide an answer to the question: how is this language choice intended to position the reader? (How is the reader meant to respond? Is that how the reader is in fact likely to respond or might there be another reaction entirely?)
(d) write a brief introduction to your analysis. The introduction should indicate that you understand the issue under discussion and the main contention of the editorial.

Strategies | Analysing persuasive language

Some sentence structures that you might use when analysing the use of language to persuade:

- The author seeks to persuade his reader by . . .
- Appeals to the reader's sense of justice are intended to make the reader feel . . .
- Words such as . . . have a positive connotation and therefore position the reader to feel . . .
- The author taps into the reader's respect for tradition when he refers to . . .
- The disappointed tone adopted by the author (. . .) is designed to make the reader . . .

Assessment tasks | Analysing language used to persuade

1. The following is an editorial on the subject of downloading music from the internet. It puts forward the point of view that the arguments being used against music downloading — that it is immoral because it is theft of intellectual property and it harms the music industry — are wrong.

Piracy or Progress: Is Music Downloading Immoral?

DOWNLOADING EDITORIAL, SHORT VERSION
JANUARY 2004

Roger Bohn, rbohn@ucsd.edu
University of California at San Diego

In all the publicity about the downloading of music from the internet, the view that it is immoral has gone mostly unchallenged. The two main moral arguments advanced by the Recording Industry Association of America (RIAA) are that downloading is theft, and that it harms the music industry and its employees. Yet polls show that downloading songs from the internet is widespread, with up to half of teenage internet users doing it. And for the most part the practitioners have few qualms about the morality of their actions. Even many who don't download music engage in similar behavior, such as duplicating CDs and ripping music from CDs to their computers.

Most commentators conclude that downloaders are moral illiterates, who either don't understand what they are doing is wrong or just don't care. But a better explanation is that the RIAA's arguments against downloading, although they have been implicitly accepted by the press, have little moral validity. Downloading may be immoral in some cases, but not for the reasons claimed.

The argument that downloading is theft derives from the position that music is 'intellectual property'. RIAA ads claim an explicit parallel between downloading a song and shoplifting a CD — the implication being that intellectual property is no different than physical property, and therefore the wrongness of physical theft that we learned in childhood applies directly to electronic data files. But intellectual property is actually very different than physical property and should be treated differently. The key distinction is that intellectual property, unlike physical property, can be used simultaneously by multiple users without interfering with other users. Therefore, our natural concept of theft does not have an obvious or automatic extension to the use of intangibles like music. Walking out of a store with an album under your shirt deprives someone else of the chance to possess and use that physical album; downloading a song has no such effect, and therefore must be evaluated differently.

Societies choose certain types of ideas and turn them into 'intellectual property' by artificially restricting the rights of people to use them. To phrase it concisely, 'Intellectual property is created by Man, not God'. Society chooses rules for defining and controlling the uses of intellectual property based on its collective interests. The purpose of intellectual property laws is to encourage creation of new ideas, without going so far as to overly restrict the ability of non-creators to use and benefit from those ideas. Intellectual property in music is created by copyright laws, and the rights of music copyright owners exist only because they are defined by laws. The internet and accompanying technologies have created revolutionary ways of distributing music, and the appropriate balance between encouraging idea creation and encouraging idea reuse should shift. Just as the then-revolutionary technologies of photography, the Xerox machine, and broadcast radio did, when technological revolutions occur they create new possibilities that society must choose how to deal with. The RIAA's simplistic assertion that downloading is theft amounts to claiming that it alone has the right to choose how society handles musical intellectual property.

And what of the music industry's other main argument — that downloading is immoral because it hurts the industry? Even if true, many technological changes hurt individuals, companies, and industries, yet that is no reason to hobble them. Americans understand that new technology should not be forbidden merely because it is disruptive.

There is also a more subtle error in this argument about economic harm. Even if we accepted the premise that technological change

should be forbidden if it causes such harm, looking only at the music industry would be the wrong way to do the accounting. The overall economic impact of downloading is almost certainly a net positive. Digital music is a big driver of personal computer upgrading, broadband internet use, multimedia hardware and software, and the like. It is not facetious to say that Intel, Microsoft, Seagate, and even Cox Communications and Sony lose more from strong laws on digital copying than the music industry stands to gain.

Thus the music industry's two arguments that downloading is immoral are distorted and invalid. The basic principle behind copyright — that society will be better off if artists have some legal rights to profit from their art — is still sound. But society is also better off if the benefits of new technology are allowed to flow. There are various ways to meet both objectives, such as the new Canadian system of collecting fees on music hardware. Another approach would be modest centrally collected subscription fees for broadband internet connections — analogous to cable TV fees.

The music industry's insistence that it should have veto power over what people do with their computers is not good for the economy or society at large, and we should not take its claims seriously. Our children are not virtual shoplifters. They have a better understanding than some members of Congress that revolutionary technology causes disruption and requires adapting codes of behavior — and it should.

See page 248 for advice on making an oral presentation.

How does this editorial seek to persuade readers to accept its point of view? In writing or orally, explain how the language choices are intended to position the reader.

2. Choose another editorial or letter to the editor from this chapter or from Chapter Eight and, in writing or orally, explain how the language choices are intended to position the reader.
3. Read the following two articles on the subject of child obesity and compare the ways in which they use language to position the reader.

Don't forget to edit and proofread your written responses.

See page 202 for the criteria for assessment.

Sports Sponsors are turning our kids into junk food freaks

BY JOANNE DWYER

The half-time oranges have been replaced by chocolate bars putting children well on the road to obesity, writes Joanne Dwyer.

As a nation we are battling with childhood obesity. Authorities are looking to children's sport as the answer and parents are responding enthusiastically. However, a seedy side of children's sport is firmly and quietly marking its territory, potentially challenging the health it promises.

Children have long loved junk food. And naturally, they enjoy eating after a good sports game. But in recent times, the link between bad food and exercise seems to have grown stronger, as part of an emerging new culture in children's sport. Changes in attitudes to food have seen the humble orange at half-time replaced by lollies, chocolates, doughnuts and soft drinks. At Saturday morning soccer games, six-year-olds can be spotted downing red frogs, eating chips and sucking on Wizz Fizz.

Comments such as 'I've got a lollipop for you in my bag after the game' can be heard being called out from the sideline. It's not uncommon to see children back on the field, finishing off those chewier lollies from half-time.

The junk food epidemic is invading children's sport on all fronts. Sports club canteens are filled with a smorgasbord of sugar and fat; dance teachers are using lollies to keep order during practice sessions.

At a very early age children are learning that high fat and high sugar treats are part of sport and the reason for trying — or the expectation for simply turning up.

The multinationals are also in on the action and are making a fat living. With McDonald's 'encouragement awards' children are rewarded for playing well with some high-fat foods — free chips, hash browns or sundaes over four weeks, on the condition that a burger is bought. No mention of Salads Plus on these awards.

Cadbury has also got in on the game. Its latest international campaign, endorsed by the British Minister for Sports, aims to fight childhood obesity.

The campaign entitled 'Get Active' encourages schoolchildren to buy chocolate bars and collect wrapper tokens to exchange for free sports equipment for their school. With 5440 wrappers a school can buy a set of volleyball net posts. That's a million calories! How much volleyball would you need to play to burn that off?

To put their reward system in health terms, the 160 million tokens available equate to nearly 2 million kilograms of fat. All in the name of getting fit and healthy.

While this campaign hasn't hit Australian shores, it appears that more and more junk food companies are being welcomed by sporting associations.

Newcomer Krispy Kreme, the doughnut maker, has quickly made an impact. Only months ago, we were publicly questioning whether with our dietary problems, we should be allowing such high-fat doughnuts onto our shores. This year, however, many sporting associations are asking their young players to sell them as a fund-raiser.

I know of at least three sports groups in the Sutherland Shire which ask parents to buy 12 doughnuts for $11 — they recommend every family buy five dozen — and take a cut of the profits made.

We all now know that a poor diet leads to children becoming overweight and obese, affecting the child both in the early years of life as well as contributing to heart disease, stroke and other heath issues later in life.

However, the problem seems to be getting worse.

Not only is childhood obesity continuing to rise at an alarming rate, but a recent Australian study has shown that an unhealthy lifestyle is causing hardening of the arteries in children as young as six.

Government initiatives are looking to schools to address the problem. The Government's recent Healthy Canteen campaign is looking at getting junk food out of our school tuckshops by the end of the year.

What must be considered, however, is that children don't just learn at school and they don't just learn from teachers. The attitudes of parents and other significant people in a child's life send powerful messages.

Whether it's for reward or fund-raising purposes, a coach endorsing junk food sends a powerful message to a five-year-old.

The picture in our minds as adults is that we are providing a wonderful healthy lifestyle for our children with weekend sports and weekday training. That we are helping them to establish healthy patterns both for now and for later life. In reality we're painting a different picture.

Endorsing junk food in this 'healthy' context is crossing out the benefits. Junk food is the seedy side of children's sport. If we aim to really tackle the childhood obesity problem we need to address the problem on all fronts.

Joanne Dwyer is a lecturer at the School of Education and Early Childhood Studies at the University of Western Sydney.

The Sydney Morning Herald, 12 May 2004

Move over, boomers and Xers, Generation O is on its way

BY EDWARD SPENCE

Exploitation of children is deplorable, with junk food advertising no exception, writes Edward Spence.

The next generation is in danger of being known as 'Generation O' — as in O for obese. The World Health Organization estimates that a billion people worldwide are overweight or obese, contibuting to an increasing incidence of diabetes, heart disease and other chronic illnesses. It is the calculated targeting of children that has most critics calling for action and that action is the regulation of advertising of junk food to children.

This week, Australian advertisers are to consider voluntary guidelines on advertising junk food to children. Regulations have already been proposed, even introduced, in countries such as the US and Britain.

The Australian Association of National Advertisers claims there is no 'incontrovertible proof' of a direct correlation between junk food advertising and child obesity. Even if we accept this, there is adequate evidence of a link between the two, which would strongly suggest that serious consideration be given to regulation, especially since the exploitation of children by junk food advertising is unethical and thus objectionable.

The object of junk food advertising is to persuade children to buy and eat junk food. Advertisers spend billions of dollars each year targeting children with innumerable junk food ads which are placed in and around their favorite TV programs. Children are influenced by such ads. As a result, children consume more junk food than they would otherwise and some become obese, exposing them to health risks including diabetes and heart disease.

Adults can form their own rational judgements about products being advertised, but children cannot.

Advertisers, of course, know this and that is why they spend billions of dollars on commercial advertising each year targeting children — why else would they do it if it didn't work?

Target advertising is by design manipulative and exploitative. It manipulates children's emotions and desires by exploiting their

vulnerability and susceptibility to sights and sounds of entertaining junk food ads. Such pervasive messages have only the advertisers' interests at heart. The children as the target are merely the means to market share and profits. As such, it is ethically objectionable.

Even if such manipulative exploitation of children by advertising did not result in any measurable harm, there would still be grounds for ethical unease. Exploitation even when it does not result in any actual harm can never be condoned. However, considering the actual and potential health risks, there is a prima facie case for substantial ethical concern, not just for the children and their families, but for the whole community.

Further research is needed to establish a causal link between junk food advertising and child obesity, but in the meantime, given the high degree of harm to health that child obesity can cause, there are grounds for adopting harm minimisation strategies.

Encouraging children to exercise more and eat more healthy food, the Government's preferred option so far, is one such strategy. But it is not enough. Regulating advertising of junk food is also necessary. Given the size of the problem, co-regulation with the participation of government regulatory bodies, the advertising industry and community groups, would prove the most credible and effective type of regulation.

Edward Spence is a senior research fellow, ARC Special Research Centre for Applied Philosophy and Public Ethics, Charles Sturt University.

The Sydney Morning Herald, 24 May 2005

Criteria for assessment

Your assessment task will be assessed according to the following criteria. Read them carefully before you begin your task; while working on your task, check your progress against the criteria and then review your completed task against the criteria before submitting it to your teacher.

Understanding of verbal, visual and non-verbal language used by authors of texts to position readers and viewers in particular ways. This includes, where relevant, the identification and discussion of:

- the connotations of words
- the various appeals to the emotions and values of the audience
- the use of visual features such as design, camera angles and colour
- the use of auditory features such as music and sound effects
- the use of strategies such as repetition, pauses, pitch and volume.

Ability to create a response in the chosen mode which identifies and discusses the ways in which language is used to persuade. This includes, where relevant:

- the use of appropriate **metalanguage** to discuss the use of language
- control of spelling, punctuation and syntax
- planning and revising
- control of aspects of oral presentation including pronunciation, pace, pitch, volume and body language
- the conventions of small group discussion.

CHAPTER 7

Using language to persuade in multimodal texts

In the previous chapter we looked at how authors use verbal language in print and non-print texts to persuade readers and listeners to accept a particular point of view or to react in a particular way. This chapter will focus on **multimodal** texts to examine the choice of specific features of **visual**, **verbal** and **non-verbal language** made by authors for the same kinds of persuasive purposes.

Cartoons

In drawing a cartoon that refers to an issue or event in the news, the cartoonist expresses an opinion on that issue or event. The usual approach is one of satire. That is, the cartoonist deliberately 'sends up' the issue in order to draw attention to weaknesses in an argument or to mock a particular point of view. Politicians are often the subjects of cartoons, and caricature (exaggeration of physical features) is one of the devices employed in order to make the politician appear ridiculous. In order to understand the cartoon, readers need prior knowledge of the issue and the people involved.

Apart from caricature, cartoonists use several other devices, some of which are listed below.

- The position of the characters in relation to each other is significant. Sometimes one character is depicted as much larger or darker than another. Size can be a reference to power or perceived character. Dark colours can be a reference to evil or potential threat. Similarly a small character can be seen as vulnerable.
- Background detail needs to be examined carefully. It is usually there in order to make some extra comment or to indicate a **context**. Where there is no background detail, the reader's attention is focused on the central character or characters, and the clothing, facial expressions and physical attitudes will all be of relevance.
- Symbols are also used. Bank notes, for example, can be a symbol of greed.
- The caption directs the reader's attention to the central issue on which the cartoonist is commenting.

Following is a cartoon that appeared about the same time as the release of the movie *King Kong*. The cartoonist has used the **imagery** from the film to make a comment on the bid by the Treasurer, Peter Costello, for the role of Prime Minister.

Read the annotations carefully, to see how the cartoonist uses visual language in order to persuade the reader to accept the point of view expressed.

To be able to read this cartoon, the reader needs to be familiar with elements of the movie *King Kong*.

The dominant image is that of King Kong, with a caricature of the face of the Prime Minister. His size is an indication of his power.

The banner 'Coming Soon' not only draws on the convention of advertising forthcoming movies, but also refers to the challenge for the leadership which was a topic current in the media at the time this cartoon was produced.

In the plane, which is ancient and rather battered, indicating its lack of power, is a caricature of the Treasurer and on the side of the plane is the word 'Costello', so we cannot mistake who this is meant to be. The plane is circling King Kong and eyeing the leadership with a view to wresting her from the gorilla's grasp.

Overall, the message is that Costello's bid for the leadership seems to be against the odds.

Grasped in his hand is a very small woman with the label 'The Leadership'. That the woman is a 'prize' is indicated by her slim figure and her blonde hair. (Some readers might find it objectionable that 'The Leadership' is depicted as a woman. They might argue that this reduces women to the status of an object: something to be owned.)

Learning activity 7.1

Examine the following cartoons. In each case, use the table provided to identify the point of view being expressed in the cartoon, and the visual and verbal language used by the cartoonist. Explain how that language is being used to position readers.

Cartoon 1

Cartoon 2

	Topic and point of view	Visual and verbal language	How the language works to persuade readers
Cartoon 1			
Cartoon 2			

Photographs

Photographs accompanying an article often add information and help to influence readers' responses either by providing an illustration or by providing extra information that was not included in the article. For example, an article on the dangers of sunbathing might be accompanied by a photo which shows bikini-clad girls lying on the beach. Such a photo might persuade readers that the problem is gender-based and more likely to be of relevance to girls, rather than boys. Or an article on loutish behaviour might be accompanied by a photograph depicting individuals from a particular ethnic group, thus implying that they are the focus of the problem.

Learning activity **7.2**

See the main photo of the child on the World Vision website featured on page 179. How do you think the impact of the site might be lessened if the chosen photo had been one which depicted aid workers rather than the child?

Remember that the photographer has made a number of stylistic choices when composing a particular photograph. She or he has decided:

- whether to use colour or black-and-white film
- how to frame the subject
- whether to use a wide shot or a close-up shot
- what kind of lighting to use
- whether and how to **crop** the photo afterwards.

All of these elements work together to produce a particular version of an event, or a particular representation of a person and to position the viewer to respond in a particular way. In the case of the photos on the World Vision website, the effect is predominantly emotive, appealing to the reader's desire to protect the vulnerable.

Strategies | Examination techniques for photographs

When examining a photograph, use these questions to guide you.

1. Who is depicted in the photograph?
2. What are they doing?
3. How does the body language of the subjects contribute to the meaning that the reader creates? (Consider, for example, where the subjects are in relation to each other, their facial expressions, gestures and stance, and the focus of their gaze.)
4. Where is the central focus in this photograph? How does this affect the meaning that the reader creates?
5. On what occasion do you think the photograph might have been taken and why? Explain the clues in the photograph that help you to answer this question.
6. What might have happened just before the photograph was taken?
7. What might have happened just after the photograph was taken?
8. What might be just outside the frame of this photograph?
9. How does the way in which the photograph is lit contribute to the creation of a mood or impression?

The headlines, text and photographs on the front pages of newspapers are essentially persuasive in purpose. Their role is to encourage potential readers to buy the newspaper.

Here is a front page of the *Herald Sun* newspaper. Read the annotations to see how the various features seek to persuade.

Herald Sun
www.heraldsun.com.au
NEWSPAPER OF THE YEAR
70 DAYS TO GO
WEDNESDAY, JANUARY 4, 2006
$1*
CASINO MADNESS PAGE 11
$190m LOSER TELLS
7-DAY TV GUIDE PLUS connect
NAUGHTY NEIGHBOURS
PLUS MELBOURNE'S TOP PARKS SUMMER PUZZLES
Millionaire murder mystery
Dead: the body of Michael Griffey (right) was found on Monday night in the garage (below, right) of his family home at Pakenham.
FOUR LOST DAYS

The newspaper banner proudly proclaims 'Newspaper of the Year', which could be seen as a marketing device to persuade readers of the quality of the newspaper.

The coloured photographs and accompanying text further seek to persuade the reader that there are more interesting stories inside, as does the 'PLUS' banner.

The large headline provides little information, but combined with the smaller headline, it declares that there is a mystery to be solved. Readers' curiosity is appealed to.

The photo of the millionaire portrays him dressed casually, making a thumbs-up gesture and looking directly into the camera. He perhaps looks a little tentative. This portrayal of him as a very 'real' person further encourages the reader to satisfy his or her curiosity about what has happened.

The photo of the house provides extra context for the story and the presence of expensive, sporty-looking cars in the photo adds further interest for the reader.

Graphs

Statistical information designed to support an argument is sometimes presented in the form of a graph. Graphs create an immediate visual impression which can be very persuasive.

Consider the following information gained from a survey conducted by the Australian Bureau of Statistics on behalf of the Victorian State Government.

ATTENDED AN ANNUAL EVENT IN THE PAST 12 MONTHS BY GENDER

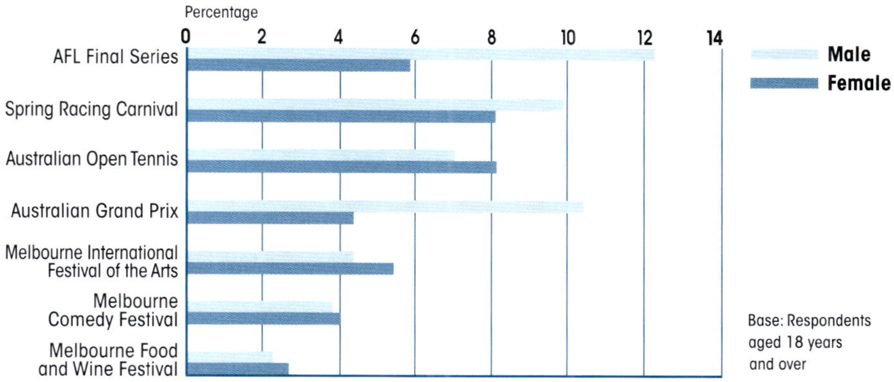

Look at the length of the coloured lines representing males and females in relation to the size of the graph as a whole. The initial impression could well be, for instance, that very large numbers of males have attended AFL matches. A closer look at the key to the figures printed on the horizontal axis tells us that in fact only a little over 12 per cent of males attended AFL matches. What would happen if we changed the intervals on the horizontal axis so that they increase in tens up to 100? How would this alter the impact of the information about attendance?

Learning activity **7.3**

1. Using the information gathered here, design another bar graph to show the percentage of males and females who did not attend an annual event in the last 12 months. Compare the original graph with the one you have created. What comments can you make about the persuasive purposes for which each of these graphs could be used?
2. Here is another graph.

PARTICIPATION IN OTHER LEISURE ACTIVITIES

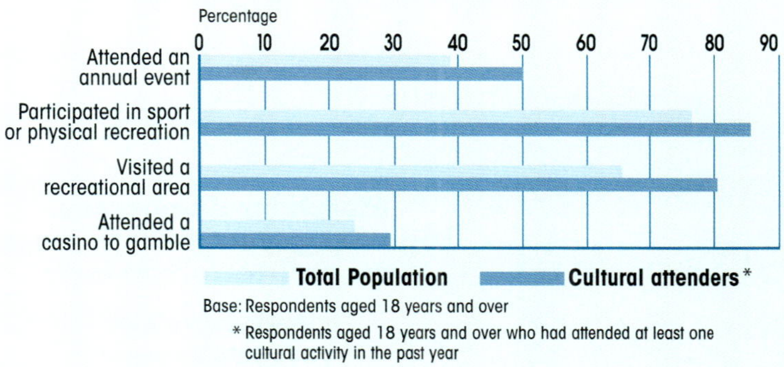

Use the information from both graphs to construct another graph which could be used to support an article arguing that gambling is a huge problem in the state of Victoria.

Posters

Posters are used for many persuasive purposes — to encourage tourists to visit a particular country or region, to persuade people to attend a concert or film and to promote a particular campaign. To do this, they use features such as colour, graphics, slogans, text and symbolism.

The juxtaposition of the petrol bowser and the bottle of water invites the reader to compare price tags.

An association with a newspaper headline emphasises the relevance of the issue to the public.

The large font emphasises the message and creates a sense of urgency.

Direct appeal to reader's sense of responsibility

'Petrol Gold' is a name that reminds the reader of how expensive petrol is.

A call to action

Designed to frighten

Learning activity 7.4

Examine the poster at left. What features of visual language are used to persuade viewers to a point of view? Work in pairs to annotate the poster.

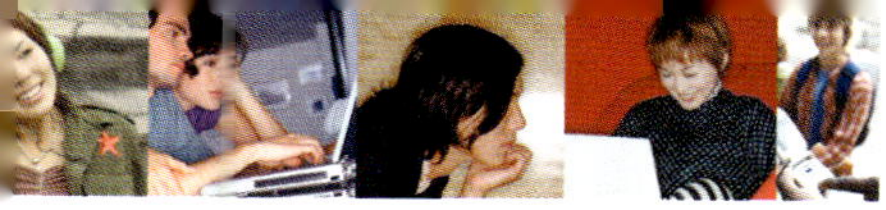

Print advertisements

Advertisers have identified a number of the values held dear by segments of our society, and many advertisements seek to promote a particular product or service by associating it with one or more of these values, which include:

- hedonism (a love of pleasure and fun)
- family life
- mateship
- freedom
- health
- beauty
- informality (a desire to be casual and relaxed)
- individualism (approval of those who are different in some way)
- humanitarianism (a desire to care for those in society who are less fortunate)
- support for the 'underdog' — the person who is not doing so well.

Learning activity **7.5**

Advertisers use verbal and visual language to appeal to these values. Select an advertisement from a magazine of your choice and identify the values to which the advertiser is trying to appeal. Present your findings to a partner to see if he/she agrees with your analysis.

The verbal language used in print advertisements

There are some common aspects to the verbal language used in advertisements, both print and non-print. They include the following:

- **hyperbole** (exaggeration) — 'the best thing that ever happened to you'
- repetition of words or ideas — The constant repetition of a word or **phrase** serves to drive home the message.
- words with positive **connotations** — stunning, revolutionary, innovative, amazing, astonishing, powerful, remarkable, phenomenal, unprecedented
- statistics — '99% fat free', 'ten times faster'
- compound words — Compound words are made up of two words joined together by a hyphen, for example, 'performance-enhancing'.
- **alliteration** — 'power plus performance'
- slogans — Many products are identified by a short, catchy phrase.
- **metaphors** — A particular brand of petrol used to be associated with putting 'a tiger in your tank'.
- rhetorical questions — These are the questions that do not require an answer because the answer is already implied. For example, 'Can you afford not to do it?' clearly implies that you cannot.
- imperatives — These are the **verbs** which order the reader to do something, for example, '*ring* now', '*contact* your dealer'.
- non-sentences or groups of words without a verb — These are usually short phrases used for emphasis and effect. 'Now you, too, can own a swimming pool. *Without the cleaning. Without the fuss.*'

Learning activity 7.6

In groups, examine a number of magazines and newspapers in order to identify print advertisements that make use of those kinds of verbal language. Cut and paste examples onto a poster and label them according to the kind of language being used.

The visual language of print advertisements

The visual language of print advertisements includes:

- photographs or sketches. A photograph of a beautiful woman, a luxury house or car implies that the product is one that is associated with that sort of lifestyle. If that's the kind of life you aspire to, then of course you should have this product. Examine the details of the photograph — the background, objects in the photo, camera angle, the clothing and facial expressions of any people in the photo, what they are doing, what age they are, their gender. All of these details are designed to contribute to an image of the product that the advertisers want to sell to the prospective buyer.
- The colours used in the advertisement are designed to contribute to the image, too. Think about the symbolism of colours — red for love, danger and passion; green for all things natural; yellow for sunshine and happiness.
- The style of font. Where print occurs in the advertisement, consider the style of font that is used. Is it formal? Playful? Hip? This is not accidental. The font, too, contributes to the image of the product.

Learning activity 7.7

Examine the following advertisements and complete the table that identifies and analyses the elements and language features.

Language features and elements of an advertisement	How the feature or element is evident in this advertisement	How the feature or element works to persuade
Main focus		
Background		
Objects		
Placement of objects in the advertisement		
Clothing, facial features etc.		
Colours		
Light		
Camera angle		
Font		
Text (verbal language) e.g. use of hyperbole, repetition, slogans		

After you have completed the table, answer these questions.

1. What image of the product has the advertiser sought to create?
2. Who do you think is the target audience for this advertisement? Explain your answer.

Television advertisements

In television advertisements, sound (such as music, **dialogue**, voice-over, sound effects) is combined with static and moving images and graphics to create a text that seeks to position its viewers in a particular way.

The music in a television advertisement, like the music used in a narrative film, is deliberately chosen to create a mood. Often the mood is an upbeat one, particularly if the advertisement is seeking to persuade readers that the product or service represents an exciting opportunity.

If well-known music is used in an advertisement, then it can evoke extra associations. For example, if the music were originally from the soundtrack of a romantic movie, then its use in an advertisement for St Valentine's Day could add an extra dimension.

Particular decisions are taken about shots and angles to be employed, framing and the use of colour. The choice of shot could depend on the type of product

being advertised. If, for example, the advertisement is for a holiday destination, it is likely that some long shots will be used. These will establish the extent of the holiday destination (for example, the wide beaches or the tall mountains) before close-up shots focus on particular elements (for example, the tourist sitting sipping a cocktail on the beach or the native flowers in the snow on the mountains).

Different camera angles can be used to emphasise certain aspects of the product. For example, a car pictured from the ground in a low-angle shot will look much larger than it actually is.

Advertisements which seek to promote an image of the product as family-friendly might be shot in warm colours, while the desire to promote a racy, exciting image might see red as a dominant colour. One particular series of car advertisements sought to portray the car as dangerous, and therefore exciting. These advertisements made use of darker colours such as blues and blacks. The car was a silvery grey.

Categories of television advertisements

In general terms, television advertisements fall into the following broad categories:

- those that rely on the singing of a jingle to sell the product
- those that use **animation** to sell the product
- those that rely on the use of a testimonial where the product or service is endorsed by an expert or important person
- those that use demonstrations of the special features of the product
- those that are presented in the form of a sales pitch, sometimes humorous, by someone actively trying to sell the product.

Learning activity **7.8**

1. Consider the different associations connected with these kinds of music:

classical	blues	folk
jazz	techno	country
heavy metal	gospel	
rap	rock	

   In pairs, decide what kind of music you would choose to be on the soundtracks of advertisements that seek to persuade viewers to buy the following products, and explain your choice.
   - a car
   - chocolates
   - a mobile phone
   - accommodation in a particular hotel
   - a film

   You will need to provide more information about the product before you decide on the music. For example, what *kind* of car? A sports car? A family car? You will also need to be able to describe your target audience.
2. Present your decisions to the class and discuss how the product and the target audience influenced the choice of music.
3. As a group, view a television advertisement and fill in the following table to identify the features of the verbal, non-verbal and visual language that are used to persuade. You will probably need to view the advertisement more than once.

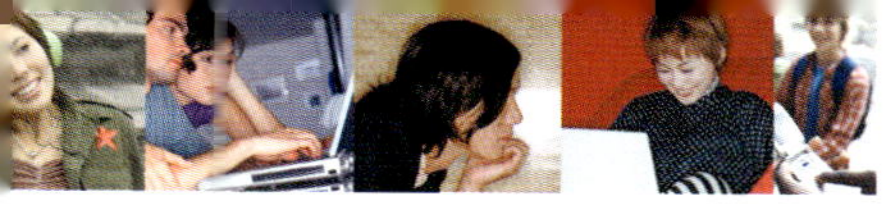

Language features and elements of a television advertisement	How the feature or element is evident in this advertisement	How the feature or element works to persuade
Category of advertisement (see page 212)		
What is said or written (Note particular words and phrases and the appeals that are made)		
Music		
Sound effects		
Gesture/movement		
Facial expression/appearance		
Type of shot		
Camera angles		
Colour		
Lighting		
Editing		
Transitions (movement from one scene to another)		

After you have filled in the table, answer these questions.

(a) What image of the product has the advertiser sought to create?

(b) Who do you think is the target audience for this advertisement? Explain your answer.

Television current affairs programs

On television, segments of current affairs programs frequently adopt a point of view on a topical issue, and seek to persuade the viewing public to agree with that point of view. The presenter, like the writer of an **editorial**, may quite clearly voice a point of view. More often, however, it is necessary to examine the language used by the presenter in order to determine whether the issue is being presented as information or whether the viewers are being positioned in a particular way. For example:

> Our next item examines a medical issue raised by doctors and families caring for AIDS victims. They claim many sufferers are being robbed of a drug that helps fight the condition. It may even keep some patients out of hospital and allow them to lead active and useful lives, yet it's not on the list of subsidised drugs, so it's completely beyond the reach of those who need it.

Clearly, the intention of the segment is to persuade the viewer that people with AIDS should have access to this drug. Describing the people with the disease as 'victims' and 'sufferers' is designed to arouse pity or compassion in the viewer,

while the use of the word 'robbed' implies that these people have a right to something that has been taken away from them. The fact that the cost of the drug is 'completely beyond the reach of those who need it' appeals to the viewer's sense of what is just and fair. The reference to 'active and useful lives' implies that not only the people themselves are missing out, but also the community.

This is an example of persuasive language being used for what is, arguably, a good purpose. Sometimes, when you become aware of how language can be used to manipulate how readers, listeners or viewers respond, there is a tendency to believe that this manipulation (perhaps because of the negative connotations of that word) is always for a bad purpose. If, however, appeals are made to the 'better' characteristics of people — such as our compassion for others — then the manipulation is not necessarily a bad thing. Many charitable organisations, for example, have become extremely good at using language and imagery to elicit our compassion and prompt us to make a donation. (See the World Vision web page on page 179.) Few people would argue against this.

Learning activity **7.9**

Rewrite the above introduction to the item on AIDS medication so that the language is more neutral. This should help you to see that deliberate language choices are made all the time. Issues don't have to be presented one way or another. Their authors choose how they will be presented.

Interviewees and setting

Current affairs programs often interview people who are involved in some way in an issue and thus provide the viewers with the opportunity to hear various points of view. But there is more happening in an interview than just what is said. Consider the following additional aspects of the interview situation.

- Who are the interviewees selected to represent various sides of an issue? Consider their appearance, their qualifications, the way they speak. For example, is one side of the issue represented by someone who is well dressed, well spoken and well qualified, while the other side of the issue is represented by someone who does not have these qualities?
- Where is the interview conducted? Examine the background for clues to the personality of the interviewee.

Professional people, such as doctors and lawyers, are often interviewed in their offices. The background is sometimes a wall of books or framed qualifications. The message that the viewer therefore receives is that this is an educated person whose opinion should not be taken lightly. If the office is a rather cold, barren place, devoid of any personality, the viewer might be expected to conclude that the opinions of the interviewee are likewise rather cold and clinical. Depending on the issue being discussed, this can be a negative or a positive thing.

If an interview takes place in a home, what is the home like? An obviously affluent home might or might not add to the credibility of the interviewee, depending on what the topic is. For example, if the interviewee is talking about the experience of unemployment, the viewers might be positioned so that they wonder what this person really knows about the issue. On the other hand, if the home is clearly that of an 'Aussie battler', then the interviewee's opinions on that issue might be seen as more relevant.

Aspects of this interview, such as the background, the interview setting, the way that Kerry O'Brien and Prime Minister John Howard are dressed and their body language, can be analysed to provide a more in-depth interpretation of the interview.

The language of the interview

The language used by the presenter in his/her introduction can position the viewers so that they endorse a particular point of view, and so too can the verbal and non-verbal language of the interview itself.

How the interviewer responds is another way in which he or she encourages (or discourages) the interviewee. An interviewer can encourage an interviewee by:

- making statements such as, 'I see' or 'yes, that's very interesting'
- smiling and nodding
- restating to show understanding ('in other words, what you are saying is that …')
- making sympathetic comments such as 'that must have been very frustrating/ upsetting/exciting'.

An interviewee who is encouraged by the interviewer is likely to perform better than one who is not. And that better, confident performance will in turn have an impact on how the viewers react to the interviewee and what s/he has to say.

The interviewer can discourage the interviewee by:

- making statements such as 'surely that's not right' or 'you don't seriously think that'
- asking the questions aggressively. The aggression might be in the **tone** of voice or in the interviewer's movements; for example, finger jabbing or pointing.
- not paying attention to the interviewee's response; for example, reading notes while the interviewee is talking
- speaking over the interviewee and not giving him or her a chance to answer questions fully
- showing facial expressions of surprise, disbelief or disapproval.

Of course, some of this 'discouragement' can happen offscreen, so it is difficult for the viewer to know why the interviewee, for example, seems to be uncomfortable or lacking in confidence.

Style of questioning

In some cases, the interviewer adopts a friendly attitude. He or she smiles, asks the 'easy' questions and often calls the interviewer by his or her first name. Naturally, the interviewee is then more at ease and is able to perform to the best of his or her ability. The viewers see someone who is confident, in control and, possibly, friendly and personable in response to the tone set by the interviewer.

Occasionally, however, the interviewer can be aggressive and 'hard-hitting'. He or she asks questions such as, 'Isn't it true that you have deliberately misled the public?' If the interviewee doesn't answer the question, the interviewer comes back to it again and again. The interviewee could be seen as evasive, deliberately avoiding answering the question, and perhaps gets a little short-tempered or flustered. The intention is probably to show the interviewee in a negative light, but the reaction of the viewers is more complex. Sometimes, the response might be the expected negative one but, at other times, viewers may react in the opposite way and feel that the interviewee has been treated unfairly by the interviewer.

Questions asked

Examine the questions that the interviewer puts to the interviewee. Are they truly probing? Are 'hard' questions asked or are they 'easy' questions that simply allow the interviewee to express his or her point of view without really having to justify it? Are the questions mainly closed questions (questions for which there is only one answer) or open questions (questions for which there can be more than one answer)? Does the interviewer pose rhetorical questions, which direct the interviewee to the response? For instance, 'Wouldn't you agree that…?' and 'Isn't it the case that…?'

The 'friendly chat' style of interview makes certain that the viewers only hear one side of the issue and that the interviewee comes across as relaxed and confident because he or she has been put under no pressure at all. It is worthwhile asking ourselves who viewers like to see put in the 'hot seat', and in what circumstances are viewers more likely to feel sympathy for the embattled interviewee, rather than the expected hostility.

Editing and juxtaposition of shots

The juxtaposition of shots refers to the way in which one shot is followed closely by another. For example, a shot of a politician assuring the viewers that schools are being well maintained might be followed immediately by a shot that shows a school badly in need of repair. The message the viewer gets from this visual material is that the politician is not telling the truth.

The commentary accompanying the visuals

Listen carefully to the commentary accompanying the visuals. Does it simply reflect what you see on the screen or does it tell you what to think about what you are seeing? For example, 'Students protested outside Parliament today' or 'Students harassed members of Parliament as they arrived for work this morning'. The word

'protested' makes the event sound like a legitimate activity, while 'harassed' implies interference and obstruction.

Learning activity **7.10**

Tape a segment of an interview from a current affairs program and work in pairs to analyse it to identify how the verbal, non-verbal and visual language work to persuade readers to a particular point of view. Compare your analysis with another pair or group.

This table can be completed as you view the program.

Language features and elements of a television current affairs program	How the feature or element is evident in this program	How the feature or element works to persuade
Topic/issue		
Introduction		
Interviewees – appearance – qualifications – the way they speak		
Setting		
Camera shots and angles		
Framing		
Verbal language of the interviewer		
Non-verbal language of the interviewer		
Style of questioning		
Questions asked		
Accompanying visuals (if any)		

Documentaries

Although we perhaps have the idea that narrative films are fiction and **documentaries** are fact, the truth is that documentaries serve many purposes. One of these might be informative, as for instance in a wildlife documentary, but certainly there are documentaries whose main purpose is persuasive. (Even in the case of a wildlife documentary, it could be that the intention is to persuade viewers. For instance, by showing elephants to be intelligent creatures who demonstrate human characteristics such as the desire to love and care for their offspring, the documentary could be persuading the viewers to believe that they should be a protected species.)

Michael Moore (see following page), writer, director and producer of the Academy Award-winning documentary, *Bowling for Columbine*, makes no secret of the fact that his purpose is to persuade viewers to a particular point of view.

View *Bowling for Columbine* and then answer the following questions that draw your attention to the persuasive ways in which Moore uses visual, verbal and non-verbal language.

Scene from *Bowling for Columbine*

Learning activity **7.11**

1. Which of the following statements do you think most accurately presents Michael Moore's point of view as expressed in this documentary? Write your own statement if you don't think any of these statements is accurate. Be prepared to provide reasons for your selection.

- The environment of Columbine (the US air base, Lockheed Martin) contributed to what happened there.
- The history of the US explains why there are so many deaths as a result of guns.
- The media plays a significant role in creating a culture where people depend so much on guns.
- The government of the United States is to blame for creating a culture of violence.
- Race relations are a major factor in the creating of a climate of fear.

2. Why do you think Moore chose to use each of the following sequences and what is their likely impact on the viewer?

- the advertisement for military and western rifle toys
- the dog dressed up as a hunter with a gun on its back
- Moore sitting in the barber's chair loading his gun
- the comic who recommended that bullets should cost $5000 each

Present your findings in a table.

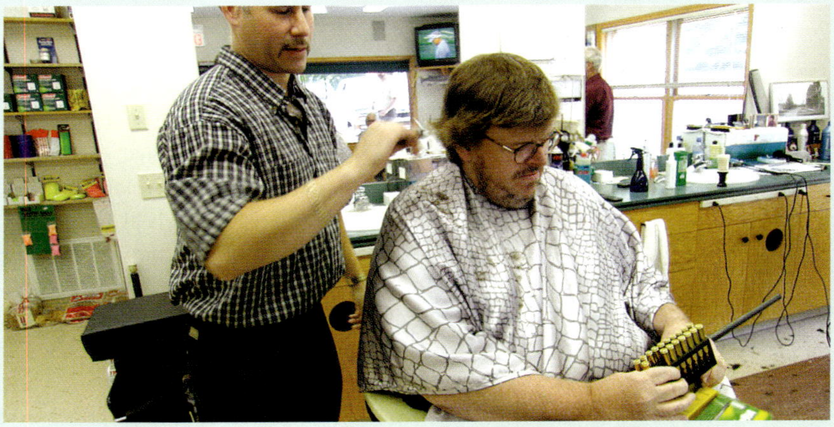

Scene from *Bowling for Columbine*

3. What effect does the soundtrack have in the following sequences?
   - the sequence beginning with the information that the city of Virgin, Utah, requires all residents to own a gun
   - the series of images that documents military incursions by the USA into other countries
   - closed-circuit footage of the shootings at Columbine.
4. One of the techniques frequently used in this documentary is the editing which follows one scene with another that provides a direct comment. For example, in one scene the Lockheed public relations representative says 'we don't get irritated with someone, and just because we're mad at them drop a bomb or shoot at them or fire a missile'. This is immediately followed by a series of clips showing footage of USA military incursions into other countries. This powerfully undercuts what the PR representative has just said. Find other examples where editing has juxtaposed particular scenes (placed scenes side by side) and analyse the likely impact on the viewer.
5. Choose two of the interviews that Moore conducted as part of this documentary and explain their purpose and how the viewer is likely to respond. What features of the interview help to create this impact? (Refer, for example, to the setting, the questions asked and the way in which they are asked, the responses and the body language of the interviewee.)
6. What are some of the ways in which Moore uses statistics in this documentary? Are you prepared to accept that they are all valid statistics? Why or why not?
7. Moore uses humour to persuade viewers to identify with his point of view. Examine the humour in the animation *A Brief History of the USA*. What is the likely response of the viewer?
8. How does Moore use the example of Canadian society in this documentary? Are you convinced by this example or is there further information that you would like to know before you make up your mind?
9. Marilyn Manson's lyrics and public behaviour are one of the factors blamed for the increasing violence in the US, yet in his interview, Manson himself talks about 'a campaign of fear and consumption'. Which point of view do you have more sympathy for and why?
10. How did you respond to the scenes in which Moore took two of the Columbine survivors to confront K-Mart representatives? (Were these effective scenes, in your opinion? Why or why not?)

Assessment task | Evaluating a controversial documentary

Although this documentary won an Academy Award, it has been the subject of much controversy in the USA. Do an internet search to explore this controversy and present a summary and evaluation, either in writing or orally.

See page 224 for the criteria for assessment.

Websites

Most websites have some form of advertising, so to that extent all websites can be said to have a persuasive purpose, but some websites have been deliberately set up with a single persuasive purpose in mind.

The PeTA (People for the Ethical Treatment of Animals) website is an example of this. This is a page from the 'campaign' section of the website which focuses on the use of animals for clothing. Like many websites, this is a very dynamic one; the content changes constantly in response to current events and updated information. You might like to look at the most recent version by visiting the website for this book and clicking on the PeTA weblink for this chapter (see 'Weblinks', page 252).

Restrained colours are reassuring to the reader, although the orange colouring perhaps implies some sense of urgency.

Top menu provides links to other parts of the website.

Design is a fairly conservative three-column approach

The tone of the writing is generally restrained (the paragraph on leather), which adds to its appeal.

'Fur too bloody' is a play on words designed to attract readers to access the link.

Left-hand menu is divided into clear sections. Readers are offered a choice of ways in which to become involved.

Asks readers to identify with the pain experienced by the animals

Text is organised into short, easy-to-read paragraphs with headings that clearly indicate the content.

Reference to 'veal' calves is designed to upset some readers.

Appeals to the desire to be attractive — and ethical

Right-hand menu provides links to some of the current campaigns being conducted by PeTA.

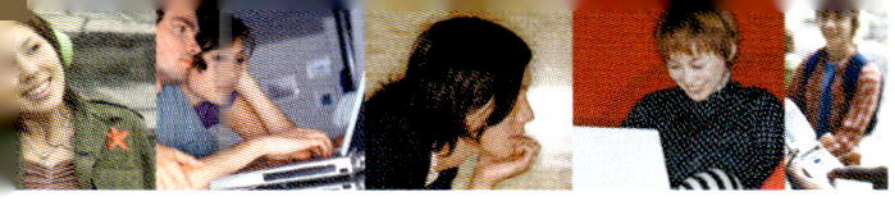

Learning activity 7.12

To view websites whose primary purpose is persuasion, visit the website for this book and click on the following weblinks for this chapter (see 'Weblinks', page 252).

- **Ausflag** (The website of an apolitical, non-profit organisation seeking to secure the popular support of the Australian people for the adoption of a truly Australian flag.)
- **Rainforests** (A website for children, designed to promote protection of tropical rainforests.)
- **Wilderness Society** (This is a web page from the website of the Wilderness Society, which promotes the saving of Tasmanian forests from logging and woodchipping.)
- **Essendon Football Club** (The official website of the club. Although apparently a source of information, the main purpose of the site is to promote the football club. Official websites of other football and soccer clubs could also be examined and compared.)

Choose another website whose primary purpose is to persuade its readers and answer the following questions.

1. What is the content of the website? (articles, photos, advertisements, interviews, reviews etc.)
2. Describe the layout (colours, backgrounds, design etc.).
3. Who do you think is the target audience for this site? (Consider age, class, gender and interests which could be used to describe the target audience.) What features of the site led you to this conclusion?
4. What is the persuasive purpose of the site?
5. What is the nature of the relationship that is created between the authors of the site and the readers? Provide examples of verbal and visual language use that create this relationship. You might begin your response to this question in one of the following ways:
   - The authors of the website clearly believe that their viewers are there to be educated. They show this by ...
   - This website preaches to the converted, those who are already supporters. This is evident in the way in which ...
   - The authors of this website see their viewers as people who are there to be persuaded. Their persuasive techniques include ...
6. Is there a dominant emotional appeal being made by the site? If so, what do you think it is?
7. Examine the verbal language used on the site. Analyse the ways in which it seeks to position the readers.
8. If there are advertisements, do they enhance the persuasiveness of the site? Explain your answer. (The nature of the advertisements will also tell you something about the intended audience.)
9. What is the persuasive effect of any photos on the site?

See page 95 for further discussion on the visual and verbal language of websites.

Assessment tasks | Analysing persuasive multimodal texts

1. Select one of the following texts and make a written or oral presentation that identifies and analyses the kind of language that the text uses in order to position its readers in a particular way.

(a) This is a brochure produced by the Commonwealth Department of Family and Community Services to promote and facilitate the setting up of playgroups.

Thousands of people just like you have started playgroups all over Australia.

Playgroups are a regular time each week when parents, carers, babies, toddlers and preschool children get together and have *fun!*

Ask Playgroup Victoria about our membership package that comes with or without insurance.

Membership benefits

- Playgroup Manual packed with information about playgroups
- Regular playgroup magazines
- Free subscription to ePlaygroup News
- Members' Hotline for telephone help on any playgroup issue
- Access to the Members' Gateway on www.playgroup.org.au
- Play training videos
- Training sessions
- Promotion of your playgroup
- Playgroup Raffle to fundraise the easy way
- Voting rights
- Parenting talks with high profile speakers
- Discounts with participating suppliers

Call Playgroup Victoria for a Membership Information brochure with all the details.

Playgroup Victoria Inc.
346 Albert St, Brunswick 3056
9388 1599
www.playgroup.org.au
Sponsored by the Commonwealth Department of Family and Community Services
ABN 13 094 186 877

PLAYGROUP VICTORIA

You can start a

playgroup!

WHAT YOU NEED TO START A PLAYGROUP

1. A few interested families
2. A place to meet
3. Some toys & play equipment

Playgroup Victoria helps you get off to a stress-free start

- New Playgroup Hotline for friendly help and advice
- Starting a Playgroup video to borrow
- Free Starting a Playgroup booklet
- Information online

Call:
New Playgroup Hotline 9388 1599
Country callers 1800 811 156

Email:
newgroup@playgroup.org.au
Visit:
www.playgroup.org.au

PLAYGROUPS ARE SO IMPORTANT...

Babies
- Enjoy the stimulation
- Learn new skills
- Meet different people

Toddlers
- Find new spaces to explore
- Discover different toys
- Develop a weekly routine

Preschoolers
- Make new friends
- Extend their skills
- Learn through play

Adults
- Develop friendships with local families
- Help run the playgroup
- Share parenting experiences

(b) This is the home page of the Incredible Adventures website, but you might like to explore some of the other pages as well by visiting the website for this book and clicking on the Incredible Adventures weblink (see 'Weblinks', page 252).

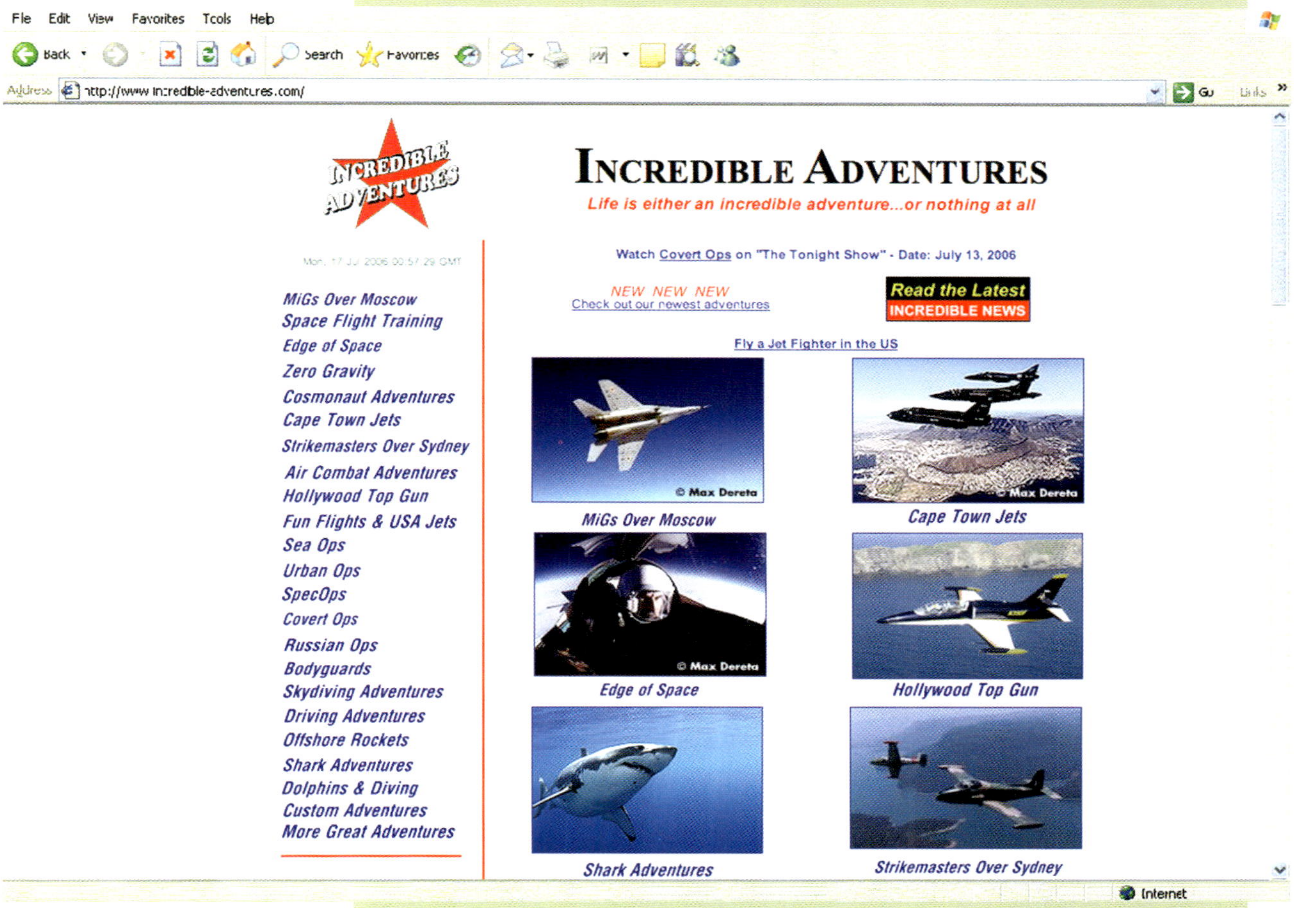

Use a **Venn diagram** as part of the planning for a 'compare and contrast' essay.

2. Compare a print advertisement and a television advertisement, both of which are advertising similar products — for example, a car or a beauty product such as hair shampoo. What are the similarities and differences in the use of language to persuade?

3. Choose two different newspapers that were published on the same day. Compare the front page in each publication to identify and analyse the verbal and non-verbal language choices made by the editors to persuade readers to buy their paper.

Strategies | Key words to compare and contrast

Use these words and phrases to compare and contrast two items such as the newspapers or advertisements:

similarly	also	compared to	as … as
in the same way	to	in comparison	as
accordingly	as well as	compared to	just as
correspondingly	like	equal to	equally
the same	similar to	while	likewise

4. Select a scene from a documentary other than *Bowling for Columbine.* Identify and analyse the ways in which verbal, non-verbal and visual language are used to persuade the readers to a particular point of view. (An episode of the SBS program, *The Cutting Edge,* or similar, could be appropriate for this task, or one of the documentaries listed on page 64.)

See below for the criteria for assessment.

Criteria for assessment

Your assessment task will be assessed according to the following criteria. Read them carefully before you begin your task; while working on your task, check your progress against the criteria and then review your completed task against the criteria before submitting it to your teacher.

Understanding of verbal, visual and non-verbal language used by authors of texts to position readers and viewers in particular ways. This includes, where relevant, the identification and discussion of:

- the connotations of words
- the various appeals to the emotions and values of the audience
- the use of visual features such as design, camera angles and colour
- the use of auditory features such as music and sound effects
- the use of strategies such as repetition, pauses, pitch and volume.

Ability to create a response in the chosen mode which identifies and discusses the ways in which language is used to persuade. This includes, where relevant:

- the use of appropriate meta-language to discuss the use of language
- control of spelling, punctuation and syntax
- planning and revising
- control of aspects of oral presentation, including pronunciation, pace, pitch, volume and body language
- the conventions of small group discussion.

CHAPTER 8

Presenting a point of view

In the last couple of chapters we looked at how **verbal**, **non-verbal** and **visual language** is used to persuade readers and viewers. Another technique authors use when seeking to convince their audience to accept a particular point of view on an issue is to combine persuasive language and techniques with logical argument supported by evidence.

In this chapter we will examine how authors construct an argument, using arguments and evidence to support their thesis or main contention, in order to convince readers, listeners or viewers of a particular point of view.

You will then have an opportunity to construct your own point of view — in oral or written form — to convince your readers or viewers to agree with your perspective on a particular issue.

Of course, this is something you do all the time. You do it when you try to convince your parents to let you do or have something; you do it when you try to convince your teacher that, for example, you need extra time to complete an activity; you do it when you try to convince your friends to go somewhere or to do a particular thing. Perhaps without even realising it, you shape the language you use, construct arguments and provide evidence. Sometimes you're more convincing and persuasive than at other times — and so you get what you want. Sometimes you're not persuasive or convincing enough.

Examining the arguments of others

In order for you to succeed as a student you will not only need to be able to construct your own well-reasoned arguments, but you will also need to be able to analyse the arguments of others. And when analysing the arguments of others you will need to use a **metalanguage** that will be understood by others. This is where we will start.

The thesis or contention

Firstly, what is an argument?

A dictionary definition tells us that it is 'a discussion in which reasons are advanced for and against a proposition or proposal'.

The proposition or proposal could also be called a thesis or, more commonly, a contention, and it is the focus of the argument. The following are examples of a thesis or contention:

- That Australia has a responsibility to fight for the global abolition of capital punishment.
- That Australia should become a republic.
- That cars should be banned from Melbourne's Central Business District.
- That governments should be doing more to prevent climate change and global warming.

Learning activity **8.1**

What are some other examples of main contentions or theses? Do a class brainstorm of issues that you think are contentious (that is, it is possible to have more than one perspective or point of view on them) and draw up a list of possible contentions.

Arguments that support the contention

For each contention there are a number of arguments for and against. For example, here is a contention:

- That cars should be banned from Melbourne's Central Business District.

In support of this contention, the author might put forward the following arguments:

- Cars cause congestion and make it difficult to get around in the city.
- Cars cause pollution, which damages city buildings and the health of pedestrians.

But of course there are also arguments that can be used against the thesis. For example:

- If cars aren't allowed into the city, this will place an extra financial burden on people who work in there.
- Exceptions would have to be made for taxis and delivery trucks and this would undermine any advantages of the proposal anyway.

Learning activity **8.2**

Select one of the contentions that you produced as part of Learning activity 8.1. In pairs, decide one argument that could be used to support that contention and one argument that could be used against it. Make a list of the arguments for and against produced by the members of the class.

Evidence and refutation or rebuttal

If an author wanted to argue in favour of this contention then s/he would need:

(a) to put forward evidence to support the arguments

(b) to refute (prove wrong) or **rebut** the arguments that did not support his or her point of view.

Different kinds of evidence can be used to provide support for arguments and to convince readers and listeners of their **validity**. For example:

- *statistics and survey results*

  89% of motorists interviewed said that traffic jams were one of the main

reasons they would avoid taking their cars into the central business district during the day.

- *expert testimony*
  Mr Jones, CEO of Hoopers International, has said that his firm will be relocating to the outer eastern suburbs. He cites increasing congestion in the city and lack of parking spaces for customers as one of the main reasons for the move.
- ***anecdotes***
  A city worker reports that when she takes her car to work, it can take her 30 minutes to travel along Collins Street from Spring Street to Flinders Street.
- ***case studies** or research*
  Research conducted by taxi firms indicates that taxi drivers are increasingly unwilling to work in the city. They believe that time spent sitting in traffic is resulting in lower takings.

It is important for authors to acknowledge the existence of opposing arguments, and just as important to refute them, if they wish to convince readers or listeners to agree with their point of view.

An argument can be refuted by:

- *clearly showing it to be wrong*
  The author produces evidence that disproves the argument. For example: Far from placing an extra financial burden on those who work in the city, the abolition of cars will in fact decrease their daily costs. Research conducted by the RACV quite clearly shows that the cost of driving a car into the city every day, and paying for parking, is far more expensive than using public transport.
- *conceding and qualifying the original argument*
  The author agrees that the opposing argument might have some validity and therefore amends the original argument to take account of this. For example: It is true that exceptions would need to be made for taxis and delivery trucks but a toll system (like that which operates on freeways), which imposes a toll on such vehicles as they enter the central business district, would see a reduction in their numbers.

Learning activity **8.3**

Select two arguments that you produced as a result of Learning activity 8.2. One argument should be in favour of the thesis and one argument should not. For each of these arguments decide what kind of evidence would provide the best support.

Following is an **editorial** from *The Age* which argues that driver education, particularly of young drivers, and education about the healthy levels of alcohol consumption are both needed in order to tackle the issue of the rising road toll. Note the annotations that identify the contention, the supporting arguments and evidence, and the use of language to persuade, and then answer the questions that follow.

Frustrating the fight to cut the road toll

'If you drink, then drive, you're a bloody idiot.' It has been one of the most successful slogans of all time. Coupled with a hard-hitting mass media campaign that showed the grim aftermath of drink-driving accidents, the slogan — introduced in December 1989 when the national road toll was 776 — has been the impetus for a reduction in road deaths. The Transport Accident Commission has kept the 'bloody idiot' message in a variety of road campaigns since but has moved away from the 'shock and awe' images of its previous advertisements. Its most recent campaign focuses on 'low-level' drink-drivers and shows a man haunted by a small boy he killed while 'only a little bit over' the blood alcohol limit. But the drink-driving message appears to have lost its potency. Last year, the number of drink-drivers killed on Victoria's roads rose significantly. In the 12 months to September 2005, 67 drivers or riders who were killed had an illegal blood alcohol level — a rise of 18 deaths, or 37 per cent, on the previous year. Victoria's overall road toll was 349 last year — half the toll of 1989 when the slogan was introduced but six more deaths than 2004. The number of drivers aged between 18 and 25 killed on the roads also increased slightly, from 47 in 2004 to 50 last year.

The increase in alcohol-related deaths has led to a call by the TAC for alcohol interlock devices to be standard features in all cars, beginning with fleet vehicles. The devices, which require a driver to pass a breath test before allowing a car to start, have been compulsory for all repeat drink-drivers since last year. It is a measure of the TAC's frustration at the increase in drink-driving that it is prepared to propose such an intrusive measure. *The Age* understands this exasperation but, while supporting the use of these devices for repeat offenders, does not back such intervention for all drivers, most of whom are law-abiding. Rather, this newspaper believes the answer is education, particularly for younger drivers, and a return to the compelling anti-drink-driving messages that simply cannot be ignored. It is apparent from the increasing alcohol-related deaths that a new generation of drivers has failed to hear the messages about the dangers of drink-driving.

Background

Argument: the new ads are not working

Statistical evidence to support argument

Use of statistics to emphasise the seriousness of the problem. The reader is meant to be swayed by this objective evidence.

The use of the passive voice in this sentence puts the 'increase in alcohol-related deaths' to the fore and emphasises that this is what the editorial is concerned with.

This description is likely to make the reader agree that the TAC proposal is wrong because it will intrude on drivers' rights.

The attempt to show that *The Age* is reasonable in its attitude is intended to persuade the reader that the point of view of the editorial is a carefully considered one.

Authoritative **tone** — '... this newspaper believes' carries a lot more weight than an individual who says 'I believe'.

Implies unfairness

Repeats argument more clearly

Contention

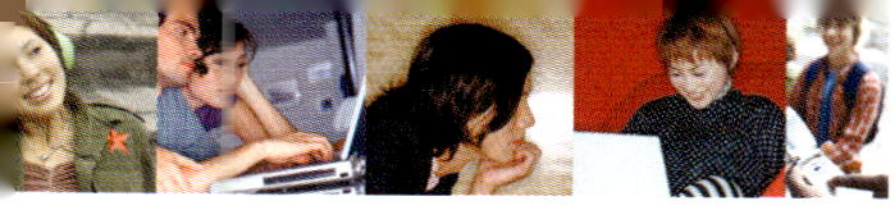

A case in point is Colac P-plater and accused serial drink-driver Dak Gatkouth, 20, who was arrested this week after allegedly being pulled up by police for drink-driving and other driving offences six times since Boxing Day. The war against drink-driving is unrelenting and the messages must be constantly reinforced. Many young people do not understand how much alcohol will take them to a blood alcohol concentration of more than 0.05 or the factors, such as eating or body mass, that can affect their blood alcohol reading. NSW Police Commissioner Ken Maroney this week called for driver education to begin in primary school. 'It's not the car that speeds, it's not the car that crosses double yellow lines, the car doesn't get drunk — it's the person behind the wheel,' he said. In Victoria, pre-licence driver education begins in Year 10.

It's not just on the roads that the message about safe alcohol consumption needs to be reinforced. Australian life revolves around a culture of alcohol and binge-drinking, particularly among young people. A recent report by the ANZ bank showed Australians were spending more on alcohol despite reining in spending on other extravagances, with alcohol expenditure up 4.8 per cent in the past nine months compared with the past four years. It has also been noted that the Victorian Government has focused more on speeding-related issues in recent years, perhaps to the neglect of drink-driving. If the road toll is to drop significantly — it hit a low of 330 in 2003 and has averaged 384 over the past five years — driver education and healthy levels of alcohol consumption must be tackled. The State Government must also act on its discussion paper, released in August, which looks at measures to improve safety for young drivers. The national holiday toll stood at 67 yesterday, with Victoria's 15 fatalities the second highest in the country. This is no time for complacency.

The Age, 6 January 2006

More evidence

This extreme case is designed to shock the reader and persuade him/her of the seriousness of the situation.

To describe the campaign against drink–driving as a 'war' is to evoke **connotations** of a series of battles. 'Unrelenting' and 'constantly reinforced' create a passionate tone which is designed to position the reader to disagree if he dares.

More evidence — expert testimonial

Authoritative tone again

Extends recommendation to include wider community

Evidence

Perhaps appeals to common knowledge

Reliable **source**

Use of passive voice adds to authoritative tone

Repetition of 'must' is designed to emphasise how important it is that action be taken. The reader is positioned to agree.

The overall emphasis on youth and the fact that it is youth who are dying in these drink-related road accidents is also persuasive because it taps into the reader's natural desire to protect the young and vulnerable.

An appeal for responsibility, designed to make the reader feel that she or he must agree — or otherwise be labelled as 'complacent' and irresponsible

Learning activity 8.4

1. How, according to the editorial, has the nature of the TAC drink-driving advertisements changed?
2. At the end of the first paragraph the editorial quotes a number of statistics. What point is it seeking to make by doing this?
3. How does the editorial view the call by the TAC for alcohol interlock devices to be standard features in all cars?
4. Why does the editorial regard the education of young people to be so important in the fight against the road toll?
5. How does the editorial link Australian culture and the road toll?
6. What was the impetus for this editorial? (Why was the editorial written at this particular time?)

Are you convinced?

Perhaps you are convinced to accept the point of view put forward by an author, but should you be convinced?

Here are some things to look out for:

- Does the author make statements of fact or opinion? If they are statements of fact ('Juvenile crime in our society is increasing'), are they supported by evidence? ('Statistics show that in 1998, 30 per cent of crimes were committed by persons under the age of 20. In 1966, fewer than 5 per cent of crimes were committed by the same age group.') If they are statements of opinion ('Public nudity is not acceptable on any beach, as far as I am concerned'), you may choose to agree with them or not, but they are not statements which prove an argument.
- If statistics are cited, is the source of the statistics also given? Is the source a reputable one? The Australian Bureau of Statistics is regarded as reputable because it is independent and has a reputation for gathering statistics in a reliable way. If, however, a survey conducted by a tobacco company produced statistics which said that the majority of people did not believe passive smoking contributed to lung cancer, you might be wise to question the validity of the source because of the possibility of bias.
- If an 'expert' is quoted as supporting an argument or giving a testimonial in support of a product, you should examine the credentials of that expert. Is the expert's name given? Is he or she truly an expert in this field? Does the expert's field of expertise relate directly to the product? For example, if a general practitioner endorses a skin-care product, is his or her medical knowledge specialised enough? Would a dermatologist's opinion be more reliable?
- Is the argument based on particular statements or on generalisations? Generalisations are easily recognised by the use of words such as 'most' and 'no-one', as well as sweeping statements such as 'Commuters are fed up with a transport system that simply does not work'. There is nothing wrong with a generalisation, as long as its truth can be demonstrated or the generalisation asserts something that is generally accepted by the readers to be a fact.
  In putting forward an argument, it is up to the author to produce evidence to support the generalisation. If he or she says that 'Commuters are fed up …', then he or she should produce evidence to show this. Appropriate evidence

might be the results of a survey conducted at a variety of stations, tram stops and bus stops in a number of different suburbs over a given period. The important thing is that the survey must have sampled a range of people who would be representative of the entire number of people who use public transport.

- Is there a proven link between the stated cause and effect? For instance, if an author claims that 'Juvenile crime is increasing. The government must introduce financial inducements to encourage mothers to stay in the home rather than enter the workforce', he or she has made a direct link between working mothers and juvenile crime. The author is claiming that working mothers are the cause of juvenile crime (the effect). Without further evidence we could not accept this as a logical argument. Examine this statement: 'Australians are becoming very bad-mannered. They are watching too many popular television programs that portray bad manners.' Do you think there is a proven link between the stated cause (television programs) and the effect (an increase in bad manners among Australians)?

Learning activity **8.5**

Examine the arguments and evidence put forward in *The Age* editorial. Are they convincing?

The answers to these questions might help you form an opinion.

1. The editorial asserts that 'the drink-driving message appears to have lost its potency'. Is this a fact, supported by reliable evidence, or is it an opinion? The statistics quoted indicate that there has been a rise in alcohol-related deaths on Victorian roads since the nature of the advertising campaign changed. Is there a direct and proven relationship between these two facts? Or could there be another explanation for the increase in alcohol-related deaths?
2. NSW Police Commissioner Ken Maroney is quoted as an expert who calls for driver education to begin in primary school. Is this evidence that should convince you to accept the point of view put forward by the editorial? Why?
3. The editorial makes the following generalisations. Which of these do you find convincing and why?
   - Many young people do not understand how much alcohol will take them to a blood alcohol concentration of more than 0.05.
   - Australian life revolves around a culture of alcohol and binge-drinking, particularly among young people.

Pre-reading: scan the texts for words with which you are unfamiliar. Make a list and find out what they mean.

Learning activity 8.6

Here are some other texts, each of which argues a particular point of view. For each text, identify the thesis and supporting arguments and evidence. Say whether or not you are convinced by the arguments and explain your reasons. (There are also many additional texts in Chapters 6 and 7 that you could use for the same learning activity.)

The first text is a review of a book by a young Australian writer, Markus Zusak.

Markus Zusak: The Book Thief

REVIEWED BY GAIL BAILEY

Here is a small fact: you are going to die. So says Death, the narrator of Markus Zusak's novel, *The Book Thief*.

The story begins with this ominous piece of information, delivered by an irreverent (and a tad overzealous) Grim Reaper. Best known for his children's books, Zusak, an award-winning Sydney writer, has chosen a serious topic for his first adult novel.

At the gravesite of her younger brother, 9-year-old Liesel Meminger spots a book in the snow, *The Gravedigger's Handbook*. Death watches on as Liesel's 'illustrious career' as a book thief begins and will several years later snatch the book of Liesel's life story from the rubble of a bombed city.

It is 1939 in Nazi Germany and Death is extremely busy. If you are not instantly put off by the thought of having Death narrate a story about a little girl growing up in Germany during World War II, then *The Book Thief* will surprise you with its endearing tale.

'It's just a small story really, about, among other things: a girl, some words, an accordionist, some fanatical Germans, a Jewish fist-fighter, and quite a lot of thievery.'

After her father is deemed a communist by the Nazis, Liesel's mother delivers her to a small town on the outskirts of Munich to the poor but loving Hubermann household.

A kind-hearted accordion-playing painter and a foul-mouthed laundrywoman raise Liesel as one of their own. On Himmel St, Liesel spends her days with a motley crew of friends and develops a penchant for stealing: apples, potatoes and books (her favourite).

Whether bought with rationed cigarettes, surreptitiously taken from a Nazi book-burning, stolen from the mayor's library or written for her by the Jewish man her foster family hides, every book that crosses Liesel's path is treated with obsessive care.

Books become a way to deal with grief. Liesel also extends the power of words to others in Himmel St, as they attempt to come to terms with the destruction of war.

The Book Thief is Zusak's first attempt at adult fiction, but his experience as a children's writer can be acutely felt. His characters are sensitively conceived and depicted — almost at if they have stepped out of a fairy tale.

And although Death is dour as a narrator (he runs his mouth with as much fervour as he wields his scythe), the story truly belongs to the resilient spirit of young Liesel. Zusak, who uses some true events told to him by his European parents, has penned a simple and compelling story.

The New Zealand Herald, 1 February 2006

The following text is an opinion column.

A phrase that is toxic and all good for nothing

GABRIELLA COSLOVICH

THERE'S a saying in current usage that I despise more than many of the other contemporary abuses of the English language, a phrase I detest more than 'like, whatever', more than managers 'actioning' some new scheme, more than chief executives 'growing' their businesses, more than politicians 'going forward'.

'It's all good' — this is the phrase I detest most of all, that I abhor with a passion I usually reserve for the latest affront to tolerance and civil liberties. Whenever I hear someone say 'It's all good', I want to shake them until their ear lobes start to wobble and scream. 'It's not all good, admit it!'

'It's all good' is the most suppressed, pent-up, toxic, hollow phrase ever coined. It is the opposite of what it purports to be and it's lazy. What does it actually mean? Things are so-so? Tolerable? Challenging? Life affirming? Character building? Relaxed and comfortable and I've got the right colour skin so I really can't be fussed changing things? Messy? Confused?

Tell me 'she'll be right', tell me 'it'll be fine', tell me 'such is life', but don't give me this mealy-mouthed 'it's all good' garbage. In his youthful heyday, Bob Dylan would never have used so vacuous a phrase.

'Happy? Anyone can be happy. What's the purpose of that? All my life I've been fighting to be miserable.' That's what Dylan said, and if anything is all good, those words are.

I wonder whether the disciples of 'it's all good' belong to the same church as those irritating people who insist I 'enjoy!' whatever it is they are plonking before me, even when it's a bottle of home-brand spring water.

Enjoy? For lucidity's sake! It is a bottle of water, not some prize-winning, multi-layered chardonnay with complex jelly bean and musk stick notes melded with perfumed Old Spice elements, an undercurrent of Lindt chocolate and a hint of Heaven caramel fudge ice-cream. As long as you're not handing me a bottle of H2S, I'll be satisfied.

Or is the 'it's all good' school of thought part of the academy that believes honesty is not the best policy, and that spin-doctoring will get you everywhere? A panel of American linguists recently decided that the word that most summed up 2005 was 'truthiness', which they defined as the quality of stating concepts one wishes or believes to be true, rather than the facts. Truthiness, to use the words of Michael Adams, a professor at North Carolina State University, means 'truthy, not facty'.

Herewith some pertinent examples. This recent celebrity mag headline: 'Stars with cellulite. But we think they're hot anyway.' No you don't! You think they look like crap and they'll make the rest of us feel better about the fact that we don't get to swan around on yachts in the Bahamas.

Or Premier Steve Bracks banging on about how Melbourne is the world's most liveable city when anyone who tried to catch a train home from the tennis or work last week knows that the world's supposedly most liveable city has an abominably dysfunctional public transport system.

But the straight-shooters are not extinct: endangered, yes, but not departed. I shared platform four on Flinders Street with one on Thursday night. The platform was packed with sweaty commuters and ruddy-faced tennis fans waiting for the late 7.05 pm to Sandringham, only to find said train divided into three stingy carriages heading to Werribee, and three stingy carriages heading to Sandringham. One woman did not stand there droning 'It's all good'. She was furious.

'All they do is fine Connex and put the money in their coffers. What do they do with it? They're not putting it back into the trains. Meanwhile, we pay $6 to get squashed in like sardines. There's no way I'm voting this Government back in if they don't fix the trains.'

It's not all good. Enjoy.

The Sunday Age, 22 January 2006

The text below is another opinion column.

Let humanity prevail

We must decide how radically we want technology to change the way we live, says Joel Garreau.

In the next few years, your child will come home from school in tears. He'll say, once again, that he is unable to compete with the children who are brighter, better behaved and physically more capable than he is because their parents have bought them technological enhancements and you have not. What will you do?

You could say, 'That's all right, dear, we don't care what other parents do with their children's minds and bodies, we love you just the way you are.'

Or, you could remortgage the house, again, to try to allow your child to keep up with the human enhancements that ever so rapidly are coming onto the market.

What you and your children can't do is ignore the enhancement products that are already realigning our concept of what it means to be human.

We are at a turning point in history. For millenniums our technologies — fire, clothes, agriculture, cities, space travel — have been aimed at modifying our environment. Now, for the first time, our technologies are increasingly aimed inward — at altering our minds, memories, metabolisms, personalities and progeny.

This is not some science fiction future. Inexorable increases in ingenuity are opening vistas, especially in what we may call GRIN — genetic, robotic, information and nano — technologies.

The curve of innovation is rising exponentially. The significance of all this is in how we will wrestle with what this means to relationships, loves and lives. The scientists, engineers and philosophers pondering the reshaping of humankind see three scenarios.

There are those who think we're bound for a near-future technological 'heaven' in which we conquer suffering, stupidity, ugliness, even death.

Then there are those who think such powers could be used for supreme evil in the next 25 years, threatening the existence of our species — the 'hell' scenario.

Finally, there are those who have sufficient faith in human cussedness, who think we will be able to control our futures rather than be pawns of technology — the 'prevail' scenario.

Ethically, intellectually, technologically, it won't be an easy path for us to choose. Yet we must.

Scientists' understanding of the human genome and the proteins that control all cellular processes in the body are leading to the creation of remarkable pharmaceuticals. One example is the pain vaccine being tested by a San Francisco company. It would cancel acute suffering for a month. Five companies in the US alone are competing to bring memory pills to market. They promise not only to ease the senior moments of the baby boomers but to revolutionise education of the young. Think of what it will do to language acquisition alone. Robotics is enabling unprecedented connections between the human brain and our machine creations. Matthew Nagle, a paralysed young Boston man, last summer became the first human to send an email with his thoughts. A computer device implanted into his brain by a company called Cyberkinetics can read his neurons as they fire. This also allows him to control a robotic arm.

Nanotechnology refers to building objects and substances one atom or molecule at a time. The results can be amazing, including forms of carbon that exist by the beakerful that are 60 times stronger than steel, have the weight of plastic, sport the clean electrical conductivity of diamond and display the precision of DNA.

Nanotechnology is projected to be a trillion-dollar industry by 2015. Some say it will revolutionise everything: warfare, energy use, medicine.

These GRIN technologies, in short, mean that every power of our comic-book superheroes from the 1930s and '40s either exists or is now in active development. A technique called 'gene doping' for example, produces such muscle strength in rodents that some University of Pennsylvania researchers doubt we'll ever have an Olympics again that does not involve genetically altered humans. Advocates of the 'prevail' scenario think back to the Dark Ages. Humans then were beset by apparently insurmountable trials similar to our own. But with the rise of the printing press, we could store and share our ideas in ways never before possible. Print allowed the rise of institutions beyond the imagination of one country, much less one person: global trade, and then the Enlightenment, which gave us democracy and modern science.

There's reason to hope that such co-evolution is occurring again. In the '70s, if you had been told that there would be a ceaseless rain of computer viruses and worms attacking the guts of our most sensitive computers, you might rationally have assumed the human race, or at least technological progress, to be doomed. In fact, the signs that humanity can make good use of technology to thwart the bad abound. On 9/11, the fourth plane didn't make it to its target. Why? Because dozens of ordinary people on that plane, empowered by mobile phone technology, in less than an hour analysed, diagnosed and solved their society's problem, at the greatest cost to themselves.

Still, we have many questions with which to grapple.

Already we see people living much longer, healthier lives than in the past. Researchers at the US National Institutes of Health think that the first human to robustly live 150 years is already alive today. What will it mean to marriage and parenting, not to mention social security, if this increased longevity continues?

What will it mean to your family if your kids are greatly more capable mentally than you are? And what does it mean to the institutions we cherish, like democracy, if it is no longer clear that all men and women are created equal?

The measure of success in the 'prevail' scenario that I hope for would not be how many transistors we can get to talk to each other. Rather, 'prevailing' in the midst of such radical evolution would be measured by the richness, depth, variety and ease of the most important connections — the ones among unpredictably clever humans like ourselves.

Joel Garreau, a *Washington Post* reporter and editor, is the author of *Radical Evolution: The Promise and Peril of Enhancing Our Minds, Our Bodies — and What it Means to Be Human.*

The Age, 11 August 2005

Constructing a written argument

Reviewing, editing and proofreading

Refer to pages 97–8 for information about reviewing, editing and proofreading your written argument.

Written arguments can be structured in a variety of ways. Not all written arguments necessarily adopt the form of an essay, as we shall see later, but in this section it is the argumentative essay that we will focus on.

The following table shows how an argumentative essay could be structured. This essay seeks to prove that schools should operate throughout the year and not just during term time, as is presently the case.

Introduction (containing contention)

Can you imagine what would happen to a business if it functioned for only 200 days in each year? How profitable do you think it would be? Yet that is exactly what happens in our schools: they are open and operating for 200 days a year. For 165 days each year they are empty and both teachers and students are idle.

It makes no sense: schools should be open and operating all year round.

Background

Schools are business enterprises. They have premises (the school buildings) and equipment (furniture, fittings, books, electronic equipment) representing a considerable

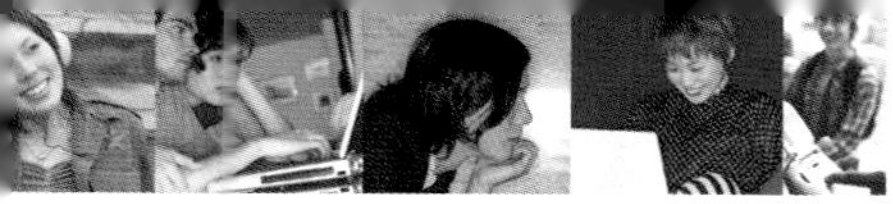

Other ways of structuring an argumentative essay:

Introduction and contention

Background

Opposing arguments and **refutation**

Your own arguments plus evidence

Conclusion

or

Introduction and contention

Background

Argument and evidence

Opposing argument and refutation

Another argument and evidence

Opposing argument and refutation

Conclusion

financial investment by the government and the tax-paying public. They have personnel (teachers and ancillary staff) who are paid salaries and provided with superannuation and sick leave, and they produce a very valuable product: educated people who can contribute to the progress, happiness and well-being of our society.

Arguments and evidence

(1) It is therefore the huge financial investment in education that presents a powerful argument for keeping schools operating throughout the year. Empty buildings and holidaying staff do not yield any return on investment. But if schools were open during the holidays, learning could continue and student results could improve. Mr Ken Logan, a representative of the Principals' Association supports this argument, arguing also that continued occupation of the premises would lessen the chances of vandalism. Vandalism frequently occurs during holidays and, of course, presents a financial burden for any school affected.

(2) In addition, in an era where accountability is the keyword and student achievement a measure of how well schools are performing, it makes perfect sense to provide students with extra opportunities to consolidate the knowledge they have gained or to make up for any deficiencies in their achievement. Indeed, research shows that student achievement slips backwards during the long summer breaks, and teachers waste precious time in the new school year trying to bring students back to where they were before they went on holidays.

(3) Holidays, in fact, are friendly to neither students nor parents. For parents the holiday period represents a time when the family often has to perform contortions in order to make certain that younger children are supervised. A parent has to take holidays, a grandparent has to be dragooned into helping out, or some other arrangement — which inevitably costs money — needs to be made. And there is no peace of mind for the parents of older children who are left home alone, unsupervised. Realistically, given an economy that functions on the basis of both parents working, parents should be able to rely on schools remaining open and functioning, rather than 'going on holiday' every ten weeks.

Opposing arguments and refutation

(1) No doubt some will argue that both teachers and students need holidays, that 'all work and no play makes Jack a dull boy' and perhaps there is some truth in this. What is not necessarily true, however, is that they need as many and as long holidays as is presently the case. The occasional long weekend, scattered throughout the year, as well as the Easter and Christmas breaks and the odd community holiday such as Anzac Day, really should be enough — for the children, at any rate. Any parent will tell you that children find long holidays boring, that they miss their friends and long to be back at school.

The situation is probably different for teachers. Given that the job is said to be a stressful one, they will need student-free time. But if teachers taught in teams, rather than individually, provision could be made for them to take holidays at different times throughout the year, so that teaching continued uninterrupted.

(2) Perhaps it could also be argued that such a system would interfere with parents' ability to take holidays, but in fact it would free parents to take holidays whenever they wanted and not just during the very expensive period of school holidays. As a result the tourist industry would see a more balanced use of its resources throughout the year, rather than having to cope with periods of intense activity interspersed with very slow times.

Conclusion

The idea has much to recommend it. Initially governments might need to put more money into the system to employ more teachers, but the serious educational and economic benefits that would follow are ones that we can well do with.

Learning activity 8.7

1. In your own words, what is the first argument put forward in favour of the contention and what evidence does the author use to support it? Do you find this argument and evidence convincing? Explain your answer.
2. In your own words, what is the second argument put forward in favour of the contention and what evidence does the author use to support it? Do you find this argument and evidence convincing? Explain your answer.
3. In your opinion, does the author successfully refute or rebut the opposing arguments? Explain your answer.

Voice, tone and word choice

The effectiveness of a written argument depends not only on its content and structure, but also on how it is written — the language choices that the author makes.

We have looked at how an author can choose a particular voice (page 94) and tone (pages 187–8) to suit the selected audience and purpose. In writing an argumentative text, similar decisions can be made. Are you going to put forward a point of view in your own voice or the voice of someone else? Who are the stakeholders in the issue about which you are going to write? Is it possible for you to assume the persona of one of these people? For instance, an argument in favour of logging, written from the point of view of someone actively involved in the industry, could have particular potency.

What tone will you adopt? If you have decided to use the persona of a stakeholder in the issue, your tone could be more emotional than if you decide to write in an objective and formal manner.

Your decisions about voice and tone will influence your choice of words, sentence structure and persuasive appeals.

Coherence and fluency

An argument that is coherent (all parts of the essay are relevant and linked to each other and to the thesis) and fluent (the individual sentences read smoothly and 'flow' from one to another) is more likely to convince the reader than an argument that is not.

There are certain words that act as signals to show how the essay is structured. Some of these words appear at the beginning of paragraphs to make a link to the ideas in the previous paragraph or appear within paragraphs to show how an idea is being developed. For instance, words and **phrases** such as however, on the other hand, moreover, thus, lastly, hence or in addition can be used in this way.

Other words and phrases are also used as signals.

Signal words	
Cause	because, for this reason
Effect	consequently, therefore, as a result
Comparisons	comparatively, by comparison, similarly, in the same way
Emphasis	and, also, in addition, not only ... but also, furthermore, moreover

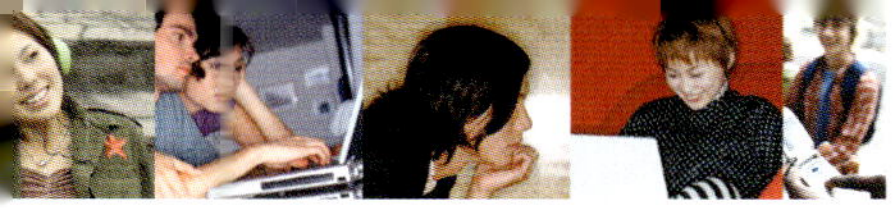

Signal words (continued)	
Clarification	for example, such as, in other words, to put it another way
Concession	admittedly, obviously, however, although, even though
Qualification	but, however, despite, while, alternatively, although
Contrast	but, alternatively, on the other hand, nevertheless, nonetheless

Learning activity **8.8**

Use words from the above examples to write sentences as indicated.

A sentence that shows cause	
A sentence which shows effect	
A sentence in which a comparison is made	
A sentence that is intended to emphasise a point	
A sentence that qualifies a point previously made	
A sentence that makes a contrast	
A sentence that makes a concession	
A sentence that clarifies	

Other ways of arguing in writing

As noted above, not all written arguments have to be in the form of an essay. We've already seen an example of an argument in an editorial, and of course letters to the editor are usually arguments written in response to an issue which is currently the subject of media attention. But it is possible for an author to argue very powerfully for a point of view using other forms such as the **feature article**, a short story, a personal recount or a poem.

Here is a short story by Richard Yaxley about a mythical animal, its situation and the narrator's reaction.

The Last Squoob

There is an assumption among some human beings that because we are exactly that — human — we are innately superior to all other living things. This assumption is based on the idea that superiority is measurable in human terms — progress, technology, science, cultural advancement — and makes it easy for us to forget respect, both for other creatures and for the environment generally.

Human beings have a long history of slaughtering, eradicating and domesticating other animals, sometimes to satisfy their own needs, sometimes because of a dangerous situation, sometimes because it is regarded as fun or sport. While this story does not advocate total animal liberation, it does perhaps suggest that respect, and space, be given to those non-human creatures who happen to share our world.

One sunny Tuesday, the only squoob left in the universe found its way to the centre of a huge tangle of wet sclerophyll bushland. There stood a vast, ancient King Billy pine, which the squoob clambered up without difficulty to rest at last, exhausted but happy, amid the silent blue leaves and cooling winds of the crown. Being the last of his species, the squoob was old and tired and lonely, and he wished to survey the world that had confounded him one last time before slipping without fuss into the gentle release of death.

Squoobs were never well-known or particularly well-documented creatures. My only photograph, taken six years ago from the edge of a walking track in the misty lakelands of central Tasmania, shows a shuffling, ponderous animal, heavy legged and tired looking, with mottled, dirty-looking fur. That squoob was nearly, unfortunately, shot. It was late afternoon, the air was murky and we imagined him to be a roo. But then he had loped clumsily from the undergrowth and we identified his flat, grey tail, the flecked belly matted with plant litter, the short, powerful arms and that distinctive squat, bullish head. For the briefest moment he looked at us, so I quickly fired off the photograph, mindful of the rarity of the beast.

Squoobs were listed as a protected species, which was, frankly, more dangerous than being allowed to live freely in the wild and take your chances. Being 'protected' meant being captured and interned in a laboratory; it meant being poked and prodded and x-rayed and jabbed and tested and swabbed. From such studies ridiculous ideas can emerge. The world's foremost 'expert' on squoobs, a Dr Clifford Farley-Jones, once informed a press conference that they (meaning the prodders and jabbers) were now 'certain that this unique creature is related to the prehistoric giant ground sloth and had somehow mutated into a smaller, Australian version after the separation of the continental plates'. These conclusions, he said, were based upon an 'exhaustive' study of the teeth, vertebrae and highly developed cheek muscles shared by squoobs and sloths. Many people found Dr Farley-Jones and his proclamations deeply engaging — I was not one of these people.

Zoological records indicate numerous squoobs at the turn of the century but since then, and with frightening speed, they had taken to dying. Dr Farley-Jones has never been able to say why, although he did mention that the same thing had happened to the giant ground sloth. This was a decidedly useless piece of information, particularly when the population was reduced to just one squoob, leaning on an ancient branch atop a vast tree in the middle of the bush, staring out with only vague interest at the universe beyond.

The universe at that time was blank and unceasing — except for a whirring spot that darted madly across its face like a bug caught in torchlight. The squoob watched the spot and, after a while, the spot caught sight of the squoob and decided to zoom in for a closer look.

The spot was actually a brand-new, bright-yellow helicopter occupied by six bright-red people who were drinking champagne and gaping at the vast sweep of bush beneath them. The man who had paid for the helicopter tour was named Wilson, and it was he who first spotted the squoob.

'What the heck is that?' he asked.

They all looked obediently to the top of the King Billy pine.

'A monkey?'

'A koala?'

'Maybe it's some sort of bear?'

'There are no bears in Australia. Bears are Canadian.'

'Not if they're polar bears.'

'There are no polar bears in Australia either, Daphne.'

'Shut up,' said Wilson, his voice taking on an impressive new authority. As his wife squeezed his knee adoringly, he told them: 'Now we're closer I can see what it is. It's a squoob, that's what.'

They looked again, oohing and aahing reverently.

'There's only one squoob left on Earth,' said Wilson. 'I saw stuff about it on a TV special last month. They've all died out, except for one. This must be it.'

He ordered the helicopter pilot to hover beside the tree. It hung there, quivering like an obscene, metallic dragonfly, while they took turns video-camming the patient, immobile squoob.

'Maybe it's dead?' speculated Wilson's wife. 'I mean, look at it. It doesn't move or swing on the branches or anything.'

'Rubbish!' snapped Wilson. He had seen the TV special, so he knew more than any of them. 'Squoobs never move much. Besides, look at its face. Its eyes are open.

Looking back, their fuss was excessive. A genuine squoob expert — I myself, for example — could have told them how unremarkable squoobs were. They were unintelligent. Their behaviour — eating, sleeping, eating again — was dull. Their lives followed a predictable course from birth to death some thirty years later, with nothing much in between. Their only unusual feature was their near-extinction. People wondered and cared about them in the same way that the last clothes-peg on Earth would become an object of curiosity.

Wilson's modern, highly trained capitalist nose had already sensed money, prestige and his chance at fifteen minutes of fame. Soon after the helicopter returned to earth he contacted the same TV channel that had run the special the previous month. They agreed to buy his video footage of the last squoob on Earth and run the story on national news bulletins, current affairs programs and a children's nature-watch show. Wilson was paid ten thousand dollars so he took his wife for a trekking holiday in Africa, where they both stepped into quicksand and were never seen again.

Following the TV coverage, thousands of earnest tourists chartered helicopters and light planes and flew out into the bush to view the squoob. Enterprising companies ran special tourist deals (Squooby Dooby Tours, Ride the Squoob Tube and so on), and the once-blank universe was soon dotted with jostling, bustling, loud-mouthed entrepreneurs polluting the air and the land. Rockets flew overhead, hot-air balloons drifted by; there was even a special satellite dish erected to bring 24-hour squoob viewing to the Internet (www.squoobviews.com). On the ground, four-wheel drives bashed ragged tracks through the bush, followed by chugging buses and singing people in old Volkswagens and officials and scientists in white government cars. One sharp-eyed developer soon hacked out a ten-hectare space next to the King Billy pine for car parking; others set up stalls and outlets for T-shirts, plastic squoob replicas, postcards, trinkets, keyrings, jewellery, large furry squoob-family teddies, soap, perfume and even monogrammed nail clippers.

The people flocked.

Such was the squoob's amazing popularity that the Minister for Tourism, cutting short her bed-and-breakfast tour of the Siberian hinterland, decided that the last squoob on Earth should be 'rescued' from the top of the tree in the middle of the bush. She told the assembled world media that the squoob would be placed somewhere 'safer' and 'more accessible'. Then she announced the creation of a Save the Squoob Society to raise funds for its extradition. Someone murmured something about Queen's Birthday Honours.

The Save the Squoob Society project made alarmingly rapid progress. Huge roadways were forged through the wet sclerophyll forest by tree-busting bulldozers specially imported from North America. The King Billy pine was secured by high-tensile steel cables to guard against wind sway that risked tossing the squoob to the ground. Scaffolding was erected around the tree and a security service was contracted to stop any would-be millionaires or animal-traffickers from attempting to steal the squoob. Scientists worked day and night to develop a serum that might extend the life expectancy of the squoob. DNA specialists ordered the exhumation of dead squoobs in order that a female clone might be developed in time for squoob mating season (usually the third weekend of September). In the city, amidst the noise and disorder of normal human life, a task force had been commissioned to construct a large, clear-plastic bubble in which, it was planned, the squoob would eventually reside and perhaps mate. Oxygen valves were sunk into the bubble's surface, hectares of eucalyptus trees were uprooted and replanted around the habitat for forage, and the plastic branches that interconnected the walls were painted in a variety of soothing, sensual pastels. The entire extravaganza was built inside an enormous viewing cage equipped with closed-circuit television, computerised entrance points and supervision towers manned by SAS sharpshooters.

The squoob, meanwhile, had shown little or no interest in the proceedings. Occasionally it chewed a leaf; two or three times each week it completed its toilet behind a convenient curtain of foliage.

The day I crept unnoticed into the compound was the day they had begun excavating the tree. Eventually it would be lifted out of the ground and gently transported to the bubble in the city. Giant excavators were ripping the soil away from the area surrounding the tree; the transportation was planned for two days hence.

'Stop it!' I yelled.

No-one heard, or even appeared to listen.

'Stop it!' I tried again.

Still there was no response. The great machines pulled and tore, scientists tossed thick folders of data at each other, people in suits and hard hats wandered around in groups, pointing and gesturing and rubbing their chins thoughtfully.

I climbed a small tree, stood with my feet balanced in two creaking forks.

'Leave it alone!' I screamed as loudly as I could. 'Can't you see, it just wants to stay there and die! It wants to die in peace! Leave it alone!'

A man saw me, listened for a moment, grinned then tapped his friend on the shoulder. 'Nut case.'

They both began to laugh. The second man extracted a walkie-talkie from his jacket and punched a button. 'Security? Got a protester in the northern sector. Eh? No, harmless enough … just a bloody greenie, I suppose.' They turned away, watching the diggers dip and screen as the earth was split and discarded.

That's when it happened.

The pistol had been hidden carefully in my underwear. I had developed it myself out of plastic in order to defeat the metal detectors. Plastic case, plastic mechanism, plastic bullets ejected with sufficient velocity to take effect from a distance. I clicked off the safety catch and took careful aim. From the corner of my eye I saw the two men turn, brace, begin their frantic scramble.

I breathed deeply, once, twice. Then I pulled the trigger. There was a flash, the briefest moment of clarity then, with dignity and grace, the last squoob on Earth tumbled from his leafy perch, rolled in gentle ovals and fell to the bush floor, a sad memento to a now-extinct species.

I am writing this from my cell in the most escape-proof prison of Australia. I was allocated twenty-five years without parole for the murder of the squoob, all of which I will spend in maximum security. According to the primitive and brutal system of justice of my fellow inmates, I am ranked beneath murderers and rapists.

Of course, I know something they do not. That bullet, that speeding, whistling projectile, missed the squoob by a considerable distance. He had tottered before I had even pulled the trigger. He fell of his own accord, probably because he had had enough of the fuss, and because he was old and tired and lonely. Had they examined the body ... but, amidst the hysteria and accusations and general hubbub, they did not.

Still, I'm content to play the scapegoat. It's not such a bad life. They feed me occasionally, I am allowed enough air to breathe, and for my own protection I am constantly monitored on closed-circuit television. There have been interviews and television profiles, inquiries into my background and psychological condition, interviews with past teachers and friends. Once a week members of the public are allowed to pay a fee and view me; and at last count, there were 1247 websites dedicated to my case. I have, I suppose, achieved a kind of notoriety similar to that of the squoob. Knowing this, I can allow myself a quiet, sleepy chuckle, for I have inadvertently taken the squoob's place in the scheme of things. I too, it seems, will grow old and tired and lonely in my prison ... before slipping without fuss into the gentle release of death.

Richard Yaxley

Learning activity **8.9**

1. In pairs, identify the thesis of this short story and the way in which the author seeks to prove it.
2. Consider the way in which the short story uses satire in order to make its point. Do you think this is an effective way to put forward an argument? Explain your answer.

Constructing an oral argument

Oral arguments can be presented informally in discussion groups, or more formally in a speech, presentation, debate or forum. Each of these forms has its own special features, which need to be considered when you are presenting your view.

Discussion groups

Discussion groups can be structured or unstructured. Structured discussion groups have a leader who has prepared a list of questions for discussion by the members of the group. The leader's role is to manage the discussion, propose questions, guide the discussion, keep it on track, encourage members of the group to contribute, and round off the discussion with a brief summary at the conclusion. In an unstructured discussion group there is no appointed leader and members of the group interact without any particular guidance.

The positive behaviour described in the strategies box on the opposite page is particularly important in an unstructured discussion.

Learning activity **8.10**

1. In pairs, brainstorm a list of factors that you think would make a discussion an effective one. Share your list with the class.
2. The cartoon above illustrates some of the roles that people play in discussion groups.

   Match the behaviour of each character with the following descriptions:
   - the one who gets things going and asks the first question
   - the one who knows everything and wants to do all the talking
   - the one who is keen to be a facilitator and to make sure that everyone gets a go
   - the one who isn't really interested in the group succeeding, does nothing to help and disrupts whenever possible
   - the one who wants everyone to work together and smoothes over any misunderstanding
   - the one who clarifies or explains
   - the one who offers information to help the discussion along
   - the one who accepts others' ideas, but doesn't necessarily have any of his or her own to add.

Strategies | Contributing to group discussions

Positive behaviour in a group discussion includes:

- making sure everyone gets a turn
- using positive body language such as smiles and nods
- making positive comments
- adding to what other people have said
- asking questions
- offering an opinion
- offering extra information
- suggesting new ideas
- summarising a point of view.

Formal speeches

Any type of formal oral communication requires preparation. Just as you plan your written responses, so too must you plan your speeches. This does not necessarily mean that you write out word for word everything you are going to say. If you do that, you may be tempted to read the material rather than give a speech. It is also likely that you will become flustered if you lose your place. The best approach is to plan the structure of your speech by writing down headings on pieces of card (cue cards) that will fit comfortably in your hand. (If you are speaking from behind a rostrum, then your headings can be written on sheets of paper, but if there is nothing between you and your audience, the sheets of paper will be less manageable and could be a distraction to your audience.) The headings on the card act as prompts to remind you of the points that you wish to make.

Of course, you will need to practise your speech before the actual delivery. Try it out on a parent or friend. You should also time yourself, so that you know how long the speech is going to last.

In your speech you will make use of many of the strategies that we discussed in chapter one. You will:

- make use of special appeals to the emotions of your audience
- use personal stories, case studies, statistics and quotations in order to support your stance
- ask rhetorical questions
- make direct appeals or pleas
- use repetition to emphasise key points.

In addition, you will:

- pace your speech so that you don't appear to be rushing through it
- use pauses to emphasise the importance of what you have just said or what you are about to say. A pause before an important point can create a sense of suspense, which serves to emphasise the point that is about to be made. A pause after an important point can allow time for the audience to absorb it, to let it sink in. The pause is therefore a persuasive device because it forces the listener to concentrate on what the speaker believes is important.
- vary the pitch and volume of your voice. A speaker can force listeners to pay close attention to a particular point by raising or lowering his or her voice. In contrast, an inexperienced speaker can lose control of voice pitch, thereby allowing his or her anger, nervousness or irritation to become obvious.
- make eye contact with members of the audience. Eye contact with an audience is an important way in which speakers attempt to convey confidence

and an impression of sincerity. Speakers who avoid eye contact are often thought to be insincere, untruthful, lacking in confidence or simply strange! Imagine the following: a speaker who looks at the wrong television camera; a speaker at a lectern who does not look up from her notes; an interviewee who closes his eyes repeatedly; or a speaker in an auditorium who focuses his gaze on the back wall somewhere. As members of an audience we tend to find these habits unsettling, so we are less inclined to listen to or even accept what the speaker is saying.

- be aware of your stance. The way a speaker stands can persuade the audience to listen to what he or she has to say. If the speaker sits or stands in a relaxed manner, the audience can interpret this as a message of confidence and authority. On the other hand, if the speaker is too relaxed — perhaps lounging in a chair — the perception of the audience might be that he or she is very arrogant.
- use clear speech and correct grammar. Clear, audible, well-constructed speech can be a persuasive technique. It lends the speaker authority and the audience may feel flattered that the speaker wants to make an impression on them. If the speaker mumbles or speaks in some other way that makes it hard to hear what is being said, then much of the speaker's message will be lost. Of course, clear, grammatical speech may not be effective for all audiences and all speakers, and you can probably think of examples where it would be less important. Nevertheless, we expect most television and radio presenters, politicians and others in the media spotlight to be able to express themselves clearly and use correct grammar.

Debating

Debating is a very structured form of persuasive speaking. The sorts of strategies mentioned in the previous sections also apply to debating, but there are certain additional rules to be observed in regard to the order of speaking and the task of each speaker.

A debate is between two teams. The affirmative team argues for the topic, while the negative team argues against it.

There are three speakers on each team. They speak in the following order and carry out the following tasks.

1. The first speaker for the affirmative team:
   - defines exactly what the topic means
   - indicates what line of argument the team will take
   - outlines what each member of the team will be discussing.
2. The first speaker for the negative team:
   - gives the negative team's definition of the topic
   - outlines what each team member will discuss
   - counters or rebuts any arguments put forward by the first speaker for the affirmative.
3. The second speaker for the affirmative team:
   - rebuts the arguments presented by the first speaker for the negative
   - presents most of the affirmative team's arguments.
4. The second speaker for the negative team:
   - rebuts the arguments of the previous speaker
   - presents most of the negative team's arguments.
5. The third speaker for the affirmative team:
   - rebuts the arguments of the previous speaker
   - summarises the affirmative team's case without introducing any new arguments. New examples that support the arguments are allowed.
6. The third speaker for the negative team:
   - rebuts the arguments of the previous speaker
   - summarises the negative team's case.

Judging a debate

When judging a debate, you need to consider three things: manner, matter and method. You can also keep these things in mind when you are preparing a debate yourself.

- *Manner.* How did the speaker deliver the arguments? Consider clarity of speech, variation in tone, forcefulness of speech, facial expression, eye contact with the audience.
- *Matter.* What was the content of the speaker's arguments? Did the arguments have substance, and what evidence was used to support them?
- *Method.* How were the speeches organised? Did they follow the rules regarding the roles of the different speakers?

When you do come to judge a debate, the assessment sheet shown below may help you.

	Manner (out of 40)	Matter (out of 40)	Method (out of 20)	Total (out of 100)
Affirmative team				
First speaker				
Second speaker				
Third speaker				
Team total				
Negative team				
First speaker				
Second speaker				
Third speaker				
Team total				

Possible topics for debate:

That the world needs more non-conformists

That charity begins at home

That Australian television is woeful

That it is already too late

Strategies | Tips for oral presentations

Certain kinds of behaviour in a public speaker are very distracting for the audience, and detract from the speaker's message. In any oral presentation, you should avoid:

- walking around as you speak, although some accomplished speakers can get away with this in certain situations
- reading from your notes
- holding sheets of papers in your hand and shuffling through them
- looking at only one part of the audience or one individual in the audience
- giggling and apologising when you make a mistake
- nervous mannerisms
- too much gesticulating.

Conducting a forum

A forum consists of a number of people who sit in front of an audience and, in turn, give a short speech about a set topic. This is often a topic of current interest in the media; for example, 'Is Australia a racist society?' There is usually a set time limit for these speeches, and the speaker may read the speech or speak from

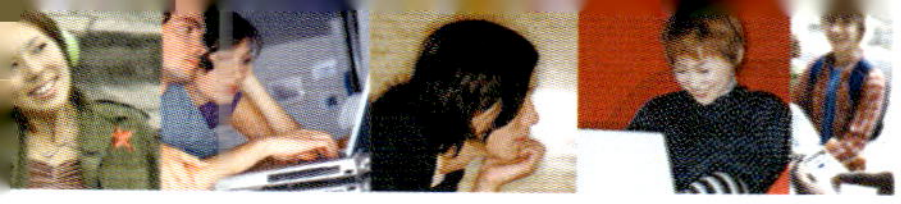

notes. The speakers do not always use visual aids. The role of the chairperson is to introduce each speaker and then, after each person has spoken, open the session up to questions from the audience. Questions can be addressed to the panel as a whole or to individual members. At the end of a set period of time, the chairperson concludes the forum and thanks the participants.

See pages 136–7 for information about making a datashow presentation

Assessment tasks |

Construct an argument on an issue of personal interest to you.

Choose one of the following forms:

- an argumentative essay on a set topic or a topic of your choice
- a **dialogue** between two people who have opposing points of view on the same issue
- a creative or personal response that presents a point of view on an issue
- participation in or leadership of a structured discussion group
- participation in a forum
- a formal speech
- participation in a debate
- an oral presentation facilitated by technology, for example, a datashow presentation.

See page 250 for the criteria for assessment.

Criteria for assessment

Your assessment task will be assessed according to the following criteria. Read them carefully before you begin your task; while working on your task, check your progress against the criteria and then review your completed task against the criteria before submitting it to your teacher.

Ability to present a reasoned point of view in oral or written form. This includes, where relevant:

- relevance of response to the set topic
- a clear and logical point of view supported by arguments and evidence
- control of spelling, punctuation and syntax
- use of the structures and features of the chosen form
- coherent organisation.

Ability to use verbal, visual and non-verbal language to position readers and viewers in particular ways. This includes, where relevant:

- considered choice of words and phrases
- calculated appeals to the emotions and values of the specified audience
- use of strategies such as body language, repetition, pauses, pitch and volume.

Weblinks

The website for this book is at: www.jaconline.com.au/englishateleven

Chapter		Page no.	On-screen text
1	Print and non-print texts	43	'I have a dream' speech
1	Print and non-print texts	43	'I have a dream' speech: audio
4	Exploring technology and communication	133	Ezine
4	Exploring technology and communication	133	Ezine
4	Exploring technology and communication	134	Tourism Australia
4	Exploring technology and communication	139	Ezine
7	Using language to persuade in multimodal texts	220	PeTA
7	Using language to persuade in multimodal texts	221	Ausflag
7	Using language to persuade in multimodal texts	221	Rainforests
7	Using language to persuade in multimodal texts	221	Wilderness Society
7	Using language to persuade in multimodal texts	221	Essendon Football Club
7	Using language to persuade in multimodal texts	223	Incredible Adventures

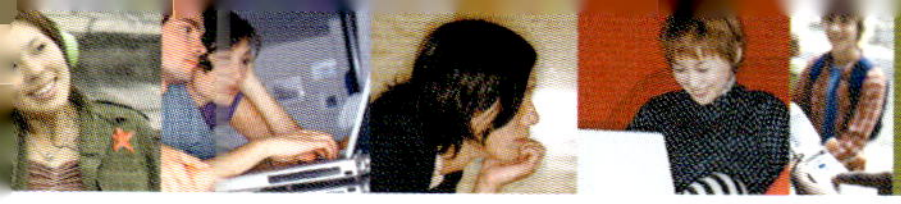

Glossary

adjective | A word which describes a noun, such as *tall* in *a tall building*.

adverb | A word which tells you something extra about a verb, adjective or another adverb, such as *beautifully* in *singing beautifully*.

allegory | A symbol representing an idea (for example, the blindfolded figure with scales used to represent Justice) or a short moral story.

alliteration | The repeated use of one consonant, as in *suspicious signs*; the commencement of two or more words of a word group with the same letter, as in *apt alliteration's artful aid*.

anecdote | A short account of an interesting or humorous incident.

animation | Cartoon-like moving images found on a website or in a movie.

autobiography | An account of a person's life written by himself or herself.

ballad | A poem or folk song, originally from an oral tradition, which narrates a story from local history or legend. The story is told in an unemotional way, often with lively dialogue, and is usually composed in quatrains with alternative four-stress and three-stress lines, with the second and fourth lines rhyming.

biography | An account or a study of a person's life, written by another.

blank verse | Unrhymed verse; unrhymed iambic pentameter verse. Shakespeare's use of blank verse, where the sentence predominated and run-on lines were used, gave a more 'natural' sound to the dialogue of his plays.

broadsheet | A newspaper printed on the standard sheet size of paper: *The Age*, for example.

case studies | Detailed analyses of a person or group, as a model or example of medical, psychiatric, psychological or social phenomena.

chronological | Arranged in order according to time: *I wrote down the most important events in my life in chronological order.*

cinematographer | A person who operates a film camera as a profession.

clause | A group of words containing a subject and a predicate, forming a sentence or part of a sentence, such as *after the boy arrived* and *She heard the news.* Clauses can be joined, and the new sentences become compound or complex sentences. Clauses are joined together using coordinating, or connecting, words such as *and, but, while* and *however.*

cliché | A saying which has become stale or dull because it has been used too often, such as *over the moon* or *as old as the hills.*

colloquial | Suitable for or marked by conversational speech or writing, in which the speaker or writer feels free to choose words from the informal, slang or vulgar elements of the language. *Arvo*, for example, is a colloquial way of saying *afternoon*.

complex sentence | A sentence containing an independent clause and one or more dependent clauses, such as *When the clock strikes* (dependent clause), *it will be 3 o'clock* (independent clause).

compound sentence | A sentence with two or more independent clauses, usually joined by one or more conjunctions, for example, *The lightning flashed* (independent clause) *and* (conjunction) *the rain fell* (independent clause).

connotation | An idea or meaning suggested by or associated with a word.

context | The circumstances for which a piece of writing is intended; a setting or situation. For example, the context for a letter might be personal as in between people who know each other well, or formal as in a business letter. Context is closely linked to audience and purpose and helps to determine the style of writing.

crop | Altering the size of a photograph by cutting.

dialogue | A conversation between two or more people, especially in a play or story.

documentary | A factual presentation of a real event, person's life and so on, in a television program, film etc.

dramatic monologue | A literary text, especially in poetry, that presents a persona, clearly not that of the writer, addressing a silent but designated audience. The dramatic monologue is distinguished from the monologue in that the persona reveals far more of his or her personality than is wise, as in Robert Browning's poem, 'Fra Lippo Lippi'.

editorial | An article written by a newspaper editor, which expresses the editor's or the paper's views.

feature article | A special article in a newspaper or magazine. Its purpose is generally informative but could also be persuasive.

figurative language | Language that involves the use of figures of speech such as similes or metaphors.

genre | Traditionally, one of the three broadest distinctions in literary texts: drama, poetry and fiction; more recently, the kinds of text within these broad classifications, such as adventure, romance, horror etc. Also, everyday texts such as letters, advertising, films, and so on.

hyperbole | [pronounced hy-per-bol-ee] An obvious overstatement made for effect and not intended to be taken literally.

hyperlink | When clicked with a mouse, a hyperlink (which might be associated with a word, a graphic or an icon) takes the user to another location in the same or a different file. A hyperlink on a web page links to other pages within the same or another website.

iambic pentameter | A common rhythm pattern consisting of five iambs (two syllables consisting of an unaccented syllable followed by an accented one), used in blank verse and used extensively by Shakespeare in his plays.

imagery | The technique through which a writer creates pictures in the reader's mind to make the words more vivid. The two main types of imagery are metaphors and similes.

information and communication technology | Information and communication technology (ICT) is the hardware and software that enables data to be digitally processed, stored and communicated. ICT can be used to access, process, manage and present information; model and control events; construct new understanding; and communicate with others. (VELS definition)

jargon | The words and phrases used only by people in a particular job or group: *computer jargon*.

linear plot | A plot that proceeds in a straight line and in chronological order.

metalanguage | The language used to describe and discuss the functions of words in sentences and the terms used to describe and categorise the structural features of different kinds of texts.

metaphor | A figure of speech in which a word or phrase is used to describe something in a way that does not fit it in reality, as a method of suggesting likeness, for example, *A mighty fortress is our God; Your bad moods are a cloud in my life.*

multimodal | Multimodal texts are those that combine, for example, print, visuals, text, sound and spoken word, as in film or computer presentation media.

non-fiction | Writing that deals with actual events and people rather than those created by the imagination of the author.

non-verbal language | Non-verbal language does not make use of words to communicate. Rather it communicates through, for example, facial expressions and gestures, sounds and music. Visual language (colour, symbols, design) is also part of non-verbal language.

noun | A type of word which names something, commonly divided into proper nouns like *Australia* and common nouns like *beauty* or *dog*.

past tense | A tense which refers to events or states in time gone by. For example, in the sentence *It happened last year, happened* is in the past tense.

personification | The giving of personal nature or character to non-living objects or abstract notions, especially as a rhetorical device, as in *The book was begging to be opened.*

phrase | A group of two or more words without a finite verb and acting as a unit, as in *by the cane chair.* They can be introduced by prepositions, as in *on the table*, or by participles, gerunds and infinitives. Phrases introduced by these three parts of speech are bold in the following sentences: (participle) ***Given your behaviour****, we will have to expel you*; (gerund) ***Giving presents*** *is something he loves*; (infinitive) ***To give them credit****, they did at least try to help.*

present tense | A tense of a verb that indicates the action or state is happening or exists at the moment of speaking.

pronoun | A word which stands for a noun, such as *we*, *her*, *they* and *it*.

prose | The ordinary form of spoken or written language, without metrical structure (as distinct from poetry or verse).

rebut | Disprove by evidence or argument, especially in law.

refutation | The process of refuting or disproving.

register | The particular kind of language conventionally deemed appropriate to a certain context or social situation. Appropriate register is sometimes determined by genre, as in a personal letter or an essay, or by the degree of formality of the communication, as in a private conversation or a public speech.

rhyming pattern | When the endings of two words sound the same, they are said to rhyme. In poetry, rhyme is usually used at the end of lines. Two consecutive lines might rhyme, or alternate lines within a verse, or even lines separated by several other lines. Some poems, such as sonnets, have quite distinctive rhyming patterns.

rhythm | A regular pattern of stressed or accented sounds, also known as metre.

simile | Figure of speech in which a non-literal comparison is made and marked by the use of *like*, as in *Viewed from the tower, the traffic below looked like a chaotic column of ants*; and by *as*, as in *Her pimple reddened as relentlessly as the sun rises in the morning.* Similes also begin with *as if* and *as though.*

simple sentence | A sentence with only one independent clause.

source | The place where something begins; a person who supplies information; a publication that is referred to.

storyboard | A storyboard is the pictorial representation of the action in a film. It depicts a series of frames, each indicating the content and camera angles of a particular scene.

subject | The part of a sentence about which something is said, such as *the roof of the house* in *The Roof of the house was red*. A sentence usually contains a subject and a predicate. In the sentence *The birds woke me at dawn*, *The birds* is the subject and *woke me at dawn* is the predicate.

tense | The form of a verb which shows the time and duration of the action or state expressed by the verb.

tone | 1. The quality of style in literature, especially as showing the author's attitude: *a serious tone*; *an ironic tone*. 2. A particular quality, way of sounding, modulation or intonation of the voice that expresses a meaning.

transitions | A movement from one scene to another or from one time period to another.

validity | The quality of being logically convincing.

Venn diagram | A Venn diagram is comprised of two overlapping circles used to compare and contrast two objects. Similarities are recorded in the overlapping area and differences are listed in those parts of the circles which do not overlap.

verb | A word which expresses the occurrence of an action, existence of a condition etc., such as *hit*, *walk*, *do*, *exist* and *be*.

verbal language | Verbal language is language that makes use of words, either in written or oral form.

verse drama | A play that is written in verse, for example, parts of Shakespearean plays.

visual language | Visual language includes visual symbols, design, colour and elements of non-verbal language such as gestures and facial expressions.

Author index

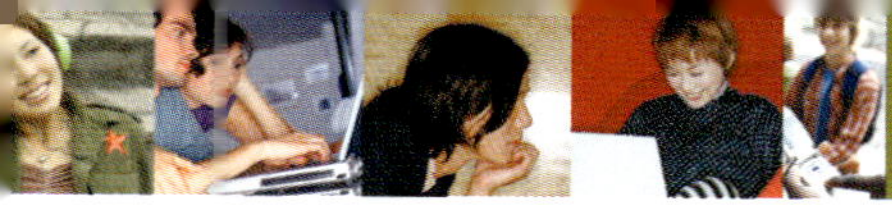

Subject index

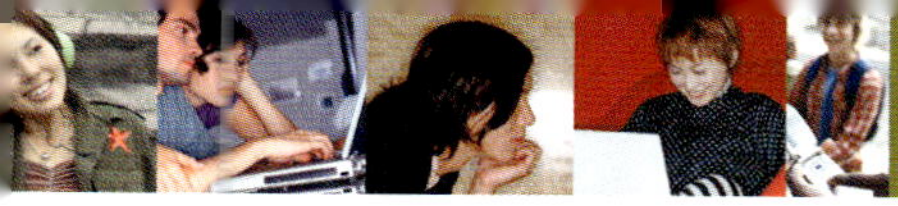

Title index